VIKINGS
OF THE IRISH SEA

VIKINGS
OF THE IRISH SEA

CONFLICT AND ASSIMILATION
AD 790–1050

DAVID GRIFFITHS

The
History
Press

For Neil,
Who found some of it, and lived with the rest

First published 2010
Reprinted 2012

The History Press
The Mill, Brimscombe Port
Stroud, Gloucestershire, GL5 2QG
www.thehistorypress.co.uk

British Library Cataloguing in Publication Data.
A catalogue record for this book is available from the British Library.

ISBN 978 0 7524 3646 3

Typesetting and origination by The History Press
Printed in Great Britain

CONTENTS

LIST OF ILLUSTRATIONS

Front Cover: The 'fishing scene' stone, Gosforth, Cumbria. Thor and Hymir ride in a boat on a fish-filled sea, as Thor hooks the world serpent. (Ross Trench-Jellicoe)

Back Cover: Sea Stallion from Glendalough, a full-size reconstruction of an Irish-built Viking Ship (*Skuldelev 2*), passes the north-west of Scotland on its way from Denmark to Dublin, 2007. (© Roskilde Viking Ship Museum)

Figures

PREFACE

I started writing this book in 2003, but little progress was made until another, somewhat larger, publication on the trading site of Meols was completed towards the end of 2007. This book's origins go back much further, however, to my schooldays. Thanks largely to some inspiring teaching, I developed an interest in archaeology and in the local history of my home area: Wirral, and neighbouring parts of Cheshire, Wales and south Lancashire. I became fascinated by what were still widely known as the Dark Ages and wondered about the role that the sea had played in those remote times. I was brought up in a house with an open view across the Dee Estuary, and my father was, and remains, a sailing enthusiast. Since he built a small plywood dinghy from a kit in the early 1970s, and later traded up to a small cruising yacht, the estuary and the Irish Sea became open to exploration. Sailing passages from the Dee to the Menai Straits, to Howth near Dublin, to the Isle of Man, to Kirkcudbright, and to Piel Island in the Barrow Channel, were all completed over the following years.

I studied history and archaeology as an undergraduate, being fortunate in that my university, Durham, was staffed with Medievalists of exceptional calibre, and I went on to write a PhD on a topic not far removed from that of this book (although this is *not* 'the book of the thesis'). I spent many hours taking up the valuable time of museum curators in Chester, Liverpool, Douglas, Carlisle, Belfast and Edinburgh, and was generously allowed by Patrick Wallace to occupy a desk in the National Museum of Ireland for a summer, in order to familiarise myself with the Dublin finds. I visited Peel and was shown the recently excavated burial material by David Freke. I saw the Peter Street and Olaf Street excavations at Waterford taking place, and I spent some weeks digging on Peter Hill's excavation at Whithorn. I was involved in creating the major 'Silver Saga' exhibition of the Cuerdale Hoard at Liverpool Museum in 1990, and contributed to the related guide, conference and book.[1] Ross Trench-Jellicoe and I spent many days on the road, visiting the churches and stone sculpture sites of Cumbria, Lancashire, Galloway and Ireland, where I benefited from his deep knowledge of early Medieval art and iconography. I owe a special debt of gratitude to my PhD supervisor and examiners, Chris Morris, Rosemary Cramp and James Graham-Campbell, for overseeing my fledgling years as a researcher. I also spent an unforgettable year as a visiting student at the University of Tromsø, Norway, under the guidance of Reidar Bertelsen and the late Olav Sverre Johansen.

Subsequently, I have been lucky to take part in Mark Redknap's splendid research project at Llanbedrgoch, supervising the excavation of House 1 in 1997–8, and to see the Cumwhitton grave finds as they were lifted from the ground in 2004. Attending the XV Viking Congress at Cork in 2005 took me for the first time to the newly-discovered Viking site at Woodstown, and across the steep Atlantic swell to Skellig Michael, the scene of a terrible Viking raid in 824. Writing this book has revealed to me not only how endlessly fascinating its subject is, but how much more there is yet to know about it, now and in the future. What follows is necessarily conditioned by my own strengths as an archaeologist, and to some extent a historian. I am not a philologist, a runologist, or a biologist. Needless to say, the mistakes are all my own.

★ ★ ★

A large number of friends and colleagues have helped me with illustrations, commentaries and technical assistance in putting this book together. Photographs and other images are acknowledged in the List of Illustrations. I am especially grateful in this regard to Patrick Wallace, Andy Halpin and Aoife McBride of the National Museum of Ireland; Mark Redknap of National Museums and Galleries of Wales; Robert Philpott of National Museums Liverpool; Eamonn McEneaney and Rosemary Ryan of the Waterford Treasures Exhibition; Linzi Simpson and Ed O'Donovan of Margaret Gowen & Co.; Ruth Johnson of Dublin City Council; Alan Lupton and Adam Parsons of Oxford Archaeology North; Peter Carrington and Simon Ward of the Grosvenor Museum, Chester; Paul Weatherall of Manx National Heritage; Mark Blackburn of the Fitzwilliam Museum, Cambridge; Roger Bland and Daniel Pett of the Portable Antiquities Scheme; Ole Crumlin-Pedersen and Rikke Johansen of the Roskilde Viking Ship Museum; Chris Lowe of Headland Archaeology; Nick Higham of the University of Manchester and Gabor Thomas of the University of Reading. I am privileged to thank Sir David Wilson, John Bradley, Richard Bailey, Ben Edwards, Julian D. Richards, John Sheehan, Richard Oram, Paul Reilly and Angus Winchester for their advice and generous permissions to reproduce images from their own publications.

  John Sheehan, Stephen Harrison, Fiona Edmonds, Ross Trench-Jellicoe and Roger White read through the text, all or in part, saving me from countless errors, lapses of style and slip-ups. The book was first copy-edited by Tricia Hallam. Advice on DNA-related matters well outside my area of expertise was given by Steve Harding of Nottingham University. Ian Cartwright and Alison Wilkins of the Institute of Archaeology, Oxford University, gave essential technical assistance with the illustrations. Several of the maps and comparative plans are the work of Peter Drake. Mike Athanson helped me prepare the distribution maps in GIS. I owe a particularly keen debt of gratitude to Robert Philpott, Roger White and Ross Trench-Jellicoe, without whose friendship, good humour, generosity, candidness and photographic skills, my efforts would have foundered a long time ago.

CHAPTER 1

INTRODUCTION

The purpose of this book is to bring together a disparate archaeological and historical subject in a region defined by common access to a relatively small and semi-enclosed sea (*1*), rather than in the more familiar terrestrial context of a country or national landmass. It is universally acknowledged that the sea was the principal highway of the Viking world. The Viking phenomenon in Britain and Ireland was primarily a maritime one. Vikings were pirates, adventurers and colonists. They also depended on the sea for trading, fishing and hunting. Early raids came from the sea. Fleets, enmities and alliances transferred easily from one landmass to another, especially when these were separated by only a day's sailing time. Trade and settlement were conditioned by maritime access and held together by seaborne contacts. The geography of the Viking world was linked by sea crossings and river passages. Islands and headlands, isthmuses, sounds, bays, inlets, portages, anchorages, eddying currents, maelstroms, sands and rocks loom large in Norse literature and place-names. Ships were amongst the most prized and animated possessions. They formed the theatre of the grandest pagan graves at Oseberg and Gokstad, and of many lesser ones such as Balladoole on the Isle of Man, and are commemorated throughout Scandinavia by the earthwork remains of the large boat-houses or *nausts* on the strands of the most powerful farms.

It is ironic, therefore, that in most of Europe the activities of Vikings have mostly been viewed in the context of territorially-bounded national historical narratives. In Ireland and Britain, as in many other European countries outside Scandinavia, Vikings have until recently been viewed as outsiders in the story of 'national races' such as Celts or Anglo-Saxons. Political concepts of nationhood, race and ethnicity, from the eighteenth century to the present, but most particularly in the nineteenth and earlier twentieth centuries, have tended to distort and manipulate the archaeological and historical past. Vikings have been used, abused or ignored within patriotic historical traditions that have been mostly concerned with explaining or excusing the rise of modern nation states. This book does not attempt to iron out differences in a search for false conformity around the Irish Sea, because many variations and differences certainly existed, but to redress the balance somewhat by placing the neighbouring areas around this small maritime zone within the context of each other.

Vikings

Vikings have become predominant in our historical perceptions of early Medieval Britain and Ireland, linking the disparate pasts of places such as Waterford, Dublin, Wirral, the Isle of Man, Cumbria and Galloway, into a common international historical theme that stretches from Greenland to Russia and beyond. Vikings are, however, far from being a unified or easily cat-

1. The Irish Sea from Space

egorised historical or archaeological phenomenon. The term 'Viking' is in part derived from Old Norse *vík* (bay or inlet), which came to mean something like 'adventurer', 'marauder' or 'pirate'.[1] It figures far more prominently as a convenient and universally understood shorthand in modern literature than as a description in contemporary historical sources where is it barely known. Rather than being restricted to its specific and historical meaning of pirate or adventurer, the term 'Viking' has now spread itself to encompass most expatriate Scandinavians in the period 790–1050, including traders and settlers, and is used in this manner here.

Early raiders and settlers from Scandinavia would not have thought of themselves as something as anonymously generic as 'Vikings'. Their identity was constituted in terms of family or wider kindred (and by implication their rank within them), their religion and home territory, and their relationship with other families in their homelands. There were linking tenets to be found in convergences of mutually intelligible language, religion and warrior ideology. Late Iron Age Scandinavia, the homelands of these raiders and settlers, was a patchwork of semi-independent territorial chiefdoms, many of which paid scant loyalty to any upstart centralising dynasty. In the comparatively kinder and more pliable landscapes of Denmark, south-eastern Norway and southern and eastern Sweden, kings had begun in the eighth and ninth centuries to assert a dynastic pressure on their compatriots, fighting and buying off rival families to elevate their own, and beginning to call on resources throughout their nascent kingdoms. The western and northern chieftains maintained a particular sense of their own independent worth. One of them, Ottar (or Ohthere), from the northernmost farm in the northernmost Norwegian province (very probably Bjarkøy, Troms county, which is part of the ancient province of Hålogaland), gave King Alfred of Wessex a memorable account of fishing and whaling, of relations with the Lapps (better known today as Saami) of the inland areas, and his trading links to southern Norway and beyond. Separated from each other by majestic but harsh topography (**2**), local centres of power in Norway are marked by clusters of monumental grave mounds, and the remains of formerly impressive buildings. These graves and settlements, particularly in the western Norwegian coastal provinces of Rogaland, Hordaland, Sogn, Møre and Trøndelag, and Vestfold in south-east Norway, have been found to include impressive quantities of Irish and British metalwork alongside iron weapons and other indigenous products.[2]

Rather than 'Vikings', contemporary historical sources in Britain and Ireland (almost all compiled by hostile ecclesiastics) preferred 'heathen', 'gentiles' (religious distinctions which largely went out of use in the 940s), or 'Northmen'. Irish annalists often used 'foreigners' (*Gaill*) as a general description, although their occasional willingness to distinguish between types of 'foreigner' – black or white foreigners, and the foreign-native hybrid *Gallgoídil* (below, Chapter 2), is somewhat more informative. Even so, contemporary references to Scandinavians are mostly implicit, rather than explicit. Were Scandinavians regarded in the west with more of a sense of familiarity than we perhaps assume? Given the contacts between an earlier, pagan, Anglo-Saxon England and Scandinavia, as exemplified in the Anglo-Saxon poem *Beowulf* and the great seventh-century ship-burial at Sutton Hoo (Suffolk), it is highly unlikely that Vikings were the first Scandinavians ever to venture towards the west of Britain or beyond. They were certainly far from the last to exert their presence, as shown by the presence of nineteenth-century Norwegian and Swedish sailors' hostels and churches in west-coast ports such as Liverpool and Cardiff.

Although 'Northmen' or 'Danes' have been of interest to antiquarians since at least the seventeenth century, scientifically grounded 'Viking Archaeology' could be said to have started with the visit to Britain and Ireland in 1846–7 of the eminent Danish prehistorian Jens J. A. Worsaae. His visit included a lengthy stay in Dublin, during which time he gave a series of lectures to the Royal Irish Academy and conferred with antiquarians such as Sir William Wilde (below, Chapter 5). Worsaae's book of 1852, *An Account of the Danes and Norwegians in England, Scotland and Ireland*, was the first of a long series of publications by Scandinavian scholars on the Viking period in Britain and Ireland. It launched a research tradition, based on typological studies of artefacts conducted with reference to museum collections in Scandinavia, which was to remain dominant for more than a century.[3] Following the writings of Sir Walter Scott, the nineteenth century also saw a rapid rise in popular interest in Viking mythology and the Icelandic sagas, some of which was little-troubled by historical and archaeological reality.[4] Nevertheless, despite the fictionalising vogue for Vikings, genuine scholars did emerge during the Victorian period. These included romanticists such as W.G. Collingwood, a follower of John Ruskin and a luminary of the arts and crafts movement, whose studies of the early Medieval sculptured stones of northern England remain a major contribution to research.[5] Viking Archaeology was, however, little more than an obscure minority interest until the mid-twentieth century. During Ireland's struggle for independence, Vikings were mostly viewed unsympathetically as villains in a national story which stressed Celtic purity,

2. The landscape of Sognefjord, Norway

and their artistic and economic contributions were generally devalued as a result. As in many other areas of cultural expression, however, such historical conservatism began to feel the effects of change in the 1960s. The later twentieth-century booms in urban development and higher education, on both sides of the Irish Sea, saw public and academic interest in Vikings rise to an unprecedented level. Major excavations in Dublin and York in the 1970s and early 1980s provided a centrepiece for renewed academic research, and in the case of Dublin, significant political controversy (below, Chapter 7). Numerous television programmes, museum exhibitions, conferences and university courses followed in their wake. Vikings have now become virtually synonymous in the popular mind with the history of northern Europe in the period 800–1100, a situation which is now producing a revisionist backlash, exemplified by Richard Hodges's recent book *Goodbye to the Vikings*, which attempts to re-cast them in a less dominant perspective, as merely an aspect of a much wider series of historical developments.[6]

As a result of the rise in Scandinavian studies, a vast number of words have been expended in 'explaining' the Viking phenomenon in European history,[7] and it is not the purpose of this book to add to them. The emergence in the later eighth century of a particular combination of circumstances in Scandinavia was accompanied by a creative and courageous opportunism. A potent brew of expansionary energy was formed by rumours and material evidence of easy pickings overseas to the west and east. This fed, and was fed by, a long-held but growing liking for foreign finery to supplement chiefly regalia for oiling the wheels of power relations at home, improving boat and weapon technology, and an increasing appetite for land-take by those disaffected with dynastic power at home and hungry for sweeter pastures. The ensuing events we now identify with the Viking period profoundly affected Britain and Ireland along with other lands across Europe. Scandinavians who raided, traded, fought and settled overseas brought ingenuity and ability to adapt to the economic, religious and linguistic circumstances in which they found themselves. Gathering new sources of wealth and power, in war, in land, and from trade in people, silver, amber, other fine minerals and many more mundane items, was the drive behind Scandinavian expansion in the west and east. Scandinavian influence did not abruptly stop or disappear at the end of the age of expansion. Vikings, and the people they settled amongst, interbred and influenced each other; a process that is in itself huge, varied, and fascinating. Much of their original cultural baggage was quickly modified, or jettisoned, as it ceased to have the same significance in their new situation as it once had in their ancestral homelands, yet other traits subtly persisted. Many people, whose ancestors had never been anywhere near Norway, Sweden or Denmark, began to identify with Scandinavian-derived cultural and political symbolism. As generation succeeded generation, the processes of cultural admixture, assimilation and transformation within those areas of Britain and Ireland where a Scandinavian presence persisted, become *the* story behind the archaeology and history.

The Irish Sea

The Irish Sea is best defined as the roughly square basin between the coasts of Ireland, south-west Scotland, north-west England and north Wales, with the Isle of Man at its centre, together with its northern and southern offshoots known as the North Channel and Saint George's Channel (*3*). There are no sharply defined geographical boundaries where the sea merges with the ocean, and nor would it be worthwhile to seek to impose them artificially. Lands within the Irish Sea region naturally include the territories bordering the central basin and channels, and inland areas that are dominated by overland or riverine access to the Irish Sea. Definitions of the Irish Sea region may be stretched further to encompass the entire Bristol Channel (north and south), the south-west and north-west coasts of Ireland, the upper Firth of Clyde, and the Hebrides (creating a much larger geographical scope which could perhaps be better termed the 'Insular Viking Zone')[8]; these are treated here as closely related, and are referred to in so far as they help to illuminate the context of the history and archaeology of the 'inner' Irish Sea region.

The present shape of the Irish Sea is a product of gradual rises in sea level since the Mesolithic period, as the influence of the last Ice Age receded and low-lying coastal lands were inundated. Its estuaries and bays are especially shallow and their upper reaches have a spring tidal range of up to ten metres. Dry land is separated from deep water by marshes and tidal mudflats, where the sea appears and disappears twice a day and navigation is fraught with shifting channels and sandbanks which change from season to season. An acute sense for the sea and land working together, which was second nature to earlier generations of coastal and estuarial communities, was needed to transit and exploit the coastal zone. Skill and resilience were required to harness wind and tide, to find reliable shelter, to anticipate changing patterns of scouring and silting in deep and shallow waters, and to follow the movements of fish and wildfowl.

Notorious for its strong tides, shallow turbulent waters and estuarial quicksands, the Irish Sea can often seem more as a grey and menacing obstacle to transit than an inviting opportunity. The open Irish Sea is most often relatively calm and nondescript with prevailing westerly breezes, but the conjunction of a spring tide and cyclonic winter storm moving in rapidly from the North Atlantic can create a hellish frenzy of short and steep seas leading to terrible conditions in coastal waters which can last for some time in winter. There are few deep-water natural harbours, although the sea loughs of Ulster, and Derbyhaven (known in the Viking period as Ronaldsway) on the south-eastern corner of the Isle of Man, are exceptions. Shelter is mostly found in deeper pools left between the sandbanks at low tide, at the heads of bays, or via intricate networks of tidal channels leading inland towards the upper estuaries and riverine waters. Patience, luck, a shallow draught, an eye and a nose for weather, and a sound and up-to-date working knowledge of the coastline and tidal flows have always been essential for navigation in this unpredictable environment. It has remained a dangerous place; records from the eighteenth to early twentieth centuries

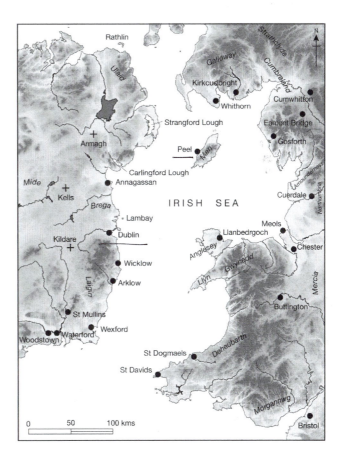

3. The Irish Sea region in the Viking period: sites and territories

show that hundreds of wooden sailing vessels were wrecked in all areas of the Irish Sea, decade upon decade, often with total loss of life, and navigational disasters continue to occur in modern times.

In reasonable visibility, at sea level few stretches of the Irish Sea are entirely out of sight of land, and on any journey across them, such as from Holyhead to Dublin, or from the Mersey to the Isle of Man, land appears ahead very soon after it is lost to sight astern. From higher altitudes, most famously from the summit of Snaefell on the Isle of Man, an enclosing circuit of mountain ranges is fully visible, from the Wicklow Hills south of Dublin, to the Mourne Mountains in Ulster, via the Southern Uplands of Galloway, the Lake District Fells and the Lancashire flanks of the Pennines, around to Snowdonia in North Wales. At sea level, where horizons are more limited, navigation by sight is marked by passage between visible mountain peaks and major coastal landmarks. The coastlines of the Irish Sea are noted for their high proportion of Scandinavian topographical place-names. Scar, Skerry, Ness, Holm, and the suffix –*ey* – all terms for rocks, reefs, headlands and islands – appear even in areas where there is little evidence for Viking settlement on land, and indeed some of these coastal landforms also retain (different) Irish or Welsh names, suggesting that seaward and landward cultures did not always fully coincide.[9] Tuskar Rock, off Rosslare (Co. Wexford), marks the south-western gateway to the Irish Sea; the islands of Caldey, Skokholm, Skomer, Grassholm and Ramsey ring the coast of Pembrokeshire. Worm's Head on the Gower Peninsula in south Wales, and the towering headland of the Great Orme in north Wales (both names from ON *ormr*, 'serpent'), dominate the seaways on the outer approaches to Bristol and Chester.

Seaways are made meaningful largely by their connection to harbours, landing places and overland routes. From the sea, the Dee and Mersey diverge southwards and eastwards into Mercia and Northumbria. Other inlets and estuaries give access to important inland routeways. The Liffey, Boyne, Barrow, Nore and Suir rivers reach deep into Ireland. The Wye and Severn open up Mercia and south-eastern Wales. The Solway Firth leads to Hadrian's Wall, with its Roman military road leading eastwards, and to the Eden Valley leading south-east towards the Pennine watershed. Morecambe Bay and the River Ribble open up the most direct routes from the Irish Sea towards York, the latter connecting to the 'Aire Gap', where a Roman road traverses a relatively low and gently contoured Pennine pass.

'The Irish Sea Province'

By the end of the Neolithic period (*c.* 2000 BC), the landscapes around the Irish Sea had seen the first permanently settled communities and the construction of spectacular megalithic burial monuments such as Newgrange, Knowth and Dowth in the Boyne Valley in eastern Ireland, and Bryn Celli Ddu and Barclodiad y Gawres in Anglesey. Archaeologists long ago began to notice the trans-Irish Sea similarities and correspondences in form, plan and artistic representation in these structures, including the geometric and spiral art carved on some of their megaliths, and speculated on the cultural links which had arisen between these lands divided by a short and shallow sea.[10] To the Edwardian Oxford geographer Sir Halford Mackinder, the Irish Sea was the 'British Mediterranean'.[11] This is not quite literally true, as it is only a semi land-locked sea, and its relationship with the ocean is more profound than its more famous (and sunnier) counterpart. The style of Mackinder's comment is imbued with the faded cartographic pink of a long-gone imperial confidence, but his essential idea has survived. The concept of a sea, rather than a landmass, being the defining geographical context of its terrestrial periphery is attractive to those who would see maritime contacts as equally important as land-based ones, and who would break away from the assumption of centrality for the land in the ancient human imagination.

The geographer E.G. Bowen, writing in the 1960s, saw the Irish Sea as a dynamic zone of contact in the prehistoric and early historic periods; he mapped and discussed the various wind and tidal streams against the geomorphological background to establish a series of 'routeways' based on best and safest passage for small boats. Bowen's article (borrowing Mackinder's phrase) 'Britain and the British Seas' helped to set the scene in a book (resulting from a conference held in Aberystwyth in 1968) entitled 'The Irish Sea Province in Archaeology and History'.[12] In chronologically-written articles (including one on the Vikings by P.H. Sawyer), its authors attempted to find common trans-Irish Sea themes and test the idea of a 'culture province' (exactly what that was supposed be, and why a maritime version would be any different from a terrestrial one, was not defined). Inevitably, significant differences in expressions of monumentality and material culture existed across time. These tended to produce a reaction against a broad-brush notion of continuity of contact. The value of studying the Irish Sea, or indeed the North Sea, Baltic Sea or English Channel, as inter-related regions of social and economic change, was only very guardedly accepted until recently. Trends in archaeological interpretation have moved on from explaining archaeological distribution patterns by migration alone, to stressing the importance of inter-communal contact, and the evolution and transmission of ideas. Barry Cunliffe's recent book *Facing the Ocean* has brought refreshed vigour to the view that the sea was at the heart of much past human experience in practical and cultural terms.[13] Despite scholarly scepticism, the concept of the 'Irish Sea Province' did take root in the 1960s, and remains in sporadic use.[14] However, to avoid entanglement with whatever its cultural implications might or might not mean, the more neutral term 'region' is adopted here.

The Irish Sea in the pre-Viking period

The north and west of Roman Britain was predominantly a military zone with little by way of villas and civilian towns, the only urbanised settlements north of Chester being the *vici* of major forts on Hadrian's Wall. Roman rule in the north and west was succeeded by a shadowy patchwork of regional British kingdoms, such as Rheged in the north (which was subsumed into Northumbria), and the constellation of small kingdoms in the mountainous west of *Britannia Prima,* which together became known to the Anglo-Saxons as Wales. The question of whether the Romans 'invaded' Ireland is one that has long been asked, but is as yet lacking a universally accepted answer. Roman coins, brooches and other portable objects are not uncommon finds in the Irish countryside. Metal detecting at an Iron Age coastal promontory fort at Drumanagh, north of Dublin, has produced a concentrated assemblage of Roman objects, leading to probably unfounded press speculation that there may have been a Roman fort on the site. The appearance of sporadic traces of Roman material culture in Ireland is most probably explained by a combination of trade, the passage of mercenaries and slaves, and informal political contacts (perhaps more likely to have been between local leaders on both sides of the Irish Sea rather than any involving imperial diplomacy).

As the tide of Roman influence rose and fell in Britain, Ireland remained a comparatively wealthy but politically fragmented society. Frequent wars of succession, cattle raids and shifting alliances produced the continual diminution and division of some dynasties in favour of the elevation of others. Before and during the Viking period, Ireland was divided into a network of kingdoms based on sub-kingdoms known as *túatha* (singular *túath*). As far as we can tell, the workings of political and landed authority were far from evenly spread or coherent; each province tended to be dominated by one, or possibly two, leading groups defined by a common kinship, and included numerous families controlling sub-kingdoms. There was much internal division and strife, even amongst groups claiming common genealogical origins under the same kings. In the aftermath of the Roman period, Irish influence and migration spread across the Irish Sea to south-west Wales, to Brycheiniog (Brecon) and to the west coast of the Llŷn Peninsula, as well as from Irish Dál Riata in Co. Antrim to Scottish Dál Riata in Argyll. The Dál Fiátach of Co. Down may have had ambitions to control the Isle of Man later in the sixth century,[15] although in the lead-up to the Viking period, Man seems to have fallen under the influence of a British dynasty with strong connections to Anglesey and south-west Scotland.

The English (or Anglo-Saxons) were latecomers to the Irish Sea region, but once established, were not slow to venture across its waters. As a sustained presence, they preceded the arrival of Vikings by little more than two centuries. Bede referred to the Northumbrian king Edwin's control of Anglesey and the Isle of Man ('the Menavian Islands') in the early seventh century.[16] Both Bede and the *Annals of Ulster* recorded that 'Saxons' attacked the Irish kingdom of Brega in 684 or 685.[17] Anglo-Saxon settlers, some of whom were still pagans, probably arrived on the Irish Sea coast of England in the sixth century, but the traditional date of their arrival in greater numbers follows upon the defeat of the Britons by the Northumbrians in 616, somewhere near Chester.[18] Less than three decades later, Mercia under Penda defeated Northumbria and took over the Cheshire Plain, establishing a coastal window onto the Irish Sea via the Dee and Mersey estuaries. As Mercia reached its short-lived peak as the dominant Anglo-Saxon kingdom later in the eighth century, Offa, and his less-adept successor Coenwulf, engaged in frontier construction and repeatedly fought the Welsh. The border earthwork known as Wat's Dyke, which may have been reused as a north-eastern spur of the later and better-known Offa's Dyke, encloses the upper Dee Estuary, terminating at the abbey of Basingwerk,[19] thus suggesting its purpose was to secure and defend the flanks of Mercian maritime access to the Irish Sea.

The spread of Christianity and monasticism had a profound effect on the Irish Sea region. The Britons defeated at Chester in 616 were aided by monks from a large monastic community nearby which Bede called *Bancornaburg* – it may have been located at Bangor-is-y-Coed on the middle Dee on the English-Welsh border, but its site has not yet been identified. In Ireland, Armagh, the shrine of St Patrick, had developed by the seventh century into a large monastery with multiple dependent houses. The circular concentric plan of the site is visible even today in the topography of the town, with the mother church at its heart (now the site of the Church of Ireland cathedral). Kildare, the shrine of St Brigit, was described in Cogitosus's *Life of St Brigit* as a *civitas* with *suburbana*. Vast and rich houses such as these held sway over large territories and resources with numerous priests of daughter-churches under their authority, and attracted and exhibited much wealth supplied by pilgrimage, industry and art. Fine objects in the form of gospel books, silver plate and jewel-encrusted liturgical equipment accumulated at these places, offering temptation to any worldly sinner unencumbered by respect for their sacred status.

Further down the scale of grandeur, medium-sized monasteries such as Nendrum (Co. Down) and Whithorn (Galloway) were sufficiently influential as economic and spiritual centres to participate in overseas trading networks and even to engage in regional dynastic politics. There were frequent rivalries and even wars between the Irish monasteries, as they were caught up in, and in some cases led, endemic power-struggles between peoples and kingdoms. A quieter and more contemplative life was sought by some, and imposed on others, in the more secluded monastic houses and individual hermitages which occupied islands, caves, coastal promontories and remote inland sites. Reference to the biblical desert of Christ's torment is marked today by the presence of 'Dysart' or 'Dyserth' place-names in Ireland and Wales. The search for extreme isolation is epitomised by the tiny monastery and 'beehive' prayer cells clinging to flat steps of rock amidst the towering offshore precipices of Skellig Michael (Co. Kerry). Although free of landward concerns and entanglements, the coastal monasteries proved to be a tempting target for seaborne Viking attacks, which began with a raid on an island called *Rechru* (identified as Rathlin or Lambay) in 795 (below, Chapter 2).

Sources of evidence for the Viking period

The early raids were dramatic but sporadic. However, the ninth century saw increasingly long-term Viking involvement in Ireland. Historically, Dublin was settled as a defended enclave or *longphort* from around 840, but archaeological evidence (below, Chapter 2, Chapter 5) is now forcing us to question whether this may have occurred in the earliest decades of the ninth century. The latter decades of that century saw reverses for the Vikings in Ireland, which culminated in their exile from Dublin during the period 902–917, although recent evidence from Temple Bar West, Dublin (below, Chapter 2), suggests that not all Viking settlers were evicted. The period 902–37, between the Viking expulsion from Dublin and the battle of *Brunanburh*, has traditionally been accepted by most historians and archaeologists as the most likely period when the imprint of permanent Scandinavian settlement occurred on the Isle of Man and the British shores of the Irish Sea. With the fugitives from Dublin seeking such territorial footholds as were readily available after 902, an intense phase of entanglement with Northumbria, the Danelaw and Mercia followed. North-west England in particular, and perhaps parts of the coast of south-west Scotland and the Isle of Man, may have already experienced some Scandinavian settlement prior to 902, coming from east of the Pennines and the Kingdom of York, which was settled by Vikings after 876 when (as recorded in the *Anglo-Saxon Chronicle*) the Danish leader Halfdan and his followers 'shared out the lands of the Northumbrians and they proceeded to plough and support themselves'.[20]

The heterogenous mixture of Vikings and their followers from Ireland and the Danelaw found new allies and adherents of English, Manx, Cumbrian and Welsh backgrounds. After 917, settlement activity in Ireland developed further, following the recapture of Dublin by returning Vikings. Dublin's development into a major trading town was accompanied by the growth of strategic and permanent coastal settlement clusters in urban hinterlands and along the major trade routes. Enclaves of Viking settlements were established in the Irish Sea coastlands at different times throughout the ninth, tenth and eleventh centuries. Some, such as attempts by Vikings to establish settlements in Ulster during the mid-ninth and early tenth century, were not destined to be permanent or long lasting. In each local and specific case, as they gained a hold on new territories, the incoming settlers appear to have struck different balances between maintaining their ancestral affiliations and maritime links to the Viking world, and assimilating the ways of life and beliefs of their new neighbours. Traditional political loyalties, as well as identities and beliefs, were far more fluid than we might assume.

Vikings who raided and settled in the Irish Sea region from the eighth to the eleventh centuries left almost no contemporary written record themselves, apart from runic inscriptions, largely concentrated in the Isle of Man and Dublin, which rarely extend to more than a few words (below, Chapter 8). The earliest developed accounts of the period actually written in the Norse language are the Icelandic sagas of two to three centuries later (their historical accuracy for the Viking period has endlessly been debated, but is coming back into fashion again after a long period of scepticism). The main source of information on Vikings is found in contemporary Irish, Anglo-Saxon and Welsh annalistic sources, which sometimes mention the same events and therefore corroborate each other. The annalists were supportive of their own rulers and patrons and therefore tended to produce oppositional and coloured accounts of Viking activity. These are complex sources which use and re-use many versions of events: the Irish annals have recently been synthesised to reconstruct what may originally have been a 'Chronicle of Ireland',[21] but this unified concept remains contentious amongst historians. Charters sometimes obliquely mention 'pagans' or 'pirates' without giving any further information (below, Chapter 4). To these we may add histories of varying reliability, composed after the Norman Conquest of England, such as those of William of Malmesbury, Simeon of Durham, and 'Florence' (John) of Worcester. Even so, large areas of the Irish Sea region remained in the historical shadows. The British kingdom of Strathclyde, which dominated the area from the River Clyde to the Solway Firth, has left little documentary record of its own, having been eclipsed in the eleventh century by the Scottish Kingdom of Alba. The Isle of Man leaves perhaps the most intriguing gap in the early historical record. Its long association with the Scottish Isles, which ended in 1266, has led many historians to assume that kings of *Innse Gall* (the islands of foreigners) mentioned in the 960s and 970s may have ruled the island (below, Chapter 3), but the Isle of Man's own Scandinavian dynasty is not recorded until the mid-eleventh century.

Warfare and dynastic competition provide an essential historical dimension to the period, which has been amply and ably covered by other recent writers.[22] The ebb and flow of high politics provides only one aspect of the picture, however. We may know who succeeded whom and the date of victories and defeats, but we struggle to find comparably informative historical accounts of the lives of lesser-ranking people, and of the topography and economy of the Irish Sea region in the Viking period. Domesday Book, composed in 1086, provides a record of English towns and manorial lordship on the eve of, and just after, the Norman Conquest. Somerset, Gloucestershire and Cheshire (which included the land between Mersey and Ribble and parts of eastern Wales) received county coverage. Under the entry for Yorkshire are the parts of central Lancashire and southern Cumbria that had previously been linked to the Kingdom of Northumbria. Domesday also provides an early historical validation for the date of place-names in the areas that it covers. Place-names are perhaps the most obvious remaining trace of Vikings in the landscape of modern Britain and the Isle of Man, and Ireland, although to a far lesser extent in the latter (*4*). The reason for this imbalance is not necessarily a mismatch of original settlement, but an indication of the different extents and ways in which Scandinavian terms have survived in different languages in later centuries.

Place-names may be divided into topographic names that denote landscape or coastal features (but which sometimes also apply to settlements), and habitative names exclusively denoting settlement. Apart from those listed in Domesday, most habitative place-names are not recorded historically until the the fourteenth or fifteenth centuries or later. Topographic names reflect the entry of Norse terms into area dialects or those of specialist occupations such as upland farming or seafaring (below, Chapter 4). Lacking the legal status of landholdings, these tend to be referred to in documents much later and are therefore harder to pin down to a specific date of origin. However, patterns of density, even of very minor topographic names, can help us to identify some of the areas where Scandinavian speakers have been more predominant in the past. Scandinavian place-names in Cumbria, Lancashire and Cheshire became fixed and accepted within the Medieval English dialects spoken in these areas, whereas in other parts of the Irish Sea region, notably Ireland and Galloway, the resurgence of Celtic languages in the Middle Ages tended to overlay and even to oust them, potentially deceiving us as to the extent of the original Viking influence on those areas. Curiously, the Isle of Man remains a halfway house with numerous Norse settlement names remaining in use, yet with a Gaelic native tongue. We are reminded that, as Vikings assimilated themselves amongst the existing populations around the Irish Sea, their input changed rapidly from a 'pure' Scandinavian one to a 'hybrid' mixture with local influences (*5*). After the mid-ninth century we are looking not for 'Viking colonists', but for 'Anglo-Scandinavian', 'Hiberno-Scandinavian', 'Hiberno-Norse', or even 'Cambro-Norse' people, who largely (but perhaps not completely) had 'gone native'. The dangers of relying on any or all of these multiple definitions are clear. 'Hiberno-Norse' is perhaps the commonest, and is used in some cases as shorthand to describe any form of Viking-Irish convergence, but is also (and perhaps more correctly) used to denote the later period of Scandinavian involvement in Ireland, from at least the later tenth century onwards. In this respect it resembles the use of the term 'Late Norse' in Scotland to denote the period of continuing Scandinavian rule in the Western and Northern Isles and Caithness after the eleventh century.

Where did the original Viking settlers come from? Certainly they did not all come from the same place. Norse Vikings from the shadowy kingdom of *Laithlinn*, possibly associated with south-western Norway (below, Chapter 2), were certainly active in ninth-century Ireland, but oxygen isotope evidence from Dublin (below, Chapter 5) confirms that two young males, born not in Norway but probably in Atlantic Scotland, were represented amongst the dead of early Viking Dublin. We have, however, to admit that we remain as yet unsure whether the Viking settlers came as small, probably elite groups, or as a larger folk-migration. Nor are we entirely certain as to the relative proportions of males and females who came from Scandinavia. Raghnall Ó Floinn estimated in 1998, based on the known sample of around 80–90 furnished Viking graves known from the Dublin area, that ten per cent of these were female.[23] It is not quite such a straightforward assumption to make on present evidence that these were all women of Scandinavian origin, but such a figure suggests that females represented a small but important proportion of higher-status individuals amongst the Viking population. The relative proportions of males and females who were not of Scandinavian biological origin, but who were accorded Viking burial rites at death, remains a fascinating and as-yet unquantifiable factor. The persistence of the Old Norse language and personal names into

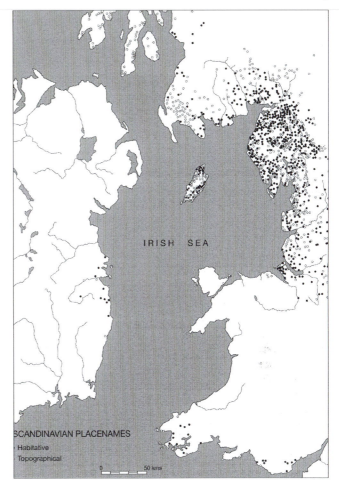

4. Scandinavian place-names, mapped from the publications of Gillian Fellows-Jensen and others

the twelfth century and beyond is perhaps an indication that the original settlers were relatively numerous, or these could owe some of their continued prominence to traditions stemming from the high rank of their originators.

Recent analysis of Y-chromosomal DNA from separately sampled populations of men from Wirral and West Lancashire with surnames recorded in documents from those regions prior to 1600, point towards up to fifty per cent Scandinavian ancestry in the male population admixture. By contrast, a similar study on a population of men from Ireland carrying Norse surnames showed relatively little trace of Scandinavian ancestry.[24] Data from Iceland (which as a place of subsequent migration, could be seen as a historical reflector of conditions in western Britain and Ireland) also suggests an emphasis on Scandinavian descent in the male line, but the Icelandic mitochondrial DNA data suggests a more 'Celtic' dominated female population.[25] Historical and biological indicators suggest that many Viking males took Irish, Scottish or Welsh wives. Particularly in cultures tolerant of polygamy, as that of pre-Christian Scandinavia may have been, fewer individual males are necessary to drive population expansion in relation to numbers of females. Projected proportions of males of Scandinavian descent in the general Medieval population in north-west England are therefore arguably significant but not overwhelming, and are perhaps to be seen as evidence of the effect of a more selective number of individuals with high reproductive potential. What DNA population sampling cannot tell us is precisely when, or how suddenly, these influences appeared in the ancestry of the modern population, nor if they were accompanied by cultural identities that matched their biology.

5. Wirral place-names: road sign at
Caldy Crossroads

To detect the extent of the early Viking presence, we must cross-reference critically all of the types of evidence available to us: this is a fundamentally interdisciplinary challenge.[26] Archaeological evidence, such as furnished burials, hoards and finds, assists us in pinning down the location of early landholdings, of economic activity, and of artistic and technological change. Runic inscriptions, and later forms of the incised linear alphabet known as Ogham, are found on stone, on wood, and occasionally on small, portable objects (below, Chapter 8). Many of the ancient parish churches around the Irish Sea house collections of stone monuments found nearby or within their bounds. Some, such as Gosforth, Cumbria (**cover**) have collections of such distinctive character that they have been labelled 'schools'. Viking-period stone sculpture includes complete and fragmentary standing crosses, recumbent grave-slabs, and the long-house-shaped monuments known as 'hogbacks', which were probably grave markers although few have been found in direct association with burials. Art and inscriptions are particularly valuable for helping us to chart changing cultures and beliefs, and in the case of stone monuments, their territorially rooted and publicly visible character maintains a vital link to place and landscape, and artistic patronage on the part of local rulers.

One major area of continuing disappointment is the limited archaeological evidence for rural agricultural settlement. Buildings, field systems, and evidence for environmental exploitation and modification have all been notoriously difficult to identify and pin down to specific innovations of the Viking period. A major problem we face with the archaeological evidence is our general inability to establish a precise date for the origins of Scandinavian rural settlement in the absence of historical evidence. With rare, recently excavated exceptions such as Cherrywood, Co. Dublin (below, Chapter 4), rural sites with buildings or artefacts of Scandinavian character or influence have not produced substantive evidence more closely datable than to a hundred year range within the period 800–1100. However, towns and trading sites have produced a wealth of structural evidence, in Dublin and Chester in particular. The ancient coastal settlement at Meols, near Chester, functioned as a beach market throughout the Viking period and beyond. At Woodstown, Co. Waterford, and at Llanbedrgoch, Anglesey, trading and manufacturing settlements have recently been discovered, the existence of which was previously unsuspected. The monastery of Whithorn in Galloway saw a small trading and manufacturing community develop in the eleventh century, which seems to have been related to contemporary Dublin. Bristol, Wexford, Waterford, Cork and Limerick have produced very limited evidence for urbanisation before the mid-eleventh century, but grew to be substantial trading settlements from the twelfth century onwards (and hence a review of their fully developed archaeological character, as for later Hiberno-Norse and Anglo-Norman Dublin and post-Conquest Chester, is somewhat outside the chronological remit of this book).

CHAPTER 2

RAIDS AND EARLY SETTLEMENT IN IRELAND

In 795, two years after the raid on Lindisfarne off Northumbria's east coast, the *Annals of Ulster* record the burning of *Rechru* (OI *Rechrann*) 'o genntibh' - by the 'gentiles' or 'heathens'. Two islands can be identified with the ancient name *Rechru*: Rathlin Island, off the north Co. Antrim coast near the mouth of the North Channel, and Lambay, off the north Co. Dublin coast. A possible echo of *Rechrann* survives in the parish name Portrane, which covers both Lambay and an adjoining portion of the mainland. Both Rathlin and Lambay have traces of an early Christian monastery, and both have attracted advocates as being the location of the raid. A third possibility, Ram's Island in inland Lough Neagh, was identified alongside the other two by Richard Warner,[1] but may be considered less likely on the grounds of its inaccessibility from the northern sea routes.

Further plundering in 795, reported by the *Annals of Inisfallen*, occurred on the west coast of Ireland at Inishmurray and Inishbofin, but gentiles or heathens are not specifically mentioned there.[2] In 798 St Patrick's Isle or Holmpatrick was burned by the heathens (*combustio Inis Phátraic o genntibh*) and the shrine of *Do-Chonna* was broken. Holmpatrick was almost certainly the place of that name in Co. Dublin, near Lambay, although there have been some suggestions, now largely discounted, that it could have been St Patrick's Isle at Peel, Isle of Man.[3] These events were accompanied by wider looting and extortion of cattle tribute, and 'great incursions both in Ireland and in Alba'.[4] The latter part of the report perhaps implies greater numbers and more extensive involvement on land than could be accounted for by a short and destructive seaborne raid.

The attacks of the 790s were, however, far from the first recorded seaborne attacks on the Atlantic fringes of Britain and Ireland. Seaborne raids from the Irish Sea were a problem for later Roman Britain in the third and fourth centuries, when a string of Roman coastal fortifications with renewed communications was constructed at Cardiff, Caernarfon, Holyhead and Lancaster.[5] For 617, the *Annals of Ulster* recorded the burning of Donnán on Eigg in the Hebrides, with 'one hundred and fifty martyrs', and in the same year a slaughter occurred on Tory Island off Co. Donegal. There is no suggestion that the raiders of Eigg or Tory were Scandinavians, but the entries show that seaborne raids, involving considerable casualties, had occurred long before the traditional start of the Viking period in the 790s.

The Irish raids of the 790s occurred alongside a spate of similar activity on the west coast of Scotland, and there is every reason to suppose the two were connected. Alex Woolf, in a recent review of Viking raiding, has suggested that the Vikings who attacked Ireland in 795 and 798

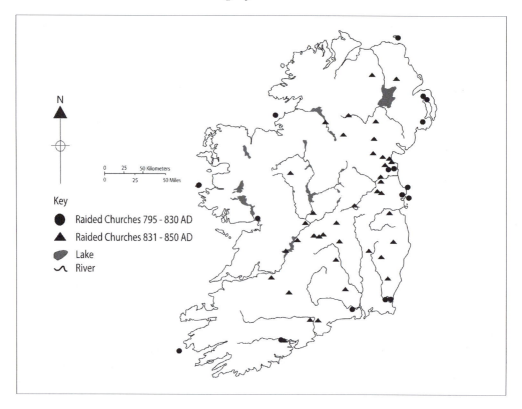

Key

● Raided Churches 795 - 830 AD
▲ Raided Churches 831 - 850 AD
🖝 Lake
〜 River

6. Viking raids on churches in Ireland

were probably the same group, or at least closely associated with, the attackers of Lindisfarne, and also 'the three ships of northmen from Horðaland', which had slaughtered the king's reeve (at Portland, Dorset), as recorded in the *Anglo-Saxon Chronicle* for 789.[6] The reference to *Rechru* in the *Annals of Ulster* is tied to a reference to the laying waste of *scrī*, normally translated as 'Scí', (The Isle of) Skye, although this has recently been questioned and the alternative *scrin* ('shrine') proposed, which could be taken instead as a reference to the destruction of the shrine at *Rechru*.[7] Less ambiguous reports occur in the *Annals of Ulster* for 802 and 806 of attacks on the great Columban monastery at Iona, the latter raid being a massacre of sixty-eight by the heathens. The following year Abbot Cellach moved to construct a new *civitas* for the monastery on land given by Armagh at Kells, Co. Meath, and to re-locate the monastic community into what must briefly have seemed comparatively safe inland pastures.

After 807, the next mention of raids in any of the Irish annals is in 821, when Beggerin and *Dairinis Cáemáin* (possibly in Wexford Harbour), were plundered. The years 823–25 saw severe raids on monasteries at Bangor, Downpatrick and Movilla in north-east Ireland. Lusk and Clonmore on the east coast were raided in 827–8. At this time there were also the beginnings of concerted Irish resistance and a growing military flavour to the conflict: in 825 the Ulaid of eastern Ulster inflicted a defeat on the heathens in Mag Inis, and the Osraige were routed by heathens in the same year, whereas an encampment of the Laigin was overwhelmed by the heathens in 827. It is interesting that in the mid-820s the *Annals of Ulster* begin to use the word *gaill* (foreigners) alongside, and as an alternative to, *gennti*, perhaps indicating that the nature of the challenge posed by the invaders had by that stage taken on an ethnic as well as a religious dimension in the minds of the Irish. From the beginning of the 830s there are increasingly detailed and extensive annalistic reports of attacks throughout the eastern and central areas of Ireland, with amongst others the monasteries of Armagh, Glendalough and Kildare being raided on a repeated basis, sometimes several times in the same year. There was also a shift in the 830s away from largely coastal raids to more inland involvement (**6**).

It is not easy to distil a broad synthesis of historical development from a succession of glimpses of sudden and chaotic events, yet events in the 830s point to Vikings becoming an increasingly long-term and numerous presence in Ireland. What had begun as a series of external attacks carried out from bases elsewhere, probably in Scotland or Norway, by the end of the 830s had taken on the character of a locally resourced and semi-regular role in the ancient and ongoing internal power struggle in Ireland. The events of the 830s, whatever their unsavoury character, must have introduced greatly increased contact between the Irish and their (largely) unwelcome visitors, and seem inexorably to point towards semi-permanent settlement and cultural intermingling, which was characteristic of the Viking presence in the middle and later ninth century.

It is now many years since the Vikings or heathens have been seen by Irish commentators as an exclusively destructive and alien force wreaking sudden terror upon a pure and righteous Christian country. The ancestral self-image of newly independent Ireland in the early to mid-twentieth century was one of Celtic prestige and serenity, contrasting sharply with the barbarism of the invading foreigner. Yet a cursory reading of any of the annals in the eighth century reveals the extent to which early Irish society was internally and often violently divided. Battles were commonplace as secular rulers pressed rival claims to territory and resources, and indeed the church itself was riven with violent disputes that sometimes escalated into slaughter. Hostage-taking and cattle-raiding, accompanied by wanton slaughter, were also present in pre-Viking Ireland, and doubtlessly also in pre-Viking Britain, although here the nature of the sources is less explicit. Endemic violence continued at varying pace throughout the ninth, tenth and eleventh centuries, drawing in Vikings as allies, clients, mercenaries, and even victims, to what were essentially internecine conflicts. Vikings seem to have learned some of their infamous tactics (such as enslaving or ransoming captives) not so much from established customary behaviour in the Scandinavian homelands, but from experiencing a rush of new opportunities in Ireland and elsewhere in Western Europe.

A wind of revisionist thinking on the Viking presence began to blow through Irish history in the 1960s with an article by A.T. Lucas, which pointed out some (to some at that time, uncomfortable) facts about the indigenous climate of division and violence prevalent in Ireland, thereby countering the prevalent view that the Vikings were new, unusual or even unique in their predilection for pillage and slaughter.[8] Even so, the heathenism of the Vikings does seem to have been a new and disturbing factor which rated repeated mention in the annals, particularly concerning their apparent lack of scruple about attacking and destroying the holiest relics and shrines in churches and monasteries. In some extreme cases, an appetite for sacrilege extended to what can only be described as sadistic attacks on Christians.[9] Some of these were on the most isolated and ascetic communities, where there could have been little hope of pecuniary reward, although their associations with Irish dynasties may have also been a reason to attack them. The notorious raid on the tiny monastery high upon the precipitous Atlantic island of Skellig Michael, which was recorded by the *Annals of Ulster* for 824, is a case in point. The abbot, Étgal, was carried off (taken hostage) by the heathens and 'died shortly afterwards from hunger and thirst.'[10]

The texts described above are generally clear about location and date (assuming the place-name given is recognisable in modern terms), and sometimes mention burning, hostages and the destruction of shrines. There are, however, chronological and geographical emphases, biases, and gaps in the historical record of Viking raiding that caution us against 'absence of evidence being evidence of absence'. Periods of apparent relief when no raids are mentioned may be misleading. Colmán Etchingham has contributed a useful statistical study of the patterns of raiding on the Irish church in the ninth century.[11] He points out that the twelfth-century saga-history *Cogadh Gáedhel re Gaillaibh* ('The war of the Irish with the Foreigners'), despite the fact that it is generally reputed to be a less reliable record than the annals, contains references to raids in the periods (e.g. 807–21) when other sources are silent, and that these are likely to have had some basis in substance. Etchingham's study excludes secular raids, which, given the powerful bias amongst documentary sources towards the church, are already likely to have been under-reported in

7. Inchmarnock 'Hostage Stone'

comparison. Moreover, there were significant regional biases in the coverage provided by the ecclesiastical sources. Reports of raids, when seen against the background of other regular annalistic entries such as ecclesiastical obits, put the emphasis in annalistic coverage clearly upon Leinster, especially the central/eastern part of Ireland between Meath and Wexford, and what Etchingham terms the 'Shannon/Brosna Basin' in the south/central midlands. The annals were evidently under-reporting other areas of Ireland, as, for example, between 831–850, almost no raids are reported west of the Shannon. With the exception of the early raids on Bangor and repeated attacks on Armagh, few confrontations are reported from Ulster throughout the rest of the ninth century.

The bias of surviving information in the documentary record – clearly towards Ireland, but then only towards *some parts* of Ireland and neglectful of others – raises the question: to what extent was the rest of the Irish Sea region affected by the same forces and movements which are known to us primarily through Irish texts? It seems unlikely that a sustained frenzy of attacks covering a wide swathe of Ireland, reported upon in the 830s, could have been entirely free of any entanglement whatsoever with the neighbouring lands across the sea to the east. The possibility that the *Inis Phátraic* of 798 could have been St Patrick's Isle at Peel on the Isle of Man has been mentioned above, but is generally discounted because of the lack of other such references in the Irish annals to places outside Ireland, and because there is an eminently plausible Irish alternative. Yet the coasts of south-west Scotland, the Isle of Man, north-west England and Wales had exposed ecclesiastical sites, perhaps not so many as Ireland or so wealthy, but which in situation and content were in many ways similar. For instance, the monastery at Maughold, Isle of Man, was substantial and already had connections with Irish counterparts. For the raiders themselves, a sheltered Manx bay or a Welsh tidal creek seemed an obvious alternative to an Irish river mouth for temporary shelter and recuperation.

If there were any raids or Viking landfalls on the eastern seaboard of the Irish Sea in the late eighth or early ninth centuries, such contemporary sources as there are (e.g. *Annales Cambriae*) are silent on the matter, with the first recorded trouble with Vikings occurring in Wales only as late as 850 (below, Chapter 3). Even later secondary sources are mute on the possibility of any such event. An extraordinary and so-far unique piece of pictorial evidence of a possible Viking raid was discovered etched on a slate from the early Christian site on Inchmarnock, a small island off the Isle of Bute in the upper Firth of Clyde, during excavations in 2001–2 (**7**). The 'Hostage Stone', as it quickly became known, depicts four human figures, three of which are wearing mail armour, and the fourth of whom (possibly a monk) is seemingly being led towards the boat.[12]

'Insular' material, mostly fine gilded metalwork of Irish ecclesiastical origin, has surfaced as single finds on the shores of Morecambe Bay, Wales and Cumbria (below, Chapter 6), and is found in much greater quantity in Norwegian graves of the ninth and tenth centuries.[13] This

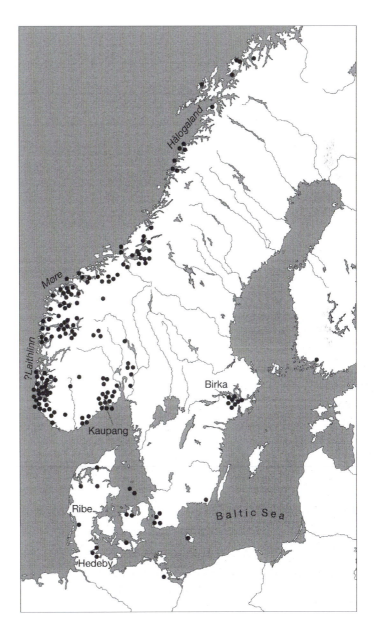

8. British/Irish 'insular' objects found in Viking-period graves in Scandinavia

material includes parts of (and in some cases complete) reliquary boxes, book mounts, ornate bowls and chalices, clearly of Christian origin. It is clear that such material, even in fragmentary form, had a powerful allure for regional Scandinavian elites, who in previous centuries had amassed Roman gold, gilt and silver finery for use in their own world of northern paganism and chiefdom politics (*8*). A trade grew up in stolen goods: the trading settlements of Ribe (Denmark), Kaupang (Norway) and Hedeby (formerly Denmark, now Germany) have all produced finds of such material in market and trading contexts (below, Chapter 6). Where disunity exists, so does opportunity, and Vikings were consummate opportunists to whom raiding and trading were interdependent activities.

Longphort and *dún*: the Viking base on land

Raids increased in ferocity and in geographical penetration of the Irish interior in the early 830s. The year 836 marks a further change in the scale of Viking activity reported in the annals, with raids in Kildare, Brega, Carlow and Connacht. In 837, sixty ships of Norsemen were reported on the Boyne and on the Liffey.[14] The Carlow raid (on Clonmore) occurred on Christmas Eve 836, which led the historian Donnchadh Ó Corráin to suggest that the raiders were already overwintering by this time, perhaps on offshore islands, and stressed the importance of captives and slavery in the developing scenario.[15] It is clear that such levels of involvement could not be sustained without at least semi-permanent land-bases at which ships could be repaired, stores replenished and captives imprisoned. Unlike the more sporadic raiding patterns of the 790s and early 800s, these more frequented landing places could not feasibly have been several days' sail away, but would have had to exist at accessible points on the periphery of Irish territory. One such location could have been Dalkey Island, at the southern limit of Dublin Bay, which had been an offshore (probably seasonal) trading site since the fifth century (below, Chapter 6). It was attested as a location for the holding of hostages in the tenth century, when an Abbot, Coibdenach of *Cill-achaidh*, was drowned escaping from the foreigners.[16]

   The first mention of a Viking base at a named place in Ireland is at *Inber Deá* (possibly somewhere near the mouth of the Avoca River at Arklow, Co. Wicklow) from which the 836 raid on Kildare was mounted.[17] The Irish term *longphort* (OI 'ship-fortress', plural: *longphuirt*) was applied in 841 to *Linn Duachaill* (Linns, Annagassan, Co. Louth). Dublin was mentioned in 841, and also termed a *longphort*. Annagassan lies between the mouth of the River Boyne and the coastal havens of Carlingford Lough and Strangford Lough to the north. Dublin, on or close to the existing Irish settlement of *Áth Cliath* ('the ford of the wattles'), lies on the tidal estuary of the River Liffey. There are signs in historical references from the early 840s onwards that Vikings were setting up camps and bases for ships alongside rivers, inlets and loughs in several strategic locations in Ireland. In the north-west, a naval force on Lough Swilly (Co. Donegal) is mentioned in 842; Lough Neagh in the centre of Ulster in 839–841; and Carlingford Lough in 852. In the midlands and east, apart from Arklow, Dublin and Annagassan (mentioned above), there was a group at Rosnaree, Co. Meath (842), and one led by *Tuirgéis* (below, Chapter 3) on Lough Ree (844–5). Further south and west, Limerick was a ship-base in 845, and Cork is mentioned in 848 and again in 867. In 860, we hear of Waterford (mentioned again in 892). The turnaround in historical fortune which saw the Vikings become the victims of sustained attack in the later ninth century reveals further named sites, some of which may already have been in existence for several decades. A *longphort* at Dunrally, Co. Laois, on the River Barrow (which meets the sea near Waterford), was destroyed in 862, as was a *longphort* at Youghal on the south coast in 866. In 867 the *Annals of Ulster* note the burning of Amlaíb's (Óláfr's) Fort at Clondalkin, Co. Dublin, and another site on the Barrow at St Mullins, Co. Carlow, was destroyed in 892. A base in Wexford was mentioned in 892, and Strangford Lough and Lough Foyle in 879 and 898 respectively.[18]

   The term *longphort* is not used consistently, and not all Viking camps are named as such – some others are referred to using the term *dún*. This term is used in the *Annals of Ulster* in the year 845

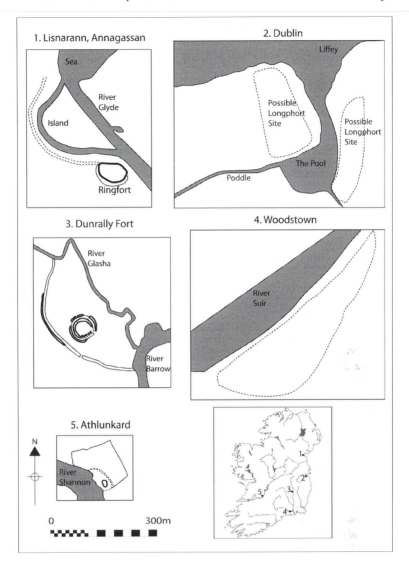

9. Longphort
Comparison

to describe Dublin and its satellite camp at *Cluain Andobair* (Cloney, Co. Kildare).[19] What do these terms denote? Can we even be sure that they had any fixed meaning? Some of the sites mentioned were evidently occupied for very short periods, even down to a few days, taking advantage of natural defensive features such as islands or bends in rivers, with their occupation leaving little or no recognisable archaeological trace in the landscape. Others became the nucleus from which more extensive and long-term occupation grew.

Many such sites mentioned in annalistic sources have yet to be identified on the ground, including some (e.g. Youghal, Cork and Limerick) where the presence of a later town obscures and complicates the archaeological picture. Those probable *longphort* or *dún* sites that remain in rural settings could therefore provide perhaps the most straightforward impression of their initial form (*9*). At Linns, Annagassan, a small but prominently sited D-shaped earthwork ring-fort, measuring 73m by 34m, known as Lisnarann ('fort of the promontory') overlooks a small eyot and sheltered anchorage close to the mouth of the River Glyde as it enters Dundalk Bay. This is a tempting, but perhaps not conclusive, identification as the *longphort* first mentioned in 841. The earthworks here could also be of native Irish origin. An early monastic site is located less than 500m to the north-east of the earthwork, and in a field in its immediate vicinity, two decorated copper-alloy mounts, one of which is enamelled, have been found.[20] Ó Floinn argued that these (Irish) objects had been looted by Vikings and were apparently intended to be refashioned into brooches. The vicinity has not so far produced any Scandinavian burials. More fieldwork would be required to demonstrate a definite link between the earthwork fortification and the *longphort*, which could equally well be associated with the monastery, as also seems to be the case at St Mullins.

The Dunrally (Co. Laois) *longphort* was mentioned in the *Annals of the Four Masters* (*Longphort Rothlaib,* 'the longphort of Rudolf') as having been destroyed in September 862 by Cennétig, the local King of Lóigis.[21] A probable site on the west bank of the River Barrow near Vicarstown was tentatively identified by the antiquarian John O'Donovan in the 1830s, and received further archaeological attention from Eamonn P. Kelly and others in the 1990s.[22] It is located on a bend of the river, alongside a tributary, the Glasha, which forms one side of the site. A low bank and ditch earthwork encloses a D-shaped area 360m NW-SE by 150m SW-NE fronting the Glasha. Towards the centre of the large enclosure is a more pronounced oval earthwork with a raised interior measuring 52m by 41m, surrounded by a water-filled ditch and a counterscarp bank. The investigators suggested that the marshy ground protectively surrounding the site would have been at its driest in early autumn, possibly explaining the date of the successful attack. The easily navigable Barrow seems to have been something of a Viking highway in ninth-century Ireland, connecting a chain of vulnerable monasteries and rich local kingdoms far into the south-east midlands.

The plan of Dunrally, comprising a large outer D-shaped riverside enclosure, marked by an earthwork or minor watercourse, with a smaller round or oval-shaped stronghold within, seems to be echoed in riverside camps elsewhere in the western Viking world. Kelly suggested a parallel in a Viking fortification on the River Dyle, near Louvain, Belgium, which was destroyed in 891. This broad form is echoed in several sites on the major rivers of central and eastern England which have in the past been tentatively associated with ninth- and tenth-century Viking activity, such as at Stonea Camp, Wimblington, Cambridgeshire, and Church Spanel, Shillington, Bedfordshire.[23] A more convincingly demonstrated example of a winter camp dating to 873–4 on the River Trent at Repton, Derbyshire has a D-shaped enclosure measuring 70m by 55m, a size which is more comparable with the inner stronghold at Dunrally.[24] Associated burials and structures lie outside the ditch defences at Repton, and this begs the question as to whether there may once have been a much larger and less well-defined outer enclosure there too.

Another (somewhat smaller) possible *longphort* site has been identified at a bend on the River Shannon, at Athlunkard, Co. Clare, on the northern outskirts of Limerick City. This also makes use of the main river and a small tributary to form two sides of a D-shaped outer enclosure measuring 75m by 30m, surrounding an oval, flat-topped mound (22m by 12m) which survives 0.4m above the surrounding ground surface.[25] Like Dunrally, it is surrounded by marshy ground. Unusually (despite excavation not yet having taken place) there are a number of potentially significant finds associated with the site including an iron ring from the interior, and an axe and two silver ingots from its vicinity. The name Athlunkard embodies *longphort* with *Áth* (OI 'ford'), although this is not necessarily a good guide to the presence of a Viking site. *Longphort* is applied (usually in the modern anglicised form 'Longford') to many locations which otherwise need have no particular early Viking association, and is liable to be confused with later fortifications such as Anglo-Norman earthwork castles. Athlunkard's claim to Viking *longphort* status has been questioned, although it remains one of the more convincing examples.[26] Kelly associated Athlunkard with a two-year Viking campaign on the Shannon in the mid-840s, perhaps as a staging post on the way inland to the *longphort* on Lough Ree in the upper Shannon, founded in 845. A possible site on the south side of the lough at Ballaghkeeran Little was identified by the late Tom Fanning in the 1970s. This consists of a marshy triangular area protruding into the lough, measuring approximately 200m by 100m, defended by low banks on the landward side. It has the remains of an apparently ancient wooden jetty and a feature interpreted as a possible boat naust. Excavation by Fanning was inconclusive, but more recent finds of gold and silver nearby have revitalised the possibility that this was a *longphort* (below, Chapter 6).[27]

Significantly, all of the five locations that would later see the growth of towns (Dublin, Cork, Limerick, Waterford and Wexford) were associated with river-camps before 900. However, to therefore assume continuity of site location is fraught with pitfalls. Cork, mentioned as a *dún* in 848,[28] is an archaeologically unproven case, not unlike Limerick, in that a likely site was on one of the low-lying estuarial islands that formed the commercial focus of the later town (which became demonstrably urbanised only from the mid-eleventh century onwards). An alternative and equally unproven site is the hill overlooking Cork, dominated by the monastery and cathedral of St Finbar. Wexford has produced good, if limited, evidence for eleventh- and twelfth-century urbanisation (below, Chapter 7), but despite speculation, the site of the camp mentioned in 892 has yet to be identified.

Waterford, on the River Suir close to its confluence with the Barrow, is mentioned in 860 when *loinges Puirt Láirge* (the fleet of Waterford) was defeated by the King of Osraige. Excavations in Waterford City (below, Chapter 7) revealed no significant remains earlier than the mid-eleventh century, with the emphasis in urbanisation falling upon the later eleventh and twelfth centuries. The location of an early Viking fleet base close to the strategic Suir/Barrow confluence was a matter of inconclusive speculation until mid-2003, when a project to build a major new bypass road through the Suir valley brought about an archaeological evaluation of the planned route. On the river bank at Woodstown, 8 km upstream from Waterford, test trenching in 2003–2005 (initially by machine and then selectively by hand) revealed over 600 features including pits, hearths, stake-holes, post-holes and kilns.[29] Geophysical investigation confirmed that a line visible on aerial photographs was a ditched enclosure defining an area 460m in length, forming an elongated D-shape along the south-east bank of the Suir. Within the interior of the enclosure, post-hole alignments visible in trial trenches were interpreted as parts of oval and rectangular houses and industrial structures.

10. Woodstown finds: a silver ingot, decorated and polyhedral weights, amber beading and a Kufic coin fragment

Over 4600 finds from the network of features in the trial trenches, including a furnished Viking burial (below, Chapter 5), left no doubt as to the predominance of the early Viking period (*10*). Domestic artefacts included hones, pins, a gaming piece, amber beads, knives, decorated bone and spindle whorls. Iron clench bolts, widespread amounts of iron slag, and fragments indicating craft working in stone, bone, antler and amber showed the presence of diverse industrial activities – of exactly the kind which would be needed in a base supplying a fleet and servicing a trading community in generally hostile territory. Melted silver, a Kufic coin, ingots and hack-silver indicate the presence of silver-working, perhaps linked to tribute payments or commerce, itself suggested by a small silver polyhedral weight of a type recognised in the Baltic region and the Danelaw. The metrology of a group of lead scale-pan weights is currently being studied.[30] A copper-alloy stud mount with gold foil decoration, and a gilded copper-alloy book clasp – both Irish-made fine objects – were argued by the excavators to be the possible result of monastic raiding.[31] On the basis of evidence procured so far, the inhabited area seems to have been abandoned before the mid-eleventh century (around the time that Waterford had begun to experience significant urbanisation), but the emphasis in the dates of the finds is firmly on the ninth century.

The archaeological evidence gained thus far at Woodstown is tantalising. The finds from the preliminary investigations are extremely rich, but as a result of deep ploughing, and the presence of a railway along the Suir waterfront, structural definition is limited and partial, and many essential questions about the site remain currently unanswered. What was its internal plan in relation to settlement and industrial zones? Is there an inner stronghold within the outer enclosure? Are there more burials? Few details or images are yet available in the public domain, partly because the Woodstown site has been the subject of intense national and international controversy since its discovery. The original route of the bypass meant that much of the site would have been destroyed and replaced by concrete and tarmac, but a major public and academic campaign was mounted to save it. Its discovery coincided with the peak of the Irish Republic's road-building boom, which prompted a series of rancorous disputes over the preservation of archaeological monuments across Ireland. After much invective in the press, in 2005 the Irish government agreed to re-route the Waterford bypass to the south of the site, although controversy continued even about the revised route. Further archaeological investigations took place in 2006 and 2007, including an underwater survey of the riverbed, and another test excavation of an area that produced further Viking metalworking debris. The site is now protected as a national monument, and plans for further investigations await the production of a research design and an international conference planned for 2010.

The site of Dublin's *longphort* has been a matter of great uncertainty. Past suggestions have touched upon almost everywhere within the inner estuary of the Liffey, most notably west of the current city centre in the vicinity of the Kilmainham and Islandbridge Viking burials (below, Chapter 5), the existence of which has been widely known since the 1840s (see below). However, a major clue is in the name *Dubh-linn* ('black pool'), which is mentioned specifically as the location of the camp in the *Annals of Ulster* for 841. This takes on a more specific meaning when applied to the former pool in the River Poddle, a minor tributary of the River Liffey on its south side. The Poddle, now culverted underground, is almost invisible except as a slight dip in the modern urban topography. The site of the former pool is now dry. At its centre is a low-lying semicircular lawn to the rear (south) of the Medieval and Georgian architectural array of Dublin Castle, which until independence in 1922 was the seat of government in Ireland, and is probably on the site of the stronghold of the tenth- and eleventh-century town. The pool in its natural state formed a sheltered (if shallow and muddy) tidal haven. To the north, the Castle and the Temple Bar district lie between the pool and the Liffey.

Perceptions of 'Viking Dublin' have been heavily conditioned by the major discoveries in the 1960s and 1970s of tenth-, eleventh- and twelfth-century buildings and urban topography, in a large cluster of excavations around Christchurch Cathedral and Wood Quay (below, Chapter 7). Little or nothing of pre-tenth-century date was found on the sites in the Wood Quay district, and the '*longphort*' question was not answered at that time, as the archaeological sequence appeared

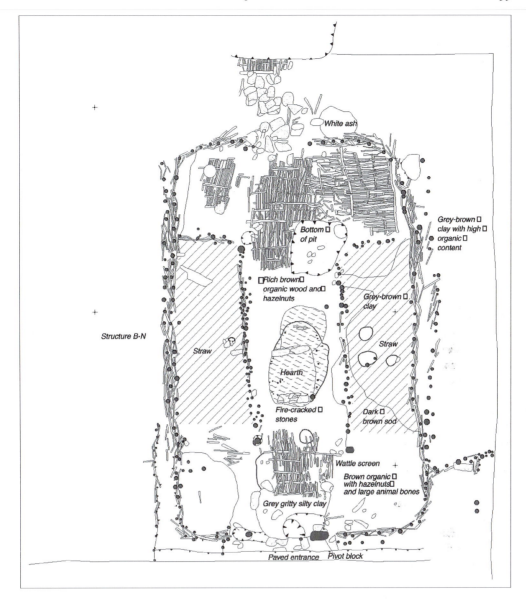

White ash

Grey-brown
clay with high
organic
content

Bottom
of pit

Rich brown
organic wood and
hazelnuts

Grey-brown
clay

Structure B-N

Straw

Straw

Hearth

Fire-cracked
stones

Dark
brown sod

Wattle screen

Brown organic
with hazelnuts
and large animal bones

Grey gritty silty clay

Paved entrance   Pivot block

11. Type 1 building plan, Temple Bar West

to confirm that post-917 Dublin had been founded on a new site. However, excavations nearer
the Poddle/Liffey confluence at Parliament Street and Temple Bar in the 1990s began to show a
stronger picture not only of ninth-century occupation, but of ninth- to tenth-century continuity. A former flood-bank along the Poddle was associated with three early sunken-floored wattle
structures, which were replaced by four houses aligned east-west towards the Poddle, radiocarbon
dated at eighty-two per cent probability to pre-917. The four houses had central hearths, side
benches and internal roof supports corresponding to Wallace's Type 1, a type that had hitherto
only been applied to buildings of the tenth century or later (**11**). These were surrounded by staked
wooden animal pens and irregular plot boundaries, indicating that occupation had become dense
and was on a more permanent basis than previously suspected. These buildings were partly refur-
bished later in the late ninth century, before the site witnessed a more extensive reorganisation in

the early tenth century, presumably coinciding with the new influx of settlers after 917. This is the first evidence to indicate some continuity of settlement through the period 902–917, even though this may have been only for a reduced and possibly lower-ranking element of the population in conditions of political adversity.[32]

Perhaps surprisingly, in view of the morphology of the other probable *longphort* sites, almost no evidence of ninth-century defences (above the status of flood banks at least) has yet been uncovered at Dublin. As a result, some scepticism continues as to whether the Temple Bar West and Parliament Street sites are genuine evidence of the *longphort,* or should perhaps be seen instead as extra-mural occupation of lesser importance. In this scenario, the Liffey Estuary could have had several linked satellite settlements of the *longphort* at strategic points, marked by discrete clusters of burials (below, Chapter 5). Until unambiguous evidence of ninth-century defences is found, the precise location and extent of the *longphort* itself are unlikely to be universally accepted (although in the opinion of this author, the site of Dublin Castle overlooking the pool is the most obvious possibility).

'Dark' and 'fair' foreigners, and the '*Gallgoídil*'

We do not know exactly who the raiders of Irish monasteries of the 790s and early 800s were, nor where they came from, although Alex Woolf suggests that the attackers of *Rechru* might have been the same group as the men of three ships from Horðaland who had recently caused unexpected strife at Portland, Dorset, when the reeve of Wessex was killed. When the 'foreigners' became a more familiar presence in Ireland, the details of their names and identities became of greater interest to the annalists. In 837 one 'Saxolb', chief of the foreigners, was killed by the Cianacht.[33] In 837, 'Turges' or 'Tuirgéis' was the leader of the encampment on Loch Ree, and was soon after taken prisoner and drowned, and 'Agnonn' (ON *Hákon*) was routed with 1,200 casualties by Cerball, son of Dungal in 847.[34] The annalists were beginning to treat 'foreign' chieftains as newsworthy personalities comparable with native kings and abbots, accustomed as they were to naming these and often adding a brief supporting note as to their patrimony. 'Tuirgéis', probably a translation of ON *Þurgestr,* became a hero-villain in Irish history, mainly due to the legendary and probably fantastical role he was accorded by the later history *Cogadh Gaedhel re Gallaibh* ('The War of the Irish with the Foreigners'), written as anti-Scandinavian propaganda for the descendants of Brian Bóru in the early twelfth century (below, Chapter 3). In this, Tuirgéis was described, amongst other probably embroidered exploits, as having desecrated the monastery of Clonmacnoise and made himself Abbot of Armagh.

Whatever the truth attached to these shadowy personalities, there can be little doubt that, as Viking activity in Ireland became more widespread and long term as deeper incursions were made into the interior of the island in the 830s and 840s, dynastic politics amongst the 'foreigners' themselves were fast-changing and developing. From the foundation of the permanent presence in Dublin in 841, there are increasing references to kingship and formal noble status amongst the newcomers. In 848 the Jarl 'Tomrair' (probably ON *Þorir*) was slain at Castledermot, Co. Kildare. He was described as *Tanist* (heir or deputy) to the King of *Laithlinn*.[35] The identity of *Laithlinn* (which may be the same kingdom later referred to as *Lochlainn* in Irish and *Llychlyn* in Welsh) has been the subject of heated debate amongst historians. There is no doubt that the term *Lochlainn* was used in later centuries to refer to Norway.[36] Was the *Laithlinn* of the mid-ninth century, therefore, a direct reference to Scandinavia? A persistent but not widely supported case against this has been made by Ó Corráin, who sees the shadowy entity as a Viking sea-kingdom of the Scottish Isles stretching from Orkney to the Hebrides, although he concedes that *Lochlainn* later referred to Norway.[37] Mary Valante has made a case that *Laithlinn* was located in Vestfold, the area of south-eastern Norway which was under Danish control in the mid-ninth century and has produced rich archaeological evidence from the trading centre of Kaupang (below, Chapter 7).[38] In the opinion of this author and numerous others, the most likely location is on the south-west coast of Norway, around the powerful Iron Age chiefdom centres of Avaldsnes on Karmøy, and Jaeren south of modern Stavanger – the area with Norway's densest concentration of insular material from ninth- and tenth-century graves (*8*).[39]

Emergent in annalistic accounts in the early 850s is a sense of political and dynastic division and competition amongst the groups of 'foreigners'. This cannot have been new, as there is no reason to suppose unity or commonality amongst Viking raiders of previous decades. However, at this stage, coincident with the development of *longphuirt* and alliances with Irish rulers, it does appear that certain leading groups of 'foreigners' were getting the upper hand to the point that they were becoming political rivals within the ongoing internal power-struggle in Ireland. Interventions by external forces added to the mix. In 852, the *Annals of Ulster* record:

> The dark heathens (*Dubh gennti*) came to *Áth Cliath* [Dublin], made a great slaughter of the fair foreigners (*Finn gaill*), and plundered the *longphort*; the dark heathens then made a raid on *Linn Duachaill* where many were slaughtered.

This is the first of many references to the 'dark' and 'fair' (often translated as 'black' and 'white') heathens (*gennti*) or foreigners (*gaill*), who are mentioned as such in both Britain and Ireland, indicating that this perception was widespread and lasting. It was accepted almost without question for many years amongst historians that dark/black and fair/white were ethnic denominators, on a general scale distinguishing Dane from Norwegian, or as Alfred Smyth argued, distinguishing the (dark) Danes of York (i.e. after the Viking takeover of the city in 876) from the (fair) Norse Vikings of the western isles and Ireland.[40] Further revisions have been contributed in recent years by David Dumville, amongst others.[41] Dumville argued, picking up an observation made by Smyth, that 'dark' and 'fair' within the Irish annalistic tradition are more appropriately to be seen as terms for 'new' and 'old'. Thus Dumville argued, supported by Clare Downham, that the dark foreigners were newcomers arriving in Ireland in the early 850s (Downham argued they were from *Laithlinn*) who attacked and subsequently imposed their rule on the burgeoning and increasingly intermixed *longphort* settlers.[42] Óláfr (OI *Amlaíb*), son of the kings of *Laithlinn* and brother of Ívarr (OI *Ímair*) (who would found a great dynasty of Dublin and York) received the submission of the foreigners in Ireland and tribute from the Irish in 853.

Óláfr's overlordship in Dublin soon drew him into violent conflict with the most assertive of neighbouring Irish kings, Máel Sechlainn, king of the southern Uí Néill, in a series of internal wars that lasted throughout the late 850s and early 860s. These ranged across much of eastern and southern Ireland and brought about alliances with powerful Irish magnates such as Áed Finnliath, king of the northern Uí Néill. A further group is identified in the annals in the late 850s as allied with Mael Sechlainn against Óláfr and Ívarr – the *Gallgoídil* – literally the 'foreigner-gaels'. This shadowy group, which is only identified between 856 and 858 until the name recurs again (in a different context) in 1034, has been the subject of much debate amongst historians.[43] Were they Irish people who had adopted Scandinavian ways, or Scandinavian settlers who had intermarried with the Irish and begun to speak Irish or Gaelic and raise 'mixed-race' families? The first sons of these, born in the early 840s, would have been of fighting age by the late 850s.[44] The *Gallgoídil* may perhaps be seen as the 'fair' foreigners in another guise. Their principal interest to the annalists was that they were distinct from, and opposed to, the 'dark' foreigners. This very minimal definition could potentially encompass people of both Irish and Scandinavian origins (indeed to stretch a point, perhaps even a few individuals of other origins such as English, Welsh or Pictish). Many traditional historical views of the *Gallgoídil* do not sufficiently appreciate the potential for ethnic convergence and the creation of new identities within individual lifetimes, even very early in the history of Viking activity in the west. These have mostly remained locked into a binary opposition of clearly defined categories of 'Viking' and 'native' – something which is an increasing hindrance to understanding as the depth and complexity of inter-communal relationships are becoming clearer (below, Chapter 8).

CHAPTER 3

EXPORTING VIOLENCE AND SEEKING LANDFALL c. 850–c. 1050

The 'dark' foreigners of Ireland, under Óláfr and Ívarr, together with Ásl, another foreigner king mentioned in 853, became thoroughly immersed in the internal Irish power-struggle. This, however, did not prevent them from exporting violence eastwards across the Irish Sea. Transporting a force of armed warriors by sea from Dublin to Anglesey would have taken little more than a full day's sail, and was therefore approximately equivalent in time to an overland march of only 10–15 miles (16–24km) at most. In 856 the *Annals of Ulster* record that Horm (ON *Ormr*), a chief of the dark foreigners, was killed by Rhodri Mawr (Rhodri 'the great'), son of Merfyn, King of Wales and Man.[1] This Welsh victory reversed attacks recorded by *Annales Cambriae* in 850 when a king named Cyngen or Cinnen was killed by heathens,[2] and in 853 came a more ominous and specific mention of 'black heathens' ravaging Anglesey. A charter granting lands along the Welsh border in Gloucestershire by the Mercian King Burgred in 855 mentions 'pagans' in the district of the Wrekin (Shropshire), although it makes no explicit link to dark foreigners.[3]

Rhodri Mawr's reign was characterised above all by conflict with the Mercians, who had destroyed the neighbouring royal house of Powys in the 850s and attacked Glywysing in south Wales and Gwynedd in 865,[4] the attack on the latter occasion being recorded in the *Annals of Ulster*, where the Britons are described as having been placed in bondage in Anglesey. Rhodri Mawr was killed by the English at Degannwy in 878, but the Welsh avenged his death in 881 with a victory over the English on the River Conwy. The next serious Viking inroad into Wales occurred in 893–4, not as a result of Irish Sea attacks, but as an extension of the exploits of the Danish 'great army' in England. A group under Hástein clashed unsuccessfully with Alfred's forces on the border at Buttington (Montgomeryshire) in 893, an event reported in the *Annals of Ulster* as one when 'countless multitudes fell'. Remnants of the defeated Viking force occupied the 'deserted city in Wirral which is called Chester' (**12**) for the winter of 893–4, presumably sheltering within the broken-down but still-substantial Roman walls.[5] They were chased out in 894, to raid and pillage in north Wales, before heading back towards the Viking-held east coast of England.

Lesser, unrecorded raids and skirmishes on either side of the Irish Sea by medium-ranking Viking leaders may have led on to more substantial campaigns where rulers became involved, which was usually the point at which events merited the attention of annalists. The Britons of Wales, Cumbria and south-west Scotland seem to have been a particularly vulnerable target. The opportunist nature of the attacks is clear: Mark Redknap has shown that from 850, the incidence

12. Chester from the air from North; the city walls echo the Roman plan

of Viking raids on Wales mirrors almost precisely in number and severity the incidence of English attacks or internal clashes reported in the Welsh annals.[6] The Viking presence in York, which they had initially entered in 866, became more firmly established from 876 onwards. Routeways connecting Northumbria to the Irish Sea through central Scotland and northern England took on greater strategic importance after this date, although Alex Woolf argues that the Forth-Clyde isthmus has been overrated and prefers to emphasise the importance of land routes directly east–west via the Pennine valleys.[7]

The Isle of Man, at the centre of the Irish Sea yet also often mist-shrouded and easily bypassed, may have held out against any Viking influence until the 870s, perhaps emboldened by its dynastic links with Gwynedd, but the death of Rhodri Mawr in 878 probably undermined its long-term chances of continuing to do so. The (admittedly weak) traditional historical consensus is that the Isle of Man probably became a Viking possession, or even possibly a kingdom in its own right, by the beginning of the tenth century, but the earliest historically attested link with Viking dynasties operating in the 'Isles' does not occur until the 940s. Clare Downham argues that British control of the island was not fully eliminated until after a raid on Anglesey by the Dublin Vikings in 918.[8]

Weakness and opportunity: Galloway and Cumbria

Throughout the Viking period in the west, increased resistance in one area was a factor in producing greater raiding and land-take elsewhere. It is likely that, during the later ninth century, documented raids and battles in Ireland were followed by raiding and some settlement on the British seaboard of the Irish Sea. This need not have been a major geographic departure from existing activity – the coast of Galloway, for instance, is easily inter-visible from the Down and Antrim coasts, and possession of territories there would have served the same purpose of overseeing and controlling the North Channel.

Can we find any evidence for Vikings attempting to force their way into possession of lands in south-west Scotland before 900? An intriguing possible hint of deliberate destruction at an ecclesiastical site was discovered during excavations in the 1980s at the early Christian monastic site of Whithorn in Galloway, which, although originally an early post-Roman British foundation, had since the early eighth century been an important western offshoot of the Anglian church of Northumbria. There was a clear discontinuity observed in the sequence of buildings and occupation between Periods II and III, marked by a fire and destruction layer that was dated by the excavator to 'probably around 845' (which, given the difficulties of obtaining a precise dating, could be a fair match for any time in the middle three or four decades of the ninth century). The existing church and adjacent burial chapel appear to have been stripped of their internal fittings after burning, and the church was arguably deconsecrated during a short intermission of occupation on the excavated site; nearby areas formerly used for domestic dwellings were put down to cultivation.[9]

The eventual replanning and rebuilding of Whithorn happened not in fact at the start of Period III, but some way into it, towards the end of the ninth century. Peter Hill, the excavator, tentatively associated the apparent mid ninth-century disaster with accounts of shaky authenticity mentioning the devastation of Galloway by Cináed MacAlpín, King of Alba. Perhaps Viking activity seemed to Hill to be too obvious an explanation for the Period II destruction layer, and unwilling to see Whithorn's reverse as merely a series of localised setbacks following an accidental fire, Hill took recourse instead to the internal narrative of Scottish History. Nonetheless, the site lies only 5.5km from the Irish Sea, and, given the apparent desecration of its church, and the Vikings' acknowledged presence upon the waters between Ireland and Scotland at this time, their involvement cannot so easily be discounted.

The involvement of Dublin Vikings in south-western Scotland gathered pace in the later 860s. In 866 Óláfr and Ásl, together with Scottish-based Vikings, invaded southern Pictland (the kingdom of Fortriu) and raided widely. In 870 Ívarr returned to the Irish Sea to join Óláfr, and the Dublin Vikings launched a devastating four-month siege on the British Kingdom of Strathclyde at *Alt Clut,* Dumbarton Rock, in the lower reaches of the Clyde. The attack on the great rock-citadel was a success, and the two leaders returned to Ireland the following year replete with booty and hostages. It opened the way to further involvement by the Dublin Vikings in central Scotland between the Clyde and Forth, which brought them into conflict with the Picts north of that area.[10]

The fortunes of Vikings in Ireland were on the turn at this point. The southern Viking camps at Dunrally and Youghal were defeated by the kingdom of Osraige in 862 and 866, and the raid on Óláfr's fortress at Clondalkin in 867 has already been noted in Chapter 2 (above). As Óláfr and Ásl raided Pictland, their erstwhile Irish ally Aed Finnliath began a comprehensive campaign to rid the lands of the northern Uí Néill of the foreigners. Ó Corráin has drawn attention to the reference in the *Annals of Ulster* for 866 to Aed taking away their 'flocks and herds' after conquering their strongholds in the north, suggesting this implies that they had extensive farmed lands at this point.[11] The evidence of the pagan graves from Counties Down and Antrim, which are coastal and unconnected to later burials (below, Chapter 5), does indeed suggest that a small number of short-lived Viking settlements along the Irish shores of the North Channel and Strangford Lough were probably brought to a premature end in the later ninth century, and not revived in the tenth.

'Galloway' is derived from *Gallgoídil*. Controversy surrounds its origin and date as the name for the south-westernmost corner of the Scottish mainland, including the Rhinns and Machars peninsulas. *Gallgoídil* resurfaced as a term in the 1030s, used in a broader sense to denote Norse-Gaelic peoples of western Scotland (some of whom at this time were linked politically to Dublin), but Galloway may not have acquired its current territorial meaning until as late as the twelfth century.[12] Cumbria, and the historic county name Cumberland, derive from *Cumbraland,* the Old English term for the Kingdom of Strathclyde, which echoes British or Old Welsh *Cymry.* The lands on either side of the Solway Firth fulfilled very well the definition of a political periphery. In contrast to Ireland and Wales, Strathclyde largely lacks a surviving documentary record, further

reducing the kingdom's historical profile. In the early tenth century, Strathclyde's notional boundaries stretched from the area around Dumbarton and Govan on the Clyde, to the north-western
edges of the Pennines, probably extending south to the River Eamont in Westmorland (Cumbria)
where its rulers met Æthelstan in 927.[13]

The collapse of Northumbria towards the end of the ninth century allowed the Strathclyde
Britons briefly to dominate areas on their southern fringes that had formerly been under
Northumbrian rule, and may already have seen some early Scandinavian settlement. Strathclyde's
hold on lands south of the Solway lasted a century at most, but it is still marked by dedications to
the British Saint Kentigern or Mungo, at Aspatria, Bromfield and Dearham. Sparse and spread-out
populations on either side of the Solway Firth existed within large and poorly defended British
and Anglian landholdings.[14] Opportunities for Vikings must have depended principally on local
circumstances – the varying ability of indigenous lords and abbots to hold together their estates
whilst maintaining nominal allegiance to their distant rulers. Some appear to have managed this;
others evidently did not. Such a weak and diffuse pattern of landed power presented the incomers
with an unrivalled opportunity for intrigue, conquest and land-take, by purchase, agreement or
merely by threat.

From Dublin to *Brunanburh*

A promising scenario for the Dublin Vikings in Scotland in the 860s and 870s was matched by
retrenchment, betrayal and defeat in Ireland. In retrospect, it can be seen that the chain of events
that led to the defeat of Dublin in 902 was already taking shape by the 860s. Ívarr died in 873 and
Óláfr probably in 874. Thereafter the leading families of Viking Dublin descended into internal
rivalry, competing for control of a diminishing power base, as their Irish enemies opportunistically
divested them of their assets. The *coup de grace* occurred in 902, when a coalition of Irish forces
from Brega and Leinster converged on Dublin. Mac Airt and Mac Niocáill's translation of the
Annals of Ulster describes it thus:

> The heathens were driven from Ireland, i.e. from the fortress of Áth Cliath … they abandoned
> a good number of their ships and escaped half dead after they had been wounded and broken.

The archaeological evidence for occupation in Dublin (above, Chapter 2) suggests that not all the
inhabitants left, but it appears that the leading families and their associates did depart peremptorily,
some possibly for south-west Scotland where 'two grandsons of Ímair [Ívarr]' are recorded as
having killed a king of the *Cruithentúath* (OI 'Pictish nation') in battle in 904.[15]

The disaster that befell Dublin in 902 almost certainly had the effect of fragmenting what was
already a divided and fractious population. Irish people who had owed political allegiance to the
defeated leaders were suddenly bereft of their right to live in their own land, whereas some individuals of Scandinavian descent no doubt remained behind as a result of their duplicity, or merely
their inconsequence as a result of gender, age, sickness or poverty. There seems to have been little
coherent strategy to the exodus: despite the ominous signs that had been building for decades, the
rulers of Dublin were probably caught unprepared when the moment came. York would perhaps
have been the most obvious destination for Dublin's leaders to make for. The most direct route is
via the Lancashire coast to the Ribble-Aire gap through the Pennines. The vast silver hoard found
at Cuerdale, dated to around 905–10, on the banks of the Ribble in 1840 (below, Chapter 6) has
led Nick Higham to propose that the Ribble acted as a base for the Dublin fleet in the period
immediately following the expulsion.[16] Other seaborne groups under middle-ranking leaders
probably headed in many directions from the Liffey mouth; loyal retainers with the descendants of
Ivarr north to the Clyde, those attracted by Viking Northumbria east towards the Lancashire estuaries, and the disaffected, unaffiliated or merely adventurous south towards the Bristol Channel,
Cornwall and on to Brittany.

The shortest sea crossing – from Dublin to Anglesey – was the most obvious immediate step to take, and we are fortunate that a corroborated account survives of just such a venture. Two historical sources, of greatly differing style and length, mention the exploits of a Dublin Viking leader (possibly not a particularly senior one) called Ingimund, in the period 902–05. The much briefer and more to-the-point of the two accounts is in A-text of the *Annales Cambriae* for 902: '*Igmont in insula Môn venit et tenuit Maes Osmeliaun*' [Ingimund came into the island of Môn (Anglesey) and seized 'Maes Osfelion'].[17] The location of Maes Osfelion (otherwise rendered *Maes Ros Melion* and *Mays Meleriaun* in other Medieval Welsh sources which rely on the *Annals* account) is unclear, but Mark Redknap has suggested it was on the Penmon peninsula jutting out from the east of the island.[18] (The important Medieval settlement of Llanfaes, near Beaumaris, where metal detecting has produced a Viking sword pommel and a piece of Viking hack-silver, is probably the strongest candidate for its location.)

Another, more extensive, version of the Ingimund story comes from an Irish source known as the *Fragmentary Annals* or *Three Fragments,* which was collated and copied by the Irish historian Duald MacFirbis from (now lost) vellum scraps of annalistic writing in the mid-seventeenth century. Although edited and translated in 1860, it remained in relative obscurity until the 1940s when the English historian F.T. Wainwright argued that it represented a genuine account of early Medieval events.[19] In what is almost certainly a reference to the events at 'Maes Osfelion', the *Fragmentary Annals* tell us that Ingimund's group of Norsemen landed in Wales but was repulsed, and continued eastwards towards English Mercia. Here they successfully sought land for the building of huts and dwellings 'near Chester' from Æthefflæd (daughter of Alfred the Great), who was ruling Mercia as her husband, the Ealdorman Æthelred, was dying of disease. After an interval, Ingimund was tempted by the riches of Chester, and the prospect of gaining better lands, to betray the generosity shown to him by Æthefflæd, and persuaded his followers to mount an attack on the city. A legendary (and probably to a great extent imaginatively-described) siege ensued. The Mercians tried to appeal to the honour and good nature of the Irish amongst the pagans (an interesting detail which probably reflects the prejudices of the Irish authorship of the tale), and even to split Dane from Norseman in the *melée*. The Mercians and renegade Irish threw down rocks onto Norsemen attempting to scale the city walls upon wooden hurdles, poured boiling beer from the ramparts. The end came when the defenders let loose swarms of angry bees that stung the invaders into a humiliating retreat, although the story ends ominously, saying: 'it was not long until they came to wage battle again'.

We hear no more of Ingimund after the successful Mercian defence of Chester. Nevertheless, the enduring Scandinavian presence on the lower Dee and Mersey, and indeed within the city of Chester (see below, Chapter 7), indicates that the Vikings did not go away, far from it: they established a permanent and lasting community. On the basis of a dense cluster of Scandinavian place-names and its proximity to Chester, Wainwright suggested that the land given to Ingimund comprised the northern half of the Wirral peninsula. The Danes who had entered Chester in 893–4 had come across a 'deserted' city, yet by the time Ingimund arrived we are told by the *Fragmentary Annals* that it was 'a city full of wealth with the choice lands around it'. The Dee/ Mersey basin was subjected to a systematic re-militarisation by the English authorities in the early tenth century. An addendum to two versions of the *Anglo-Saxon Chronicle* called the 'Mercian Register' lists a series of places that were accorded the status of a *burh* (initially meaning a militarised, defended enclave, but later meaning a town). Chester was named as having been 'restored' as such in 907 (possibly a reference to its former Roman status rather than a more recent Anglo-Saxon version).

Burhs were established at Eddisbury in mid-Cheshire in 914, and at Runcorn, a prominent bluff that controlled the lowest tidal crossing-point of the Mersey, in 915. On the death of Æthefflæd in 918, control of Mercian affairs passed her brother, Edward the Elder of Wessex, and Mercia effectively ceased to exist as a separate political entity. Edward maintained the policy of constructing *burhs* on his north-west frontier, adding Thelwall (near Warrington) and Manchester in 919, and finally *Cledemutha* (Rhuddlan, near the mouth of the River Clwyd in north-east Wales) in 921.

With the exception of Chester, the north-west Mercian *burhs* were small by southern standards; some were merely temporary forts which have left little permanent trace, notably Eddisbury, which was probably a very superficial and short-term re-use of the Iron Age hillfort known as the Castle Ditch (*13*), and Thelwall, which remains an unidentified site (unless it has become confused with Warrington, which was later to be the site of a Norman castle). Manchester, along with all of Lancashire, was Northumbrian territory, and the lands between the Mersey and Ribble in south-west Lancashire were soon added to Edward's territorial gains. Other *burhs* not mentioned in the *Mercian Register* may have extended Edward's power northwards. Nick Higham has argued persuasively that a *burh* was probably founded at Penwortham, on the south bank of the Ribble near Preston, around 920, which would have extended Edward's realm to within a stone's throw of the Viking settlements in the territory of Amounderness on the north bank of the river (below, Chapter 4).[20]

The establishment, over fifteen years, of a string of defended places across the Dee/Mersey lowlands from north-east Wales to the Pennines, which were hinged upon the strategic centre of Chester, does not seem to be a proportionate response to a threat posed by relatively small groups of Vikings. These were evidently allowed to remain in their settlements. Surely if the presence of these incomers had been the prime motivation for Ætheflæd's and Edward's policy, it would have been more straightforward and decisive to try to emulate the Irish success of 902 and drive them away onto the sea. Instead, it seems that local Viking settlers were seen as a nuisance with potentially dangerous external affiliations, but strategically secondary to the more fundamental English aim of re-establishing secure rule north of the midland gap, and using this strategic position to push for new territorial control westwards into Wales and northwards into Northumbria.[21] Edward had to concern himself with more than merely the Viking threat. Rule from Wessex was seemingly resented widely in north-western Mercia. William of Malmesbury mentioned a revolt of the citizens of Chester in 924 in alliance with the Welsh, which, it seems, nearly destroyed all the previous strategic gains. This was suppressed by Edward, who died shortly afterwards at the royal estate at Farndon, on the Dee south of Chester.[22]

13. The Castle Ditch Hillfort, Eddisbury, Cheshire from North, the site of the *burh* founded in 914

The exploits of Ingimund, despite being our only historical record of a post-902 migration from Dublin, were almost certainly not unique. Other medium-ranking leaders, some probably maintaining links with the exiled ruling clan of Ívarr, almost certainly made landfall on the coasts of Galloway, the Isle of Man, Cumbria and Lancashire. They may have sought to join kindred settlers already in these areas prior to 902, or, like Ingimund, to establish new settlements either by conquest, or, equally likely, by treaty and payment. They may have come to terms with some local lords, but evidently displaced others. Two western Northumbrian nobles, Abbot Tilred of Heversham (Cumbria), and Alfred, son of Brihtwulf, are recorded by the anonymous *History of St Cuthbert* as taking refuge east of the Pennines during the reign of Edward the Elder; the latter is described as 'fleeing from the pirates'.[23]

The deposition of the Cuerdale Hoard in the period 905–10 (below, Chapter 6) adds significance to the Viking presence on the Lancashire estuaries, which formed the most direct strategic links between York and the Irish Sea. The fact that the vast treasure was never retrieved by its owner implies serious problems and reversals for whatever enterprise it may have been intended to finance. The re-grouping of the Dubliners took longer, and was perhaps trickier than expected. In 913–14, a naval battle between 'heathens' and a fleet of Uí Néill occurred off the English coast, another inter-Viking naval battle took place off the Isle of Man, and a fleet of 'sea-pagans' appeared in Waterford Harbour.[24] Ragnall of York, who had styled himself King of the Danes, captured a base at or near Waterford, at which in 916 the *Annals of Ulster* recorded 'a great and frequent increase in the number of heathens arriving'. His (probable) brother Sigtryggr (OI *Sitric Caech*) went to Dublin, where the resistance of the Leinstermen was quickly overcome and Viking rule re-established in 917. The failure of an Irish counterattack by Níall Glúndub in 919 consolidated the renewed Viking presence on the Liffey. There were also repeated attacks on Wales at this time, which culminated in attacks on Anglesey and the Isle of Man in 918. Ragnall departed from Ireland once again to Northumbria, subsequently fighting the Scots and Northumbrians at Corbridge on Hadrian's Wall and retaking York, whilst leaving a small but presumably well-armed group of followers behind in Waterford. Excavations in the city have not so far shown occupation earlier than the mid-eleventh century (below Chapter 7), although it is possible that the *longphort* at Woodstown was re-used at this point.

After the defeat of 902 was avenged, Sigtryggr was impatient to return eastwards across the Irish Sea to reclaim his status and power at York, leaving a more junior kinsman, Guðrøðr (OE *Guthfrith*), in charge of Dublin. Another, more shadowy, band of Vikings took over Limerick and sniped constantly at Dublin's back until they were routed by Dublin Vikings in 937. Dublin-sponsored fleets on Carlingford and Strangford loughs in Ulster attacked the Ulaid in 923 and raided Dunseverick – a native Irish fortress on the Antrim Coast – in 926, but were defeated by the northern Uí Néill; there was to be no resumption of the 'flocks and herds' in north-east Ireland which were ousted in the 860s. It is hardly a surprise, therefore, that when Dublin saw further opportunities for aggrandisement and expansion under Guðrøðr's ambitious son Óláfr in the 930s, these were not in the contentious and difficult arenas of Leinster and Ulster, but on the other side of the Irish Sea.

Sigtryggr, according to the *Historia Regum Anglorum*, raided Davenport in Cheshire in 920. The strategic significance of Davenport, a small manorial estate near Congleton, is unclear (little else about it suggests it was important, although it may temporarily have housed hostages). This was an audacious strike, well within Mercian territory on the eastern edge of the Cheshire Plain, which Edward the Elder had recently protected with *burhs* at Thelwall and Manchester. Sigtryggr then went to York where he acceded as king on the death of Ragnall. Edward's son and successor Æthelstan (924–39) travelled to Eamont Bridge in Westmorland (Cumbria) in 927, which probably then marked the border between Northumbria and Strathclyde/Cumbraland. Here he received the submissions of Constantine of Alba (who had already clashed with Ragnall at Corbridge), Hywel 'Dda' ('the good') of Deheubarth, and Owain of Strathclyde.[25]

This success, so far north of distant Wessex, under its formidable young king, threatened to strike a wedge of English power directly between York and Dublin by forming alliances with the Scots and Britons in the north. Guðrøðr rushed from Dublin to attempt to wrest control of York on the death of Sigtryggr in 927, but failed, and the city temporarily fell to the English. Ten years later, Óláfr sought to overturn his father's failure in Northumbria. The intervening decade had seen the Scots of Alba and Britons of Strathclyde turn against Æthelstan, and they joined a coalition with the Dublin Vikings. The anti-English forces landed somewhere from which they could mount an attack on Æthelstan's growing power in the north. 'Florence' (John) of Worcester, writing after the Norman Conquest, stated that the landing was on the Humber,[26] but the details may have become hazy over the intervening centuries. The landing quickly led to a major military confrontation. The location of the battle, named in the *Anglo-Saxon Chronicle* as *Brunanburh* (OE 'Stronghold of Bruna'), is uncertain, but there is only one surviving place-name in direct accord with it, which is Bromborough (Wirral), on the shore of the Mersey estuary and 16km north of Chester.[27] On toponymic and geopolitical grounds this is surely the most probable location for the battle, although there are also determined advocates for locations near York, relying principally on Florence's comment, and also near the Solway Firth, at the Roman fort of Burnswark near Dumfries. The battle was evidently spectacular in scale and brutality, as it receives lurid descriptions not only in English sources but in the *Annals of Ulster*: 'a great, lamentable and horrible battle'. It is arguably referred to in *Egil's Saga* as the battle of *Vinheithr*, in which Egil fought as a mercenary for the English.

Brunanburh saw Æthelstan victorious; the Scots under the 'grey and aged' Constantine suffered particularly grievous losses, and Óláfr and his surviving followers fled ignominiously by 'studded ship' across what some versions of the Anglo-Saxon Chronicle called 'Dingesmere' [OE 'the lake, marsh or sea of the Þing'] – possibly a reference to one of the two estuaries bordering the Wirral,[28] or even an incidental glimpse of a contemporary term for the Irish Sea itself. Perhaps surprisingly, Óláfr recovered his ambitions quickly and soon returned to York following Æthelstan's death in 939. The seasoned and battle-scarred campaigner was made king by the Northumbrians, who resented southern English authority. His successor, Óláfr Cuarán, son of Sigtryygr, became a powerful ruler of Dublin for most of the period 941–980, and also ruled Northumbria until 952. Thereafter followed only one more brief period of Viking rule in York, under Eiríkr 'Blood-axe', who was ejected in 954 and murdered at Rey Cross on the upland Pennine wastes of Stainmore, whilst fleeing north-westwards towards Cumbria, possibly towards embarkation for Dublin. By the mid-950s, Scandinavian settlers in Northumbria were dealing with new realities of resurgent English power, and the pendulum of Viking influence across the Irish Sea had returned permanently, and irrevocably, to Dublin.

The later tenth and early eleventh centuries

Strathclyde's hold on its southern possessions succumbed in 945, when Æthelstan's successor Edmund ravaged Cumbraland and granted it to Máel Coluim (OE *Malcolm*) of Alba in exchange for an alliance 'on sea and land'.[29] The encroachment of the nascent kingdoms of Alba and England into Cumbria and Northumbria limited the opportunities for Viking expansion in the north-east of the Irish Sea region. In particular, the loss of York seems to have blunted the ambitions of the dynasty of Ívarr in Ireland for political entanglement in England. From the 950s onwards, internal rivalries between Dublin and Limerick, and between internal Dublin factions and those of the 'Isles', were played out closer to home. Typically, the competition for influence and resources targeted the more politically divided and vulnerable areas of the region. Wales, particularly its west and north, saw a major phase of interference coming from Dublin and Man in the later decades of the tenth century, fostering a climate of renewed violence and instability. Vulnerable targets such as the monasteries at St David's and St Dogmael's were subject to seaborne raids, in the case of St David's, a wearisome eleven times between 967 and 1091.[30] The death of Hywel Dda in 950 had removed a prestigious and long-serving leader, who had presided over an era of peace bought at the cost of appeasing Æthelstan. The poem *Armes Prydein Vawr,* which was composed during

Hywel's reign, indicates that a head of steam was already building in Wales against his pro-English stance. Its anonymous writer summons the men of Dublin (*Gwyr Dulyn*), the gaels of Ireland and Scotland, and the men of Cornwall and Strathclyde, to unite and resist the English. When the Welsh chronicle *Brut y Tywysogion* (corroborated the following year in the Irish *Annals of the Four Masters*) tells us that the sons of 'Abloec' (probably Óláfr Cuarán) 'laid waste to' (*diffeithawd*) Holyhead and Llŷn in 961, they may not therefore have initially expected an entirely hostile reaction from the local population. In 971–2 Anglesey was devastated, this time by Guðrøðr and Maccus or Magnús, the 'sons of Haraldr' (probably the Haraldr who was Viking king of Limerick). After attacking the important church at Penmon, they 'subdued the whole island'.

The Haraldsson brothers had links with both Dublin and Limerick but were probably based in the Isle of Man in the 970s and 980s, and may, therefore, have seen Anglesey as a legitimate political objective, given the traditional political association between the two islands. Colmán Etchingham has suggested that their activities 'typify the way in which different regions abutting the Viking seaways of Britain and Ireland could be linked by the political ambitions of Viking dynasts'.[31] Their short-lived suzerainty over Anglesey in the early to mid-970s may represent a rare period of direct Viking rule in north Wales. Maccus, possibly hoping for wider recognition of his claims, was amongst those who went to Chester in the early summer of 973 to seek the favour of the new ruler of Anglo-Saxon England. The *Anglo-Saxon Chronicle* records that twenty-nine-year-old King Edgar, newly consecrated at Bath, took his retinue by sea to Chester and received the submission of six kings of northern and western Britain. Florence (John) of Worcester gave a more elaborate version of the story which named eight sub-kings: Cináed of the Scots, Máel Coluim of Strathclyde, Maccus, Dunmail, Siferth, Hywel, Jacob and Juchil, stating that these newly-subservient allies rowed the proud young king on the Dee from the 'palace' to the monastery of St John before an approbatory crowd of ealdormen and nobles.[32] This event marked the zenith of English influence in the Irish Sea region in the tenth century. A grand public spectacle on water, preceded by a royal passage by sea around Wales from the Bristol Channel, it confirms the high priority placed by the Anglo-Saxon court on the northern and western fringes of the kingdom. This event also marked the peak of confidence for pre-Norman Chester itself. Its strategic harbour and mint, with their sea-borne connections westwards and northwards, were the keys to English power in the region. The onlookers who watched the rowing could not have failed to be aware of the symbolism of the city's tidal river, which joined the heart of Edgar's kingdom to the northern and western seas.

Maccus probably derived little long-term benefit from his public display of fealty to Edgar at Chester. The Haraldssons were evidently unable to hold onto Anglesey for very long, as Guðrøðr is recorded as raiding it once again in 980 and again in 989. The 'northern naval force', which the *Anglo-Saxon Chronicle* tells us attacked Cheshire in 980, may possibly have been connected to the Haraldssons, who were perhaps frustrated by a lack of hoped-for English support for their aspirations in Wales. In the context of Guðrøðr's raid on Wales in 989, the familiar term 'black' gentiles (in this context possibly meaning Danes) was resurrected by the Welsh annals to describe Guðrøðr's allies. The attackers took hostages amongst the Welsh, some of whom were later redeemed by a ransom of a penny each paid by Maredudd, King of Deheubarth. A resurgence of interest in the Irish Sea region from Danes is possibly symptomatic of a desire to find indirect ways of reversing English encroachment on the Danelaw. Danes were reported in Ireland in the 980s, and they assisted Guðrøðr Haraldsson in winning a battle on the Isle of Man in 987. The Anglo-Danish war of the 990s saw the fighting spill over the Irish Sea, when King Svein 'Forkbeard' of Denmark attacked the Isle of Man in 995. The English monarchy was not prepared to accept that the Isle of Man might become a Danish possession, and the island was attacked yet again in 1000 by a royal fleet which had come out of Chester, shortly after King Æthelred II 'The Unready' himself had supervised the ravaging of Cumbraland.[33]

A period of relative success enjoyed by the descendants of Ívarr in Dublin during the mid-tenth century, which Clare Downham has described as a time of 'patronage and display',[34] was dealt a serious blow in 980 when they were defeated by Máel Sechnaill of the Uí Néill at the Battle of Tara.

After this, the elderly Óláfr Cuarán retired to the monastery on Iona (itself indicating that the Dublin dynasty was Christianised by this time). Máel Sechnaill kept up the pressure on Dublin throughout the 980s, although he began to lose influence to a rising power from the south, Brian Bóru of Munster. Brief periods when the Waterford dynasty held sway in Dublin were interspersed with problems with a local ruler to the north, Gilla Mochonna of southern Brega, who committed acts of humiliation on prisoners from Dublin by yoking them to a plough.[35] Dublin's ruler from 989, Sigtryggr 'Silk-Beard', rebelled against both Brian and Máel Sechnaill, becoming deeply entangled in Irish domestic rivalries in the process. The signal event in this tortuous series of rebellions, betrayals and attacks, was the battle that took place at Clontarf, on the north side of the Liffey Estuary, on 23 April 1014. Sigtryggr, assisted by a coalition of Viking allies from Man, Orkney and elsewhere, together with a force of Leinstermen, engaged the forces of Munster and Connacht under Brian (whose temporary ally, Máel Sechnaill, had withdrawn to watch from the sidelines). In a battle much hyped by later commentators seeking to glorify Brian's contribution (prime amongst whom was the writer of the *Cogadh Gáedhel re Gaillaibh*), the Vikings and Leinstermen were cut off from their ships and defeated. Brian was murdered by some of his fleeing opponents, an act which confirmed his place in the Irish historical pantheon.

Despite its traditional status in Irish history, the Battle of Clontarf was far from a final, holy, victory over heathen foreigners in Ireland, instead merely inaugurating a temporary period of hegemony for Munster. Dublin continued its attempt to remain independent by playing one Irish faction off against another. Its ability to influence internal Irish affairs was, however, on the wane. There are signs that the pressures and limitations felt in Ireland during the period 990–1030 led Dublin's rulers to bolster their footholds in other areas of the Irish Sea, to which they had unrivalled maritime access. Dynastic links between Dublin and Gwynedd were consolidated at this time, a connection which was later to produce a truly hybrid royal descendant in the person of Gruffudd ap Cynan, ruler of Gwynedd in the later eleventh century, who was born to an Irish mother and raised in Dublin. The foundation of a fortified settlement by Dublin on the north Wales coast occurred in around 1000 when, according to the *History of Gruffudd ap Cynan*, Gruffudd's grandfather Óláfr Sigtryggsson built a castle at a place called 'Bon y Dom', possibly somewhere on the Menai Straits (below, Chapter 6).[36] The spread of 'Hiberno-Norse' coin production (which had begun in Dublin in the last decade of the tenth century) to the Isle of Man in the second and third decade of the eleventh century, has led to suggestions that Dublin controlled the island at this time.

A severe blow to Dublin's political independence occurred in 1052, when Diarmait mac Maíl na mBó, King of Leinster, overthrew Echmarcach mac Ragnaill to take the city. After this, it never fully escaped the claims of Irish overlordship until the Anglo-Norman conquest of 1171. Echmarcach also had a power base in the 'Isles', probably in the Isle of Man, to which he withdrew and continued to press his claims, but without a great deal of success. After the mid-eleventh century, the dynastic and political history of the Isle of Man was closely linked to the Hebrides, eventually forming the 'Kingdom of Man and the Isles' which remained under Scandinavian rule until 1266 (below, Chapter 9). The mid-eleventh century was a watershed for Viking influence in Ireland. As the independent political role of the Scandinavian settlements became subordinated to Irish interests, their commercial roles became yet more prominent. 'Ostman' Dublin (the town of the 'East Men'), where trade rather than war defined its role and identity, was the guise under which the former Viking town survived and prospered. Waterford, and indeed the smaller town of Wexford, also began to prosper as trading towns at this time (below, Chapter 7).

CHAPTER 4

LAND-TAKE AND LANDSCAPE

In searching for patterns of early Viking settlement, we must beware of making uncritical assumptions about the available evidence. One of these is that, where Scandinavian place-names exist, this is indicative of the original location and extent of ninth- or tenth-century Viking landholding. This was probably much more restricted in scale than the spread of place-names implies (**14**). When taken as indications of Viking settlement, place-names are subject to widespread uncertainty and debate concerning their date of origin and extent. In those areas outside of the coverage of Domesday Book (Ireland, Wales beyond its borderlands, the Isle of Man, south-west Scotland and the central and northern parts of Cumbria which were outside the English kingdom until 1092), the earliest documentary proof of the presence of most place-names tends only to occur at much later dates, in the twelfth century or beyond.

There is a particularly marked contrast between Ireland, where comparatively few habitative Scandinavian place-names are found (and those almost exclusively in the hinterland of Dublin), and north-west England and the Isle of Man, where they are much more numerous. Place-names in −bý, which are commonest in Cumbria, Dumfriesshire, Lancashire, Cheshire and the Isle of Man, with a few in Wales and Galloway (but are contrastingly unknown in Ireland), have traditionally been seen as markers of Danish or Danelaw influence. However the subtly different West Norse −bœ́r and East Norse −býr, which are also rendered in modern terms as −by (or −bie in Scotland), complicate the picture. To confuse it still further, there were also plantations of people from eastern England after the Norman Conquest, who imported the nomenclature of the Danelaw, notably around Carlisle and in the Eden Valley after William Rufus took Cumbria from Alba in 1092.[1]

In the Isle of Man (**15**), within and around areas with Norse names covering parish or sub-parish extents – such as Colby, Dalby, Jurby, and Sulby – are more numerous smaller and less important Manx names which reflect the island's Medieval and later history of Gaelic vernacular speech. Perhaps oddly, with the exception of Jurby (ON *djúra-bý*, 'deer [park] farm'), the parishes and treens on the west side of the island, where most of the Viking burials and crosses are found, have Gaelic names. The rest of the −bý names are mostly found in the east and south of the island. Scholars have for many years debated the relative date and significance of the Norse and Gaelic place-names. Gillian Fellows-Jensen proposed in 1983 that the −bý names in the Isle of Man reflected a migration of settlers from the Danelaw, who subsequently moved from Man into Wirral and south Lancashire, taking their naming habits with them.[2] This sweeping model, and others like it, have since been criticised, and local variations and longer chronologies stressed.[3]

14. A working suggestion for areas of Viking land-holding and settlement before 1050

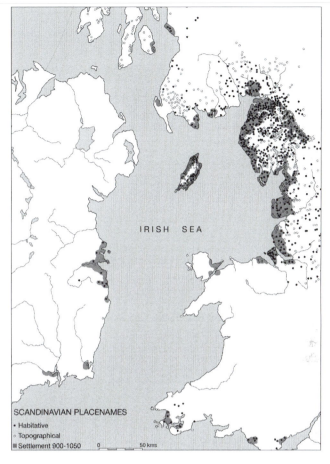

SCANDINAVIAN PLACENAMES
• Habitative
○ Topographical
■ Settlement 900-1050

IRISH SEA

0   50 kms

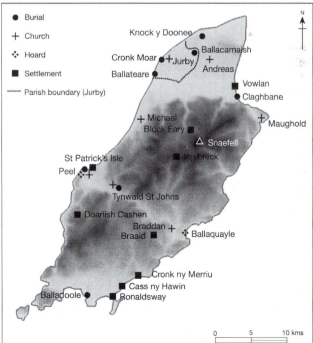

● Burial
+ Church
✥ Hoard
■ Settlement
······ Parish boundary (Jurby)

N

Knock y Doonee
Ballacamaish
Cronk Moar +Jurby   +
            Andreas
Ballateare
                        ■ Vowlan
                        ● Claghbane

+ Michael
Block Eary ■
            △ Snaefell
St Patrick's Isle   ■ Injebreck
Peel ✥+
                        + Maughold
+
Tynwald St Johns

■ Doarlish Cashen
        Braddan +
Braaid ■   ✥ Ballaquayle

        ■ Cronk ny Merriu
        ■ Cass ny Hawin
Balladoole ● ■ Ronaldsway

0   5   10 kms

15. Isle of Man: sites mentioned in text

Indeed in 2001, Fellows-Jensen partially withdrew her 1983 model, suggesting that the similarities between some of the Manx *–bý* names and those in north-west England in particular, could instead derive from Lancastrian influence in later centuries, probably during the Stanley lordship of Man which began in 1405. Even this idea has since been questioned, and the case for Viking influence to some extent rehabilitated. However, the suspicion that later influences are at play persists, as demonstrated by Snaefell, the apparently pure Viking name of the highest mountain on the island (which is often admiringly compared to Snæfell in Iceland), but which was shown by Fellows-Jensen to be a later and probably romantic adaptation of the sixteenth-century English *Snawble* ('snow field').[4]

There are, therefore, dangers in a too-easy transference of logic between the presence of Scandinavian place-names (mostly only documented in much later sources) and the assumption that these all denote early settlement. It seems that many of the original Viking estates and land-holdings, expropriated, bought or otherwise taken over from earlier owners, rather than founded anew, retained their existing pre-Viking names. Norse-Gaelic place-name compounds reflect contact with Ireland and the Gaelic-speaking areas of Scotland, although the date and direction of these contacts remain contentious. Scandinavian minor names and field names were mostly not recorded until much later than the settlement names, and in terms of their general spread were in many ways a reflection of long-term assimilation of Norse terms into local dialects. Yet distinct localised densities of these may reflect a stronger and more dominant initial settlement of Old Norse speakers, and perhaps help to make a case that the settlers were not just a tiny warrior or trading elite, but came in significant enough numbers to change permanently the detailed nomenclature of the landscape.[5]

Disentangling early settlement from place-name patterns affected by later linguistic influence is, therefore, far from straightforward. This difficulty applies both in Britain and Ireland. The Norse language was widely spoken within tenth- and eleventh-century Dublin, as shown by the number of runic inscriptions found there (below, Chapter 8). However, its influence on the wider land-scape in the form of place-names is almost indistinguishable from that of the Anglo-Normans, as a study of rural settlement in Co. Wicklow demonstrates (see below).[6] As described above (Chapter 1), place-names reflect the long filtration of terms and naming habits into local dialects, and may have been coined many decades or even centuries after the first arrival of the first Old Norse or Old Danish speakers. This is particularly so for common northern English topographical names such as 'fell', 'dale' and 'beck'. Some areas possess Scandinavian place-names yet have little or no other indications of Viking settlement. A sparse spread of Scandinavian place-names, including habitative and some minor names, in inland and eastern Cheshire, seems to lack a close relationship with Viking settlements in the county's western coastal districts, and may instead largely be the result of a long post-Norman osmosis of Scandinavian terms into the Cheshire dialect.[7] Clusters and single outliers of place-names in *–bý* which are found in coastal Pembrokeshire, and along the coast of Glamorgan, are also with few exceptions regarded as 'late' by place-name scholars, and many of them may be associated with later eleventh- and twelfth-century trade at Bristol (below, Chapter 7).

Place-name scholars have concentrated much of their attention on ethnic differences in the landscape. Many Viking place-names are hybrids, combining Scandinavian personal or topographic names with Irish/Gaelic, Anglo-Saxon or British terms for enclosures, landforms, farms, shielings or enclosures. Amongst the very few habitative Norse place-names that are found in Ireland, in the hinterland of Dublin, Scandinavian personal names are prominent (**16**). These include Ballygunner (OI *Baile*, 'homestead' + ON *Gunnar*) and Balally (OI *Baile* + ON *Óláfr*). Baldoyle (OI *Baile* + *Dubh Gall*) is an Irish name that may recall the 'dark foreigners'; Leixlip (ON *lax hlaup*, 'salmon-leap') in north-east Kildare is an almost unique example in Ireland of a purely Norse name located well inland, away from coastal features.[8]

Debate concerning the Gaelic-Norse names of north-west England has hinged on whether these are to be seen primarily as reflective of Irish influence (probably coming originally from the settlements of Dublin Vikings) or as indicative of a Scots-Gaelic wave of influence and settlers,

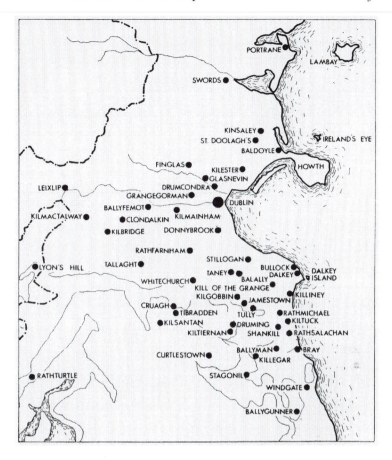

16. The Dyflinarskíri

perhaps after the cession of Cumbria to Alba in 945 (above, Chapter 3). The presence of – *óergi* names (a Norse loan-word from the Gaelic *áirigh*), denoting summer pastures, which are commonest in Scotland but by no means unknown in Ireland, has been a case in point; these occur as *–ergh* or *–argh* in Cumbria and Lancashire, *–eary* in the Isle of Man and *Arrowe* in Wirral. 'Inversion compounds', where the personal name appears second, such as Setmurthy (Cumbria) (ON *saetr*, 'shieling of Muiredach'), in a word-order which is typical of the Celtic languages, are also seen as signifiers of hybrid Norse-Gaelic influence.[9] More distinctively, Irish names in north-west England, such as Liscard and Noctorum in Wirral (OI *lios na carriage,* 'hall at the rock' and *cnocc Tírim,* 'dry hillock') occur amidst clusters of Scandinavian habitative and hybrid names in *–bý*.[10] The *Irby* or *Ireby* names of Wirral and Cumbria show that the Irish were distinctive enough within regions already dominated by Viking settlers to attract their own ethnic label, as indeed were the Scots (Scotby, Cumbria) and possibly also the Franks (Frankby, Wirral).[11] Church dedications can help to illuminate patterns of external affinities. These include Irish saints (Patrick, Brigit, Kevin or Cóemgen); British saints (Ninian, Kentigern or Mungo); Northumbrian saints (Cuthbert, Oswald); Mercian saints (Chad, Werburgh) and even Viking saints (Olaf or Olave). Although, like most place-names, dedications can rarely be traced historically prior to the later Medieval period, they can nevertheless contribute to the picture of cross-cutting patterns of historic links and allegiances found around the Irish Sea.

Habitative names in *–bý* are applied to major and minor settlements, so offer little guide to status. *Skáli–* names normally appear in Cumbria and Lancashire as *–scale* suffixes, as at Seascale, Sandscale and Holmscales. Elsewhere, such as in Orkney (where they appear as *–skaill*),[12] they are taken to indicate high-status settlements with drinking-halls, but have tended in northern

England to be interpreted by place-name scholars (following Eilert Ekwall) as the somewhat less grand alternative of a shieling hut.[13] It is difficult to see why this difference in interpretation has become so entrenched in the literature. Shielings are less likely to occupy the prime lowland sites that have *skaill* names in Orkney, but the converse, that some at least of the *skáli* names in Cumbria and Lancashire indicate high-status sites, cannot be so easily dismissed.

Estates and landholding

Historical sources convey at most a piecemeal and partial story in terms of Viking land-take and settlement around the Irish Sea. Military conquest and political hegemony, real or claimed, is not necessarily always to be equated with the establishment of permanent territorial holdings, dwellings, economic interests and agriculture. Conversely, as shown by the Ingimund episode in Cheshire, on a small scale, and by local agreement, Viking settlers could be accommodated amongst the detailed patchwork of landholding and alliances. This may have taken place within what have generally been assumed to be uniformly hostile kingdoms, especially where central political authority was permissive, distant or weak. Ingimund's opening gambit in Mercia, following his defeat in Wales, was not to go onto the attack in the first instance, but to seek terms with Æthefflæd, which he unwisely breached when he felt strong enough to mount an armed attempt on Chester. We find fleeting hints in contemporary historical sources of other apparent negotiated arrangements over territory, a practice that may have been more widespread than our few documentary survivals can demonstrate. One of these concerns the possession of Amounderness (ON *Agmundr's Ness*, 'promontory'), the area north of the River Ribble in Lancashire. The strategic significance of the Ribble in providing maritime access to the Aire Gap across the Pennines to York has been noted above in Chapter 1. This area was nominally a peripheral part of the moribund kingdom of Northumbria, which, like Strathclyde/Cumbraland to the north, was ripe for piecemeal territorial gains by Vikings in the early tenth century. As the power of Wessex extended northwards into this political vacuum, the recent territorial gains by outsiders attracted the interest of royal authority in the south. In a grant of 934, Amounderness ('this land of no small size') was given to the Church of York by Æthelstan, to hold 'without the yoke of hateful servitude' (a possible reference to it having been in pagan hands previously). The king had purchased Amounderness 'with no little money of my own' (from whom is not mentioned), but in previous grants to two of his thegns of lands in Derbyshire and Bedfordshire, of similar style and content, the purchase 'from the pagans' is explicitly worded.[14]

In Cumbria, the area that became the Norman Barony of Copeland, and the Westmorland hamlet of Coupland, both have Norse place-names implying purchase (ON *kaupa land*, 'bought land') which led Gillian Fellows-Jensen to suggest that 'not only great estates but small units of settlement passed into the hands of the Vikings in return for money'.[15] In view of the large consignments of portable wealth in the form of silver, most spectacularly the Cuerdale Hoard found on the banks of the Ribble (below, Chapter 6), which were present here in the early tenth century, it is by no means unlikely that land transfer was taking place through negotiation and purchase, amidst a (now historically largely invisible) mosaic of local allegiances and disputes, buy-offs, and transient political opportunities, rather than by armed conquest. There seems, perhaps surprisingly, to be virtually no demonstrable case of Scandinavian incomers wiping out and wholly redrawing existing local political boundaries, having achieved total conquest and subjection of the existing inhabitants.

Implicit in Fellows-Jensen's comment (quoted above) is support for a considerable measure of continuity in the shape and structures of landholding, and the view that the first Vikings to arrive took over existing estates, with secondary settlements in more marginal areas being established later. Place-names therefore present us with an interesting conundrum. We instinctively look for the densest clusters of habitative Scandinavian place-names, predominantly those in –*bý*, to signify the presence of Viking settlers, yet the earliest (already extant) estates and churches taken or purchased by Viking settlers in most cases continued to be known by their existing names. In Galloway, Cumbria, Lancashire and Cheshire these are Old English, British [Old Welsh], with the incoming Scandinavian influence at most perhaps expressed by a 'Grimston' style hybrid name, combining an existing generic place-name such as –*ton* with a Scandinavian personal name, such as at Thurstaston in Wirral (ON *Torstein* + OE *tūn*), and Ulverston in Furness (ON *Ulfarr* + OE *tūn*), although *tūns* also exist in Norway, so some of these may have been Viking imports. Later or secondary landholdings, founded anew after the Scandinavian settlers had fully established themselves, and lacking the previously established identity of many of the first Viking landholdings, may therefore be the ones with the most unambiguously Norse-sounding names. Fellows-Jensen has proposed that –*bý* names with general topographic or impersonal appellatives, including the names of peoples (Irby), animals ((West) Derby) and trees (Ashby), are older than –*bý* names with Scandinavian personal names, indicating that 'they are a result of the fragmentation of old estates and the granting of individual units to the men whose names they contain'.[16]

Some early patterns of landholding lived on in relict form as Medieval hundreds, estates, parishes and baronies long after the Viking period. The great nineteenth-century historian of Cheshire, George Ormerod, drew attention to an obsolete minor hundred in Wirral, called the Hundred of Caldy.[17] This was mentioned in the 1182 Cheshire Pipe Roll and its privileges were observed until as late as 1819. Ormerod listed the parishes and townships included in the minor hundred, the mapping of which allows us to reconstruct its extent as a series of blocks of land occupying much of the north-west of the peninsula, accounting for the majority of the Scandinavian habitative place-names in the area. J. McN. Dodgson, in his masterly argument over the location of the Battle of Brunanburh (above, Chapter 3),[18] not only realised the potential significance of Ormerod's observation for the Viking period, but suggested that the Hundred of Caldy approximated to the original extent of the Norse settlement associated with Ingimund. Dodgson drew attention to the place-name Raby (ON *rá-býr*, 'farm on a boundary'), which borders Thornton Hough, one of the townships listed by Ormerod as part of the minor hundred. Further evidence of territorial distinctiveness in north Wirral includes a Thingwall place-name (see 'things' below), which, by local tradition, is associated with Cross Hill, a modest topographic rise within Thingwall township in the centre of the peninsula. Concentrated north of the probable boundary, but also extending outside it southwards towards Chester, are numerous Norse habitative place-names that were in existence by the time of Domesday Book in 1086. These are supplemented by (generally less

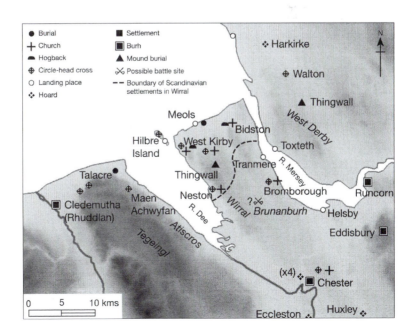

17. The lower Dee and Mersey: sites mentioned in text

precisely dated) minor field and other topographic names, such as field names in *carr* (ON *kjárr*, 'brushwood, boggy land'), and *holm* (ON *holmr*, 'dry ground in a marsh, island'). These have been suggested as indicative of a high level of vernacular Norse linguistic influence living on into the Middle Ages.[19]

A small outlying group of place-names in *−bý* are found on the edge of higher ground to the south of the Mersey Estuary, at Whitby and Helsby, and these are accompanied by a discrete cluster of minor Norse names in *−breck* (ON *brekka*, 'slope') and *−thwaite* (ON *þveit*, 'clearing'), which led Margaret Gelling to suggest that a small enclave of tenth-century settlers had established itself as an outlier of the main settlement in north Wirral.[20] The Hundred of Caldy was subsumed into the larger Hundred of Wilaveston (Wirral). The minor hundred was held as part of a single estate at the time of Domesday Book in 1086 by the Norman baron, Robert of Rhuddlan. Dodgson suggested that the boundary of Robert's lands approximated to the boundary of the Viking settlement enclave (**17**).

As his affliation to Rhuddlan would suggest, Robert also held lands in the portion of north-east Wales between the rivers Dee and Clwyd, then known in Welsh as the Cantref (hundred) of Tegeingl and in English as the Cheshire Hundred of Atiscros – a hundred name which refers to a cross (see below). This land (later called Flintshire) was peripheral and disputed territory between the Welsh of Gwynedd and the English of Mercia throughout the eighth to eleventh centuries and beyond. Domesday Book tells us that the lands held by Robert in 1086 had been held in 1066 by two individuals with Norse names, Leofnoth and Arni, both of whom had extensive possessions in Wirral.[21] These may have been leaders of the (by then) long-settled and peaceful Anglo-Scandinavian community in the area, but what happened to them at or after the Norman Conquest is not recorded. A small scatter of minor compound Norse/English place-names occur in the north-eastern corner of Flintshire, including Kelston and Axton, both of which have groups of (probably prehistoric) burial mounds near their historic focus.[22] A possible Viking grave was found in sand dunes near the shore at Talacre in 1931 (below, Chapter 5), and there is a small but distinctive collection of tenth- and eleventh-century red sandstone sculpture from churches at Meliden and Dyserth, bearing decorative motifs and images which closely resemble those from sites in Wirral and Chester (below, Chapter 8). Most impressive, and probably still in its open-air original position, is *Maen Achwyfan* in Whitford parish,[23] a free-standing circle-headed sandstone cross 3.4m high (**18**). The cross is surrounded on three sides by six burial mounds. Whilst these are probably Bronze Age barrows in origin, they form a distinctive group, and may possibly have been re-used as burial sites or the focus of a local assembly in the Viking period.[24] The cross is unlikely to date to much earlier than 1000, and it is probable that the small cluster of Norse settlers in north-east Wales were a secondary migration across the Dee from Wirral during the middle or later tenth century, rather than a landfall from Ireland or other more distant origins in the later ninth or early tenth centuries.

Amounderness, the subject of Æthelstan's grant to York in 934, became one of the hundreds of Lancashire after the Norman Conquest, and it is in this form that the name has survived.[25] The Lancashire hundred of West Derby, on the north side of the Mersey Estuary across from Wirral, may also have its roots in a Scandinavian estate founded in the early tenth century. It formed the western coastal portion of the block of land known as *Inter Ripam et Mersham* (between Ribble and Mersey). This lay north of the original line of Anglo-Saxon *burhs* in the Mersey Valley prior to 920, but which may shortly afterwards have been brought into the ambit of the English monarchy. Around 1000 this land is recorded as being held by a Mercian lord, Wulfric Spot, who also held part of Wirral. Wulfric Spot's will bequeathed his lands either side of the Mersey to his brother Ælfhelm and son Wulfheah, and interestingly lists his payments to the king as '200 mancuses of gold, two silver-hilted swords, four horses, two saddled and two unsaddled, and the weapons which are due with them'.[26] Wulfric Spot also held numerous lands in Mercia and the Danelaw, and by recent descent was probably a direct beneficiary of the reimposition of English rule in the north-west, leading Nick Higham to suggest that he or his forebears 'may have bought these estates from Scandinavian lords unsettled by the conquests of the West Saxon Kings'.[27] West Derby

18. *Maen Achwyfan* (Whitford, Flintshire), sandstone standing cross dated to *c.* 1000

Hundred has a particularly dense cluster of Scandinavian place-names, including a Thingwall name (see below) and an identical boundary name to Wirral's Raby in the form of Roby, together with other Norse place-names such as Toxteth,[28] Kirkby, Crosby and Ormskirk. Ekwall described 'proper Scandinavian names' as being very common in West Derby, in contrast to neighbouring Warrington, Newton and Salford hundreds to the east. West Derby lacks a surviving array of Viking-period stone sculpture comparable to that of Wirral, although a cross is known from Walton-on-the-Hill. An early tenth-century silver hoard from the Harkirke, Little Crosby, was recorded in the seventeenth century (below, Chapter 6) before its contents were melted down and subsequently stolen.

To the north of Amounderness lie the estuaries of the rivers Lune and Wyre, and the vast tidal inlet of Morecambe Bay, which leads north-eastwards to the estuary of the River Kent, with the Cartmel and Furness peninsulas to the north (**19**). Fiona Edmonds has drawn renewed attention to two groups of lands held at the time of Domesday apparently by the same lord, Gilemichel.[29] These included estates grouped under the manor of Strickland, along the course of the Kent leading north-east from Morecambe Bay, and another tight cluster near the mouth of the Lune around Lancaster. Gilemichel (*Gille-Míchíl*) is a Gaelic name argued by some specialists to be of possible Scots origin,[30] but Edmonds argues that it is just as likely to be an Hiberno-Norse name, and suggests that Gilemichel was a descendant of Dublin Vikings who had obtained possession of some of the best landing-places on the Morecambe Bay coast.[31] At the north-western extremity of the bay, it seems likely that the network of islands and sheltered channels around the southern end of Furness, including Barrow, Walney and Roa islands, also formed an important Norse estate on a strategic harbour. The churchyard at neighbouring Rampside has produced a probable tenth-century weapon grave (below, Chapter 5).

The historical geographer Angus Winchester, in a study of estate development in Copeland and on the Solway Plain (Cumbria), proposed that patterns of early settlement and later expansion could be detected in later Medieval records of feudal renders paid by individual estates to their baronial overlord, in conjunction with place-name analysis.[32] The ancient dues of 'Cornage'

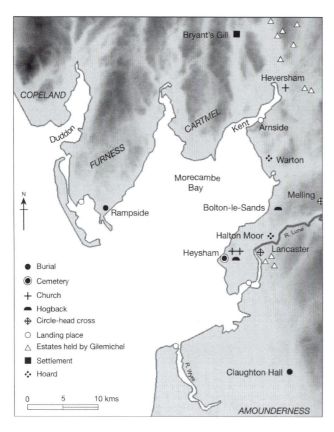

19. Morecambe Bay area: sites mentioned in text

(otherwise known as 'Noutgeld') and 'Seawake' are characteristic of coastal districts of the baronies of Copeland and Allerdale. Estates paying both renders predominate in Allerdale,[33] whereas in Copeland there is a less uniform pattern that betrays more clearly its different phases of development. Here the estates, which paid both types of renders to the Medieval baronies of Egremont and Cockermouth, cluster along the coast and in the western lowland areas bordering the Lake District fells (**20**). The place-names of the lower-lying coastal districts display a mixture of British and Old English elements combined with Norse habitative names in −bý, whereas estates further inland on higher ground which paid other dues, the place-names are more uniformly Norse, but mostly a mixture of topographic and habitative names other than those in −bý. Winchester suggested that this reflected an initial takeover by Vikings of existing estates, some of which retained their original names, followed by expansion in the eleventh and twelfth century into forest clearings on rising ground, as denoted by the place-name −thwaite (ON *þveit,* 'clearing') such as Hewthwaite, Brackenthwaite and Thackthwaite, and then on into the higher and remoter uplands where summer pastures denoted by the name suffix −sett (ON *sǽtr,* 'shieling'), such as Setmurthy, are found. A similar picture of primary habitative names occupying lower-lying coastal districts, with secondary clearance and shieling names encroaching inland onto higher land, is noted on the Isle of Man (see below).

The Cumbrian coastal estates that paid both Cornage and Seawake in the Middle Ages have a mixture of British, English and Norse place-names. Another support for the primary focus of Norse landholding in north-west England being within the existing estate structure, comes from the distribution of Viking-period stone sculpture such as circle-headed crosses, hogbacks and Norse mythological scenes (below, Chapter 8). The majority of the locations in Cumbria, Lancashire and Cheshire, where the sculpture is located, have non-Scandinavian names. These include English names, such as Addingham, Gosforth, Workington, Dearham and Brigham

(Cumbria), Bolton-le-Sands, Halton and Heysham (Lancashire), Bidston, Wallasey, Woodchurch and Walton (Wirral/West Derby); or British names such as Dacre, Carlisle, Lowther and Penrith (Cumbria). Many of these places already had pre-Viking churches with a sculptural tradition. Gaelic-Norse hybrid names such as Aspatria (Cumbria) account for a much smaller number of sculpture sites. Remarkably few sites with Viking-period sculpture have unambiguously Norse place-names, such as Crosscanonby and Kirkby Stephen (Cumbria) or West Kirby (Wirral).[34]

Not all early Viking settlement in Cumbria and Lancashire was on the outer coastal plain. As might be expected from a situation where land-take was conditional upon finding an accommodation with existing landholding interests, the Viking estates seem to have been restricted in extent and discontinuous in their spread (**21**). Some groups established themselves in strategic positions in the upper estuaries and on navigable inland rivers. Amongst the mound burials (below, Chapter 5), only Aspatria is in a coastal parish, whereas Hesket-in-the-Forest and Claughton Hall are between 15km and 25km from the nearest coast. Hesket is located beside a Roman road that leads south from Carlisle through the Eden Valley and towards the important route across Stainmore towards York. The Eden Valley has the second-densest pattern of Norse habitative names in Cumbria, after the Solway coastal plain, within which a particular cluster is visible in the middle section.[35] Dacre, Addingham and Penrith, all significant pre-Viking churches and estates dominating in the Eden Valley, attracted Norse settlers and together may have formed a localised super-estate or chiefdom. All three have Viking-age sculpture. Penrith has a group of hogback grave monuments known by the later romantic name of the 'Giant's Grave'.[36] There are two hogbacks at nearby Lowther and one at Addingham. Only a few miles downstream from Addingham, the cemetery discovered in 2004 at Cumwhitton, which overlooks the Eden from the east (below, Chapter 5), is an example

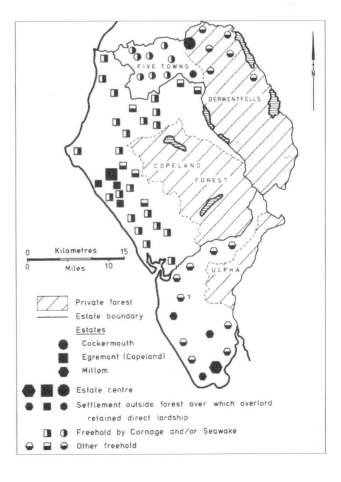

20. Land tenure and Medieval estates in Copeland, Cumbria

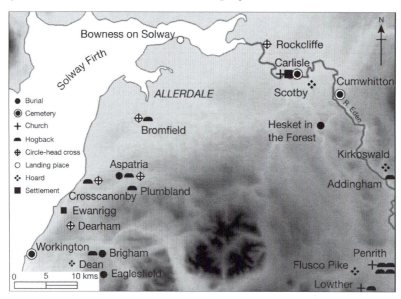

21. Northern Cumbria: sites mentioned in text

of a local burial place where Scandinavian-style furnished or pagan rites were practised, yet in a parish with a compound British *Cwm* ('glade') and an Anglo-Saxon habitative place-name, which was originally Whittington.[37]

Clusters of habitative Scandinavian place-names are found in south-west Scotland in the vicinity of Dumfries (see below), on the Solway coast near Kirkcudbright, and on the southern Machars peninsula in Galloway (*22*). A Viking grave found at Kirkcudbright (below, Chapter 5), a stray find of a Viking-style glass linen-smoother from the town,[38] and the nearby Norse place-names at Bombie, Gretby and Borgue (ON *Borg*, 'stronghold') may point towards the presence of a local early Scandinavian landholding around the mouth of the River Dee in the early tenth century. The presence of a fine Viking-period cross-slab at Kirkcolm, near Stranraer (the 'Kilmorie Stone'), which has a probable Sigurd scene (below, Chapter 8),[39] implies there may have been an early Viking estate on the northern Rhinns of Galloway, next to Loch Ryan. The *−bý* names at Sorbie and Bysbie on the southern Machars Peninsula near Whithorn were argued by Richard Oram to be evidence of new, if small, communities of Gaelic-Norse settlers from either Ireland or western Scotland gravitating at a 'generally late date' towards the monastery: 'the slotting-in of a few incomers into an already crowded landscape'.[40] Gillian Fellows-Jensen has noted how these few names concentrate around estates and centres of secular control, implying they were established by small-scale, high-status groups.[41] A further group of six names ending in *−bý*, near the Ayrshire Coast facing the island of Arran – which has a (probably unrelated) ninth-century Viking grave at King's Cross Point, Lamlash[42] – may also represent a localised Scandinavian settlement cluster on the northern fringes of the Irish Sea region, but the documentary evidence for these names begins only in the fifteenth century.[43]

In an influential paper published in 1988, John Bradley drew attention to the area around Dublin known to the writers of Icelandic sagas (such as Egil's Saga) as 'Dyflinarskíri' ('Dublin-shire'). He proposed that this, in the twelfth century at least, represented an extensive urban hinterland under Dublin's rule that probably extended throughout most of the modern counties of Dublin and Wicklow, and possibly included a coastal strip as far south as Wexford (*23*). Bradley has revised his view somewhat in a more recent paper, arguing that early Scandinavian settlement was more concentrated around Dublin and its satellite *longphort* at Clondalkin, and in smaller, discontinuous coastal enclaves to the south.[44] After the re-foundation of Dublin in 917, the Dyflinarskíri probably developed as a broader area of Scandinavian landed authority over a largely Irish population. Together with the area known as the *Fine Gall* (Fingal) to the north of Dublin, which probably extended north-eastwards to Lambay, Lusk and Skerries, Dublin's lands formed an impressive urban hinterland that supplied the city with the agricultural produce which is amply demonstrated archaeologically (below, Chapter 7). Stone sculpture, although less common than in north-west England and the Isle of Man, offers some clues to the pattern of lordship and estates. The 'Rathdown Slabs', which occur in formerly rural parishes immediately south of Dublin, bear relatively simple motifs such as roundels, and may mark a local Scandinavian tradition. A single, isolated hogback, from Castledermot (Co. Kildare), 65km south-west of Dublin, may commemorate a local Viking settler. Partly on the basis of this hogback, Bradley argued in 1988, somewhat speculatively perhaps, that Dublin's landed hegemony may have extended even further south in the tenth and eleventh centuries, although he was careful to note that nominal territorial control does not imply a dense settlement pattern of Dublin Vikings. The later 'Ostman Cantreds' – including the Barony of Rosslare south of Wexford, the territory of Gaultier around Waterford (and possibly also the Honour of Dungarvan to its west), the Barony of Kerricurrihy around Cork, and the rural deanery of Limerick – provide evidence for directly controlled urban hinterlands around the other Hiberno-Norse towns, but their origins cannot be closely linked to Viking activity before the eleventh century at the earliest. Bradley's model has provided a challenge for historical and archaeological research on the extent of Viking presence in rural Ireland.

Clare Downham has recently contributed a study, taking the *longphuirt* as its starting point, which suggests that rural Viking settlement was more extensive than previously assumed.[45] Colmán Etchingham's study of settlement in Co. Wicklow confronted the difficulty of disentangling Scandinavian influence from later Anglo-Norman influence on place-names. He drew attention to sites such as the defended enclosure of Rathturtle on the western flanks of the Wicklow mountains (the rath of 'MacTorcaill', a family name originally from the Old Norse personal name *Thorkill*), which invite further investigation, but conclusive archaeological evidence for Scandinavian settlement in the county is as yet slight. Etchingham concluded his paper by stating: 'It appears that the Hiberno-Norse presence did not involve expropriation but rather a more complex pattern of tributary relations and coexistence'.[46]

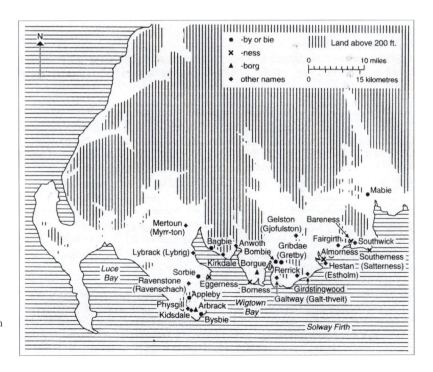

22. Scandinavian settlement in Galloway

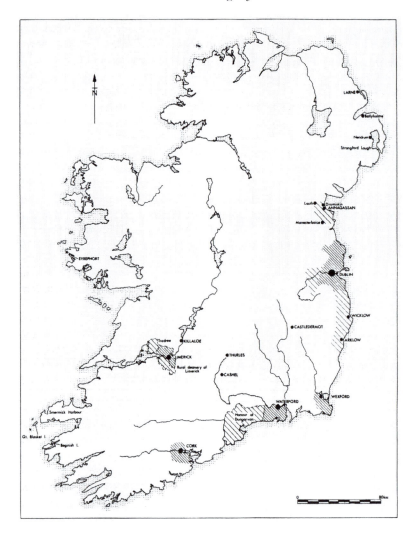

23. The Medieval
territories of the
Hiberno-Norse
towns

Territory, boundaries and defence

All available evidence points towards Viking settlers in the Irish Sea region occupying land
within existing patterns of landholding. G.W.S. Barrow argued that the territorial structures of
Lancashire and Cumbria preserved ancient 'Celtic' features well into the Medieval period,[47] and
many archaeologists now think that many of the estate structures which first become detectable in Medieval documents have an even more ancient prehistoric lineage in the landscape
going back to the Iron Age or Bronze Age.[48] A comparable case-study is the historic system of
land division on the Isle of Man, parts of which are first recorded in twelfth-century sources,
but the obscure origins of which have long been debated between advocates of 'Celtic',Viking,
and of earlier prehistoric origins.The smallest and possibly the most ancient division amongst
these are the quarterlands, approximating to a single important family farm, which, thanks to
the statistical analyses of Paul Reilly, we know vary between 50 and 180 acres in extent (average
around 90 acres or 36.5 hectares). Quarterlands, according to Reilly, display 'a marked tendency
towards equitable division when quality of land is considered'.[49] These are grouped into taxable
units known as treens, the majority of which vary between 200 and 500 acres in extent (80–200
hectares), and which form the component parts of the next level up: parishes.These are grouped

mostly in threes (with one double) into even larger units – the sheadings, or court districts – of which there are six, divided into two equal groups by a line down the middle of the island known as the 'Deemster's (Judge's) Division'.

It is clear that the rather neat Manx territorial hierarchy has evolved over the centuries, assisted by some judicious 'tidying-up' in later times, and that it is untenable to try to attribute it as a complete system to the Viking period, or indeed to any earlier period. Many theories have been advanced down the years as to its significance and date. There have been several now-obsolete nineteenth-century attempts to demonstrate it had Scandinavian origins, but quarterlands or their equivalent are not characteristic of Norway or Denmark. In the twentieth century, the Norwegian linguist Carl Marstrander,[50] following earlier suggestions by P.M.C. Kermode, emphasised the apparent coincidence between the sites of chapels (*keeills*), detached burial grounds (*rhullicks*), and the distribution of quarterlands, and the historian Basil Megaw compared the Manx shead-ings to the commotes of Anglesey, speculating on the pre-Viking political links between the two islands.[51] Hugh Marwick sought to compare the Manx land system with that of Orkney, where the Medieval system of ouncelands (*urislands*) and pennylands offered a possible parallel. Reilly's work, which was based on an early application of computer-based statistics, poured some math-ematical cold water on the theories of Marstrander and others. It is clear that only very general statements can be made about the antiquity of the island's land divisions as a whole. Nevertheless, there are hints in localised areas that Viking settlers did integrate with, and perhaps adapt, an exist-ing territorial landscape. One such is the statistically much more striking coincidence between the placement of grave mounds on the coastal ridge in the parish of Jurby (below, Chapter 5) and primary territorial units (**24**). The use of visible forms of burial to denote landholding and to mark boundaries is a common feature of prehistoric and early Medieval archaeology. Mound burial, with its pagan associations, is a clear guide to an early (i.e. pre-conversion) settlement presence, although its topographic relationships with the imprint of Christianity on the landscape are more complex than they might seem. David Wilson, in his recent survey of Vikings on the Isle of Man, was sceptical about the value of the Manx land system for telling us very much at all about the Viking period, but did accept the Jurby example as a valid indication that some of the minor ter-ritorial boundaries of the island probably do echo the pattern of Viking landholdings.[52]

The presence of 'Seawake' (Latin *Vigilia Maris* 'the vigil of the sea') in Medieval Cumbria gives us an intriguing hint of a coastal civil defence system, suggesting some political commonality amongst the coastal estates of Cumbria. It is difficult to be certain that this was a Viking-period introduction. Coastal civil defence arrangements are a long-lived tradition, and indeed, as we have

IRISH SEA

km

24. Burial mounds and boundaries in Jurby Parish, Isle of Man, located on (**15**)

seen in Chapter 1, seaborne raiders had been troubling this coast since the later Roman period. A suggestion of Marwick's,[53] taken up by Marstrander, that the Manx land system was a relic of a Viking-period *leidang* or naval militia, has tended to attract caution and scepticism from more recent commentators. This is perhaps now worth fresh attention after recent work on Irish documentary sources such as *Lebor na Cert*, which gives clear information on the ships and naval levies of Irish kings in the eleventh and twelfth centuries.[54] In this regard, it may be worth re-examining the role of coastal promontory forts which archaeological evidence suggests were reoccupied during the Viking or later Medieval periods, as excavated on the Isle of Man at Vowlan, Cronk ny Merriu, Cass ny Hawin and Close ny Chollagh (see below),[55] and also on the north coast of Anglesey at Castell, Porth Trefadog.[56] Single rectangular buildings, generally accompanied by very few artefacts with consequent problems for site dating, were squeezed onto the restricted and exposed seaward side mostly of small univallate or bivallate ramparts. There seems little indication that these were high-status or even permanent residences, but a function as coastal lookouts related to more established settlements nearby, is perhaps a more likely possibility. Former Roman signal stations, or Iron Age forts on conspicuous promontories – given Norse topographical names, such as the small ramparted point at Burton, Ness, Wirral[57] – may also have played a part in such a system.

Meetings and 'things'

The Isle of Man shows that even minor boundaries have the potential to be significant relics of the Viking period. The geography of Viking landholding was not merely a matter of abstract ownership of large and ill-defined estates, but had physical expression even down to a modest level of spatial demarcation. The Manx example may not be unique to the island. Quarterlands also occur in townships in Ireland,[58] although once again we find it hard to pin down their origins and date. The lands of Holm Cultram Abbey, on the Solway Plain near Carlisle, an area that is inter-visible with the Isle of Man, were also divided into quarters.[59] How was social and political control organised in these local territories? The Norwegian historian Per Sveaas Andersen has drawn attention to 'sociotoponyms', mostly relatively minor place-names which express a social or communal gathering, and which, he argues, indicate the presence of distinctively Norse communities.[60] These include *skeith* (ON *skeið*, 'race course' or alternatively 'boundary', the former perhaps more likely, particularly when coupled with *hestr*, horse) such as at Hesket (Cumbria), Hesketh (Lancashire) and two minor Heskeths in Wirral, and at Brunskaith near Carlisle. *Lek* (ON *leik,* 'play'), as at Laking How (leik + ON *haugr*, mound) at Seascale (Cumbria), expresses a similar communal theme.

The most significant of the 'sociotoponyms' are the *thingwall / tinwald / tynwald* names (from ON *þing-vollr,* 'meeting place of the assembly'). The best known of these in the Irish Sea region is the Manx Tynwald, which still gives its name to the island's parliament (**25**). The modern legislature meets indoors at the island's capital, Douglas, but an annual open-air ceremony takes place at Tynwald Field on St John's day in July. The assembly site consists of a flat-topped, circular, four-decked terraced mound measuring 25m in diameter, located 190m west of a Victorian chapel, which may stand upon the site of an earlier *keeill*.[61] The site has been landscaped in recent times, and today visitors can see a paved, enclosed ceremonial avenue, leading from the mound to the chapel, surrounded by a viewing area. The antiquity of the mound itself is a matter of speculation, but it is located in a rich multi-period archaeological landscape; Viking-period furnished graves were found nearby and a contemporary date for at least a reconstruction of the mound cannot be altogether dismissed (below, Chapter 5). Timothy Darvill, who recently surveyed the site, argues that Tynwald was the senior, but not the only, assembly site on the Isle of Man, presiding over a lower category of local administration at sheading level.[62] Perhaps significantly in view of the likely proportion and status of Viking settlers (below, Chapter 8), with the single exception of Nordmot (ON *Norð-mot,* 'north meeting') on the boundary between Braddan and Balwin, the minor assemblies all have Gaelic names.

25. Tynwald, St Johns, Isle of Man

Thingwall in Wirral has already been referred to above. It is locally associated with a modest rise, Cross Hill, the top of which may have been shaped and enhanced as a mound-like feature, but which is now only very faintly detectable after centuries of erosion and ploughing (**26**). Low earthworks surround the hill on its east and north sides and some of these appear to form a banked approach from lower ground to the east; there has never been an excavation here so these features are so far undated. The etymology of the Wirral Thingwall is identical to that of its neighbour across the River Mersey in West Derby (the *vollr* parts of the two names are overlaid with OE *wella*, 'spring'). The West Derby 'thing', now located amidst the eastern suburbs of Liverpool, is also associated with a low rise in the ground. Unlike Cross Hill, this site has been built upon, in the form of a large Victorian house, Thingwall Hall. Its gardens are terraced, but this is more likely to be the result of Victorian landscape gardening than Viking-period mound construction. A third name of this type, Tinwald (*vollr* is here overlaid with OE *wald*, 'wood'), occurs amidst a localised spread of Scandinavian place-names in the vicinity of Dumfries.[63] These, the antiquity of which Fellows-Jensen was very guarded about (several of the Dumfriesshire −*bý* names have Norman personal names and are not recorded before the fourteenth century), may have been the result of a trans-Solway movement of settlers from Cumbria, but further detailed research is required to distinguish Viking-period settlement from secondary immigration after the Norman Conquest. A low flat-topped mound is located in the village of Tinwald, which is listed as a Norman motte with a bailey, although the evidence for the latter is scant.[64] It has been reduced by ploughing and now stands only 2.5m high, with the area on top measuring 17m by 10m. The mound may possibly have functioned as a motte, but this does not rule out earlier origins and purposes. It may have been similar to another large mounded assembly site (now levelled and largely destroyed) at Doomster Hill, Govan, in the heart of the kingdom of Strathclyde, which is located close to a major collection of Viking-period sculpture, including five large hogback grave monuments in Old Govan Church.[65] Another terraced mound, at Lincluden on the western side of Dumfries, has also been proposed as a possible 'thing' site, although its terracing has been dismissed as a later addition to a Norman motte.[66]

The 'thing' site of Dublin could be expected, on the grounds of the city's size and power, to have been even larger and more impressive than the Manx Tynwald. Only glimpses of evidence have survived for it, and it is impossible to be certain whether it began as a pre-Viking focus, was

26. Cross Hill, Thingwall, Wirral

created during the ninth-century *longphort* phase, or, as seems more likely, it arose during the more extensive and permanent settlement phase following the recapture of Dublin and the re-establishment of Norse dynastic rule in 917. An area east of the River Poddle, beside the junction of present-day Suffolk Street, St Andrew Street, and Church Lane, was formerly characterised by at least one large mound, which many writers have referred to as the 'Thingmote' or 'Thengmotha'. It was also known as the 'hogges' (plural, probably from ON *haugr*, 'mound'). This area, now in the centre of Dublin, was extra-mural to the Viking town, and on present evidence seems to have been less densely built up. It looked out towards the 'Steine', a now-vanished stone landmark that marked the entrance to the outer harbour at the mouth of the Liffey. To the north of the 'hogges' lay an open area which is now known as College Green, but in the Medieval period was called Hoggen Green; the neighbouring monastic foundation was known as St Mary del Hogges. The main mound (there was possibly more than one) seems to have been an unusually large and prominent landmark until it was levelled in 1685, but its precise origins and date are a matter of speculation.[67] A cemetery containing at least four male weapon graves was found here, either under or beside the mound destroyed in 1685 (below, Chapter 5). Like Tynwald, the area seems to have maintained an association with political assembly in later times, which is still marked by the impressive eighteenth-century Bank of Ireland building fronting the north side of College Green, which was built to house the Irish House of Commons (abolished in 1800). The link between the 'hogges' mound(s) and the 'thing' site of early Dublin was apparently universally accepted until Seán Duffy published a revision in 1997 where he attributed the 'Thingmotte' in the later twelfth century to a small parcel of land 200m further west at Dame Street.[68] Here the victorious Henry II established his court in 1171 following the Anglo-Norman Conquest. Whatever the site of the later twelfth-century assembly (which may have changed over time), the 'hogges' mound was evidently prominent enough to have acted as a major focus of political and ceremonial life in pre-Norman Dublin.

Not all assembly sites in areas settled by Vikings necessarily had 'thing' names. Pre-Viking names survived in use for some of these, such as Moota Hill near Blindcrake in Allerdale (Cumbria),[69] or Hadlow in south Wirral.[70] Other possibilities exist on purely morphological grounds. The juxtaposition of the standing cross *Maen Achwyfan* and six prehistoric barrows in north-east Wales has been noted above. A sub-rectangular three-stepped terraced mound measuring 32m by 29m beside the farmhouse at Fell Foot, Little Langdale, Cumbria, has been suggested to be a 'thing' or local assembly site.[71] It lies on a junction of paths through the steep valleys of the Lake District, in a remote, thinly-populated location, but lacks any place-name association. A survey in 1994 provided a topographic record of the site, but did not confirm a Viking-period origin.[72] Sceptics have noted other more prosaic and recent explanations for terraced mounds.[73]

Assembly places are a well-known phenomenon in Anglo-Saxon England (where the hundred and shire 'moot' was widespread), and across the Viking world, where prominent places functioned as 'tings' (sometimes burial mounds, and sometimes prominent topographic sites, often with either a central or border location in their territories). The modern parliaments of Norway and Denmark preserve the 'ting' name, as does, famously, the Icelandic *Alþing* and its historic open-air site at Thingvellir. Tingwall and Dingieshowe (Orkney), and Dingwall, (Sutherland), show its presence in Norse Scotland. Assembly sites were originally more like courts than legislative parliaments. They were principally concerned with administering dues and justice. Markets grew up alongside some of the more important meeting sites, such as tend to be encouraged by large gatherings of people in any circumstances. In Norway, where dispersed settlement areas often existed long distances apart in a mountainous and fjord-riven landscape, the political coherence of regional chiefdoms depended on the ability of local rulers to summon those over whom they claimed to rule. Large high-status farmsteads such as Borg in Lofoten,[74] and Huseby overlooking Kaupang,[75] fulfilled a combination of political, tax-gathering, feasting and priestly ceremonial roles in pre-Christian times.

Surrounding these impressive structures were ceremonial landscapes where prominent burial mounds, byres and large boat-sheds (*nausts*) expressed the ancestral status of the chiefly lord's family and their household. It was into these rich monumental landscapes that the first churches inserted themselves, as Norway, Sweden and Denmark swung towards Christianity in the later tenth and eleventh centuries. A related phenomenon in western and northern Norway, suggesting seasonal congregations of vassals and followers, are clusters of temporary dwellings or 'booths' in the form of 'courtyard sites' (*tunanlegg*). These consist of inward-facing curved rows of small, unadorned buildings with limited occupation deposits. These consisted of three-sided walled structures to which tent-like roofs of skins supported by timber poles could be quickly added when occupied, arranged in a circle or horse-shoe surrounding a central fireplace. Most Norwegian courtyard sites are dated to the older Iron Age (*c*. AD 0–600) but several show evidence of continued occupation into the later Iron Age or Viking period.[76] Individual booths of similar type are also found at Thingvellir, although not arranged in the same closely-grouped, inward-facing way.

It is likely that Viking settlers in the Irish Sea region brought with them not only the 'thing' names but also inherited traditions and practices of chiefly power in their Scandinavian homelands. Elaborate burial, and the use and re-use of objects and art forms to create and recreate ancestral memory, were evidently essential for the imposition of authority in the new settlements (below, Chapter 8). Ongoing contacts with Scandinavia brought new stimuli throughout the tenth century, which shaped political and commemorative practice in the west. However, the experience gained particularly in Ireland during the ninth century, or more likely between the first raids in the west and the majority of consolidated Scandinavian settlement in the tenth century, must also have had a strong influence on the settlers. Vikings active as traders and warriors in Ireland during the ninth century cannot have failed to be aware of, and indeed to be drawn into, the rich and widespread culture of assembly and ceremony in Irish society. Vivid ceremonial landscapes surrounded many of the royal inauguration sites of the Irish kingdoms. At the most impressive end of the scale, at major royal sites such as Tara, Clogher and Navan, complexes of burial monuments, avenues, animal herding enclosures and buildings formed a dramatic backdrop to elaborate political and marriage ceremonies.[77] These were given dramatic meaning through verbal oration and possibly also music, and the conspicuous use of splendid garments and ornaments. Irish sources give us unparalleled colour and detail on the events that took place at these sites, but many of their impressive topographic features are also echoed in aristocratic and royal sites in Britain, such as at the citadel of Dunadd (Argyll), or at the palatial site at Yeavering (Northumberland). Even at more modest assembly sites in Ireland, as Elizabeth FitzPatrick's work has shown,[78] mounds and stone monuments continued to be used, re-used and indeed re-invented as foci of social commemoration and local political power throughout the Middle Ages. It is not difficult to envisage the Viking settlers' inherited Scandinavian traditions being adapted and reconfigured to encompass the contemporary public assembly and ceremonial practices which they had witnessed across Ireland, Scotland, Wales and England.

Rural settlement archaeology

Compared with the rich heritage of Scandinavian place-names, hoards, single finds, towns and trading sites around the Irish Sea (below, Chapter 6), archaeological evidence for rural agricultural settlement has so far been limited and disappointing in scale, especially for the first two centuries of Viking settlement. With good historical, place-name and artefactual evidence for the Viking presence in the Isle of Man and north-west England, it might be assumed that there would be plenty of recognisable settlement archaeology in the form of buildings, enclosures and field systems. This, however, has proved to be an extremely difficult *lacuna* to fill.

The Dyflinarskíri, which could be expected on the basis of Dublin's needs to have supported a vibrant agricultural hinterland, has until recently produced little clear evidence of Scandinavian settlement. The challenge of disentangling Scandinavian cultural signatures from local ones is indicated in the case of a stone cashel site at Feltrim Hill, north-east of Dublin. This was almost certainly a native Irish settlement, yet excavations in the early 1960s produced Scandinavian-style objects reminiscent of those from urban Dublin. These included copper-alloy stick and ringed pins, a bone comb, an iron spearhead and knives, beads, and a silver ingot.[79] A more recent discovery occurred in the late 1990s during redevelopment at Cherrywood, on the south-eastern outskirts of modern Dublin. A circular Iron Age enclosure, 43m in diameter, which had been re-used as a cemetery in the pre-Viking period, was reoccupied, possibly in the late ninth century. A building (Structure 1) measuring 17.5m by 6m, and displaying a slightly bow-sided 'longhouse' style shape, was constructed (*27*). Although its floor levels had been ploughed out, associated pits and foundation trenches remained. Occupation debris included animal bone and artefacts, the most striking of which is a fragment of a whalebone plaque, a rectangular, flat, bone tablet possibly used for smoothing linen, and decorated with distinctive inwardly-turned horse- or dragon-heads. These are found particularly in northern Scandinavia (a near-identical one was found in a female boat grave at Grytøy, Troms, Norway) and in pagan Viking burials in the British Isles, such as at Scar, Sanday, Orkney. This apparently early and recognisably 'Scandinavian' phase of occupation (a very rare occurrence in the Irish Sea region) was short-lived and replaced by two smaller structures, one of which (Structure 2) resembles the urban Type 1 building found in Dublin and elsewhere (below, Chapter 7). Amber and blue glass beads, a bone comb, iron objects and two copper-alloy ringed pins (below, Chapter 9) confirm the transition to a 'hybrid' cultural assemblage in both structural and artefactual terms. There is not yet a final report available for the site, so all dating remains provisional.[80]

Cherrywood Structure 1 resembles Scandinavian longhouses, in the west found more commonly at sites such as Jarlshof and the Brough of Birsay in Atlantic Scotland, than the few other domestic structures in the Irish Sea region. Another, rare example of a probable Viking longhouse in the Irish Sea region is the large bow-sided building measuring 20m by 8m at the Braaid, a settlement site located on the upper fringes of cultivated land in Marown, Isle of Man. This poorly dated structure was investigated by H.J. Fleure in 1935–7, and again by Peter Gelling in 1963.[81] No environmental or stratified dating material was reported from either of these excavations. The longhouse stands in close proximity to a rectangular stone structure, possibly a byre, and a circular one that probably represents an Iron Age roundhouse (*28*). It is impossible on current evidence to say whether all three were in use at the same time, or whether there was direct continuity of occupation between them. The Braaid was abandoned after a later phase of occupation that was

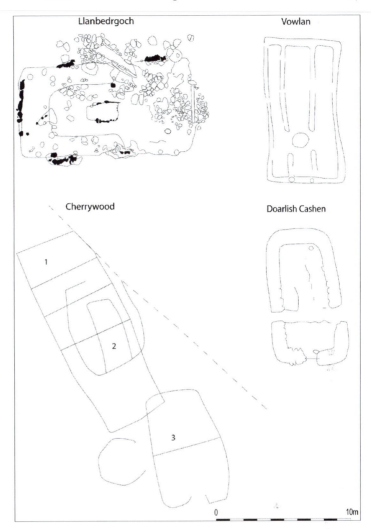

27. Comparison of buildings from rural sites

marked by small, rudimentary huts, suggesting that the earlier status implied by the size of the longhouse had declined to a mere seasonal hut or shieling.[82]

Another upland farmstead excavated in the Isle of Man by Gelling, Doarlish Cashen in Patrick, produced evidence of a smaller rectangular house measuring 7m by 3m internally, with side benches, a central hearth, and opposed doorways towards one end (**27**). An internal hollow in the east wall possibly indicated a dairy-store, and a grain-drying kiln or oven was located outside the house.[83] The building was interpreted as Viking-period, although the only datable find was a sherd of grey pottery. Doarlish Cashen was located at 210m OD within the remains of an associated field system, indicating that when it was occupied, it was part of a thriving upland economy. Gelling also excavated shieling sites with circular huts at Block Eary and Injebreck, in the mountainous central area of the island (**15**). The former bears the Norse-Gaelic toponym *óergi* and the latter Norse −*brekka* (see above), but neither site produced dating material for any earlier than the twelfth or thirteenth century. While it would be tempting to link these sites to patterns of Viking-period occupation, perhaps as a secondary movement inland from coastal estates (on the same model as proposed by Angus Winchester for Copeland in Cumbria), this is impossible on present evidence. It is a salutary fact in 2010 that we still depend largely on excavations conducted in the 1960s or before to try to build a picture of the Viking impact on the rural environment. The tiny

28. The Braaid
settlement site,
Isle of Man

and disparate amount of radiocarbon and environmental data from excavations of Scandinavian settlements on the Isle of Man, and indeed in Cumbria and other areas, needs to be comprehensively expanded and improved before we may start to create a genuinely informative landscape history for the Viking and Medieval periods in the Irish Sea region.

Dating problems have affected other sites excavated on the Isle of Man. The small coastal promontory fort at Vowlan, Ramsey, which was excavated prior to quarrying in 1946 by Gerhard Bersu (below, Chapter 5), produced a series of six building foundations preserved in the sandy soil (**29**). These, which were well defined and recorded, frustratingly lacked any finds or other dating evidence. The most complete of the buildings, A and B2, measured just over 9m by 5m, with a centrally situated hearths and side benches. Gelling's excavations at Iron Age coastal promontory forts in the 1950s and 1960s, at Cronk ny Merriu, Close ny Chollagh, and Cass ny Hawin, showed these were all reoccupied at some point in the Viking or Medieval periods, and may have been part of a coastal watch or defence system (see above). The building which Gelling exposed within the ramparts at Cronk ny Merriu bears close resemblance to the house at Doarlish Cashen, with side benches and opposed doorways. A less well preserved example of the same type was found at Cass ny Hawin, whereas at Close ny Chollagh, the building was larger and more formally rectangular (and very probably later in date). The finds indicated that the sites were occupied in the twelfth and thirteenth centuries, but Wilson does not rule out earlier occupation in the Viking period.[84] The importance of fortified Manx coastal landforms in the later Viking period and beyond is confirmed by evidence from the Peel Castle excavations in the 1980s. A tenth- or eleventh-century stone chapel (*keeill*), which had formed the focus of a major cemetery (below, Chapter 5), was demolished around the time that a hoard of Dublin Hiberno-Norse coins (dated to around 1040) was deposited near its north wall. Subsequently, there was a massive refortification of the site with a new stone rampart, within which part of a twelfth-century building interpreted as a later Norse longhouse was exposed.[85]

South-west Scotland and north-west England suffer from an even more obvious lack of coherent rural settlement archaeology for the Viking period, and more landscape research is needed (below, Chapter 9). So far, most sites which have produced any demonstrable settlement evidence of the ninth or tenth centuries in north-west England are peripheral to the region, both geographically and topographically. These include an upland settlement with a longhouse at Gauber High Pasture, Ribblehead, on the Pennine watershed, a site which is often compared with another upland settlement on marginal land at Simy Folds, Upper Teesdale, Co. Durham.[86] An excavation

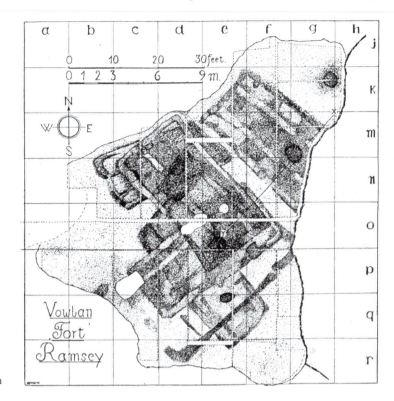

29. Vowlan Promontory
Fort, Ramsey, Isle of Man

in 1981–85 exposed parts of an upland settlement at Bryant's Gill, Kentmere (Cumbria) which may date from the Viking period. A 10m-long building with a central paved area produced a single radiocarbon date of the eighth or ninth century; finds include eight lathe-turned spindle whorls and twenty whetstones (**30**), together with iron artefacts, slag and worked stone.[87] No plan or final report on the Kentmere building has yet been published.

Older excavations and surveys have also taken place, such as those undertaken in Cumbria by W.G. Collingwood and by the Royal Commission on Historical Monuments (RCHME). Collingwood partially excavated the multi-period upland settlement of Ewe Close, near Crosby Ravensworth, in 1908, and in the 1930s, the RCHME surveyed the nearby earthwork sites Castle Folds, Cow Green, and Muddy Locks.[88] Collingwood's work at Ewe Close revealed Prehistoric and Roman finds, but later settlement potential was probably overlooked. Rectilinear buildings were mapped by the RCHME there and at the other sites, suggesting that clusters of prehistoric and Roman earthworks may have attracted settlers in the Viking or Medieval periods. In more recent times, aerial photography has supplemented earlier landscape coverage. Unexcavated possible longhouse settlements are identifiable, such as at Linglow Hill (**31**), near Great Asby in the upper Eden Valley (Cumbria). Environmental studies of vegetation histories have so far been limited in scale and generally inconsistent in their broader outcomes. Pollen evidence of upland clearance has been observed for the Medieval period in the Howgill Fells and the Forest of Bowland in the Pennine fringes east of Morecambe Bay. This may have started as early as the tenth century, but comparable studies in West Cumbria give a rather later date for the clearance phase.[89] The English Heritage-funded North-West Wetland Survey of the 1990s produced few significant advances for broader knowledge of the early Medieval landscape, despite extensive fieldwork (which did however cast considerable new light on the Prehistoric and later Medieval periods).[90] To try to remedy this chronological gap, future landscape-based environmental research should begin by targeting specific sites and landscapes which already have some proven or likely archaeological potential for the Viking period.

30. Whetstones and spindle-whorls from Bryant's Gill, Kentmere, Cumbria

31. Earthworks showing unexcavated longhouse settlement at Linglow Hill, Cumbria

32. Irby, Wirral, bow-sided buildings under
excavation in 1990

For the lowland, valley and coastal estates in north-west England where the majority of the
early settlers established themselves, we are dependent thus far on very few exposures of structures of this period. Excavations of later Medieval settlements, such as Nick Higham's work at
Tatton Park, Cheshire, may offer an indirect way forward in helping to characterise the pre-
Medieval landscape.[91] Unexpected and mostly isolated glimpses of Viking-period structures have
resulted from multi-period field projects. These included a horseshoe-shaped stone corn-drying
kiln excavated at Ewanrigg, near Maryport, on the Cumbrian coastal plain in 1987, which produced an early tenth-century radiocarbon date.[92] A small trial excavation trench in the garden of
Gosforth Hall, Cumbria, in 2004 revealed parts of a stone-walled structure and produced a tenth-
century radiocarbon date.[93] Excavations at Hoylake Road, Moreton, Wirral, in 1987–88, revealed
an enclosure ditch that had been re-cut three times, within which were detected the remains
of three timber-built structures.[94] The upper fill of the ditch produced a mudstone hone and a
mid-tenth century Anglo-Saxon silver penny (below, Chapter 6). At Irby, Wirral, excavations in
1990 produced rare structural evidence of Viking-period occupation in the form of fragments of
three probable elliptical buildings marked by gullies (*32*).[95] These have been dated to the tenth to
twelfth centuries by association with a Saxo-Norman ceramic spike lamp; an amber bead, probably of the Viking period, comes from the same site. Both Moreton and Irby are situated within
the hinterland of the trading site of Meols (below, Chapter 6). If any more general conclusion may
be drawn from these excavations as to the wider potential for identifying Viking rural settlement,
it is that lowland sites in particular tend to be associated with spreads of Roman material and
Roman structures. This is certainly the case at Irby, and some of the single finds referred to above
occurred in conjunction with Roman surface finds of pottery and coins. This observation adds
to the hypothesis that early Viking settlement in the lowland areas was most often a takeover and
adaptation of earlier or existing settlement locations.

CHAPTER 5

BURIAL: CHANGING RITES, NEW PLACES

As seen in the previous chapter, the territorial impact of the Viking presence can be traced not just through charters, land-grants and place-names, but also through the topography of burial in the landscape (*33*). Burial conducted in conspicuous and symbolic forms, such as the mound burials in Jurby Parish on the Isle of Man, or burials marked by stone monuments, were unmistakable statements of individual or communal presence (below, Chapter 8). Some of the earthen barrows on the Isle of Man referred to in Chapter 4 may have prehistoric origins, but those which have been excavated (see below) point towards a short phase of widespread and dramatic mound burial in the Viking period, so late in date as to be almost contemporary with some of the island's stone sculpture which bears vivid scenes from the Norse cultural repertoire. Furnished burial, with grave-goods, is an unmistakably new development that does not occur prior to the start of the Viking period in the west (the latest such burials from Anglo-Saxon England date to the mid-seventh century). It lasted a very short time, from around 800 to *c*. 950. Furnished burial therefore provides one of our best archaeological insights into the pagan beliefs and traditions of the Vikings. Almost from the first moment the incomers arrived, however, the new settlers began to change and redefine their traditional beliefs and customs as a result of intensive contact with the peoples they settled amongst (below, Chapter 8). A 'transitional' phase is evident, on the cusp of Christian conversion, where grave-goods representing the pagan past were reduced to a few inconspicuous items, but art on contemporary stone monuments still echoed scenes from pagan legend.

Most records of Viking burials in the Irish Sea region are antiquarian, i.e. they pre-date 1900 and lack modern standards of location, description and illustration. Human skeletal remains have rarely survived; these were largely lost or discarded, and in many later excavated examples (such as Cumwhitton, below), acid soil conditions have meant that they have decayed away to leave little or no trace. Weapon graves are traditionally interpreted as those of high-status male warriors. It is more unusual to find female burials, particularly of high enough status to merit extensive grave-goods, but the presence of Scandinavian-style oval brooches, beads and other less warlike and more domestic items have traditionally been seen as indicative of these (as noted above in Chapter 1, the male-female ratio in the Dublin area graves has been estimated at 9:1). Many such identifications are, however, based on little more than speculation and gender stereotyping in the general absence of human remains for scientific testing.

The dating of burials is dependent on relative or absolute methods, ideally, but so far rarely, used in conjunction with each other. Most common is the traditional 'relative' method, by identifying the latest-dated object amongst the grave-goods, to give a *terminus post quem* ('point after which')

33. Viking burials in the Irish Sea Region

● Burial

▲ Mound burial

■ Cemetery

0   50   100 kms

for the date of burial. We continue to depend on this for most of the Irish Sea Viking burials, but it is inexact and only produces a general indication. Coins are the most closely dated objects, but are only rarely found in graves and could have been in circulation for some time before deposition. Other artefacts are even less easy to pin down to a specific date, and in many cases have broadly-drawn chronologies covering decades or even half-centuries, such as many of the weapon and oval brooch typologies developed by the Norwegian scholar Jan Petersen in the early twentieth century.[1] Scientific 'absolute' techniques, such as radiocarbon dating, can give a probability for the date of death of people or accompanying animals, or of the biological materials used in surviving organic objects such as wooden coffins. Dendrochronology, or tree-ring dating, has been used on ships and wooden domestic structures, but has yet to make any impact on burial studies because almost no substantial surviving timbers have been found in graves. Even calibrated radiocarbon dates only give a margin of probability, which itself, unless very precise, may produce contrasting interpretations. Where organic remains are now lost, or have disintegrated beyond the point where a radiocarbon sample can be extracted, the *terminus post quem* method based on artefacts is all that we have. So far, with the notable exception of recently excavated burials from Dublin (below), radiocarbon dating has been little used for Viking burials in the Irish Sea region, although new analyses of such human bone as is preserved in museum collections may well add considerably to our understanding.

Regional surveys 1: Ireland

The single 'warrior burial' found in 2003 at Woodstown, Co. Waterford (above, Chapter 2), included a ninth-century sword of Petersen's Type U, with another lobed sword pommel, a cone-shaped iron shield boss, a spear, a battle-axe and a ferrule, a copper-alloy ringed pin and a perforated whetstone. Although the inhumation had decayed away due to acid soil conditions, the grave-goods helped to determine the early date and significance of the site.[2] The new evidence for ninth-century settlement around the Poddle at *Dubh Linn* is emphasised by the discovery of a series of inhumations for which radiocarbon and artefactual dating points towards a very early Viking presence. The Temple Bar West excavations (above, Chapter 2) produced an unfurnished child burial on the bank of the Liffey, associated with a pit in which had been deposited a complete cattle skull, similar to another pit further east on the site, where seven cattle skulls had been deposited. A series of limited excavations on redevelopment sites around the southern rim of the pool in 2003–4 discovered evidence of burials furnished with weapons and other grave-goods, some of which may date to the earliest occupation of the *longphort*.[3]

At Ship Street Great, 50m south of the pool, a truncated supine skeleton of a male aged between twenty-five and twenty-nine years was buried with two silver rings, including a fine finger ring, glass bead and corroded iron plate. A sword-blade fragment was found nearby. A larger excavation site 100m to the east at South Great George's Street included about twenty per cent of the southern and eastern margins of the pool itself, centred on a small stream inlet entering from the south-east, which had been revetted against flooding at an early stage in the occupation of the surrounding area. The archaeology on the western side of this trench was heavily truncated by later cellar-digging, but east of the small inlet four more burials were found, all buried in different orientations with head positions to the north, south-east and west. Two of these (F196 and F223)

34. Viking burial F196 with iron shield boss (centre), South Great George's Street, Dublin

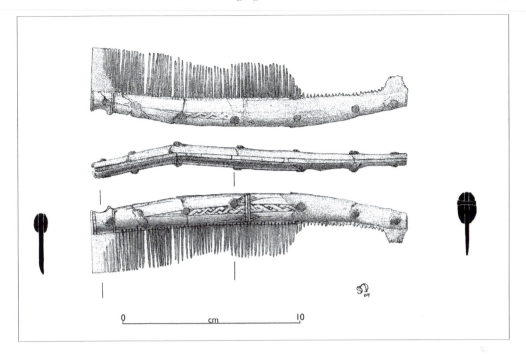

35. Antler comb from Burial F598, South Great George's Street, Dublin

had prominent weapons, including domed iron shield bosses with nails and some fragments of mineralised wood and knives, although neither had a sword (**34**). Both also had pieces of pre-burnt wood inserted in the burial, and in the chest area of F223 (which was buried on top of an existing hearth) was found a fragment of tabby-weave fabric. A third burial (F342) was represented only by the lower part of the body, and no grave-goods were found, although 151 fragments of animal bone were seemingly deliberately placed with the body. Finally a further burial (F598) produced a well preserved if truncated skeleton that had been buried with a fine antler comb (**35**), a plated iron knife-guard and a copper-alloy zoomorphic-headed pin.

These four burials were regarded by their excavator, Linzi Simpson, as an associated group, yet she refrained from using the term 'cemetery' to describe them. Only F196 and F223 can genuinely be termed full-scale 'weapon burials' but the inhumations in the other two were probably also young adult males (although some remaining doubt is attached to F342 on this due to its incompleteness). Oxygen and strontium isotope analysis (which can give a probable indication an individual's place of birth and early life by measuring traces of regionally-variable waterborne minerals in teeth and bones), suggested that F223 and F598 were probably raised in Scandinavia, whereas F196 and F342 were more likely to have been born somewhere in the Atlantic region of Britain, perhaps in the western or northern isles of Scotland. These results not only confirm the heterogeneous origins of the Vikings in Ireland, but point the way towards much more extensive studies of this kind in future.

A significant factor promoting not only an association between the four South Great George's Street and Ship Street Great burials, but a strikingly early date around the turn of the eighth and ninth centuries, was the apparent consistency of a series of radiocarbon dates. These were applied to sampled parts of the surviving bone matter that concentrates within the period AD 770–800, with only F598 of the South Great George Street burials apparently dating to somewhat later in the ninth century.

Site/Burial	Radiocarbon probability (ninety-five per cent confidence)	Intercept date	Oxygen isotope value and suggested origin	
Ship St Great	AD 665–865	AD 790	Data not currently available	
S. Great George St F196	AD 670–880	AD 770	–7.7	Atlantic
S. Great George St F223	AD 670–880	AD 770	–10.4	Scandinavia
S. Great George St F342	AD 689–882	AD 782	–7.5	Atlantic
S. Great George St F598	AD 786–955	AD 885	–11.2 to –13.8	? Scandinavia
Golden Lane LXXXV	AD 678–832	Not given	Data not currently available	
Golden Lane CXXIX	AD 680–870	Not given	Data not currently available	

Scientific analyses of recently excavated burials from Dublin, after Simpson 2005 and O'Donovan 2008

Given the recorded history of Viking Dublin, which begins only in around 840 (above, Chapter 2), these dates seem perplexingly early. However, the data presented above may not convey as simple a message as it seems to. Radiocarbon dating gives us a range of probability. The 'intercept date' is based on a statistical calculation method about which significant scientific doubts exist, and which could be substantially reworked with the benefit of new data.[4] Simpson herself acknowledged the possible influence of the 'Marine Reservoir Effect', where a larger-than-average dietary intake of marine proteins over the lifetime of an individual or an animal can give an artificially-early date of up to several decades when the consuming individual's bone collagen is dated. Scientific analysis is ongoing, so tempting though it may be to leap to premature judgment, it is too early to be certain that four out of the seven people who were buried at these sites all died in the period before 800. Their dates of death *could* have been several decades later, according more closely with the historical foundation of Viking Dublin.

Simpson suggested on the basis of the South Great George's Street burials and the surrounding evidence for occupation including flood revetments, hearths and burnt animal bone that the earliest site of the Dublin *longphort* may have been on the eastern side of the pool. In view of lingering doubt about the early radiocarbon dates of the burials, the question remains open to continuing inquiry. There is no reason in principle why the *longphort* and its associated occupation could not have encompassed both sides of the small tidal pool, perhaps utilising the southern bank as a focus for burial or industry. The Ship Street Great burial was located in close proximity to the church of St Michael le Pole, which had its own Christian cemetery. 272 burials from this cemetery were excavated in a site facing Golden Lane in 2005, including two 'satellite' furnished burials located outside the main concentration of graves (LXXXV and CXXIX).[5] The former, the truncated burial of a young, well-built male, included a belt buckle and strap end almost identical to similar examples excavated in Cumbria and the Isle of Man (below, Chapter 8), together with an iron spearhead, a knife and two lead weights. The latter, a female burial, was only tentatively associated with Viking-period finds. Another (less well recorded) burial found in 1860 at Bride Street, a short distance to the west, had a sword, spearhead and shield boss – this arguably could have been an outlier of the same broad cluster, although rather than St Michael le Pole, it may be associated with nearby St Brigit's Church.

Without adequate radiocarbon dating or stratified coin finds, however, it is difficult to be certain that most of the other furnished burials in Ireland (most of which were discovered many years ago) date from the ninth or the tenth century. The recently-excavated burials south of the Pool add to a picture of discrete clusters of burial across what is now termed the Greater Dublin area, far exceeding the geographical scope of the *longphort* or even the tenth- and eleventh-century town.[6] Further furnished burials have been found south of the River Liffey and east of the Poddle at College Green, and sword finds at Cork Street and Kildare Street. The probable cemetery of at least four male graves at College Green lay close to, or under, the mound known as the 'Hogges' (above, Chapter 4). Raghnall Ó Floinn disputed the assumption made by other scholars that the College Green burials were tenth-century in date, arguing that the presence of weapons (two swords, four spearheads and a shield-boss), together with other objects including a copper-alloy buckle and antiquarian notes of 'some silver fibulae', could as easily be ninth century.[7] On the northern side of the Liffey, antiquarian reports describe at least one female grave (with a pair of Petersen Type 37 oval brooches and a third which re-used a fragment of insular metalwork) from Phoenix Park, suggested by Ó Floinn to be in the vicinity of the Christian site of Cell Moshamóc. Nearer to the city centre but still north of the Liffey, a series of poorly-recorded furnished burials at Palace Row and Granby Row were found in the 1760s and 1780s.[8] These may possibly have represented a cluster of furnished graves in the area of Parnell Square, indicating that the 'North Side' of Dublin probably saw more intensive Viking activity than is sometimes assumed.

The largest burial cluster of all, itself accounting for a majority of Viking burials in Ireland, occurred at the western edge of Dublin, in what was either a single cemetery, or alternatively two closely related cemetery groups, stretching between Kilmainham, and Islandbridge 800m further west (**36**).[9] They lay close to the early Christian monastery of Cell Maignenn (Kilmainham), offering further possible evidence of interplay between Scandinavian pagan and Irish Christian traditions, and are, therefore, to be compared with the burials south of the Pool described above. The Kilmainham/Islandbridge burials have for many years been seen as indicative of a possible site for the *longphort* on the western fringes of Dublin, although no domestic or settlement evidence has been found in the vicinity. Indeed, Linzi Simpson pointed out that in later centuries, Kilmainham was used as a detached extra-mural burial place for the city, so there is no reason why this tradition might not have Viking-period origins.

The burials came to light in sporadic exposures over a period of around 150 years, from the late eighteenth century onwards. They were disturbed because they lay in an area of gravel quarrying which later was to lie across the line of approach to Dublin's main western railway terminus. Early antiquarian involvement, firstly by Joseph Huband Smith of the Royal Irish Academy, and later by George Petrie and Sir William Wilde,[10] ensured that many of the grave-goods were saved; these were illustrated for the Royal Irish Academy in an extensive series of fine watercolour plates known

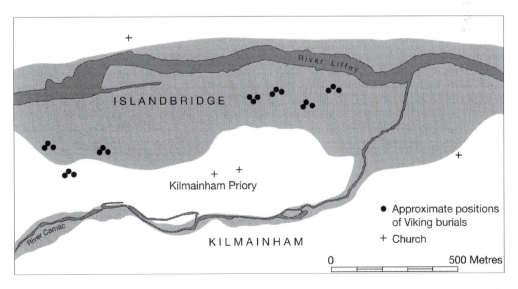

36. The Kilmainham-Islandbridge area, Dublin

as the 'Plunket Tables' after their artist (**37**). The objects were exhibited at meetings and commented upon by leading authorities of the day, most notably by the Danish antiquarian J. J. A. Worsaae, who visited Dublin in 1846–47 (above, Chapter 1). Worsaae published a description which is almost certainly based on speaking to people with first-hand experience of the discoveries:

> In constructing a railway […] workmen some years ago laid bare a number of ancient tombs. In these lay whole rows of skeletons, each in its own grave, and by the side of them many weapons and ornaments.

He went to say that:

> The great number of graves, and the careful manner in which each is said to have been set or enclosed with stones, show that they were made in all tranquility by the Norwegians and Danes.[11]

Further exposures of burials occurred during the construction of the War Memorial Park at Islandbridge in 1933–34, when the Austrian-born archaeologist, Adolf Mahr, then serving as Director of the National Museum, excavated and photographed two or three inhumations accompanied by weapons. However, the precise locations and extents of the burial complex remained poorly understood and unpublished in any detail until Elizabeth O'Brien's reappraisal in the 1990s. Despite the lack of secure antiquarian information on the precise number and extent of the burials, detailed scrutiny of the surviving information suggested that the two cemeteries together produced a minimum of forty-three furnished burials, with Kilmainham producing twenty-seven male and three female, and Islandbridge seventeen male and two female graves. The dating emphasis, based on a study of the artefacts, is on the ninth century, although some of the graves might be as late as the early tenth century.[12] It is possible that burial at the cemeteries ceased after Dublin was sacked in 902, but further detailed research is required to confirm this. The male

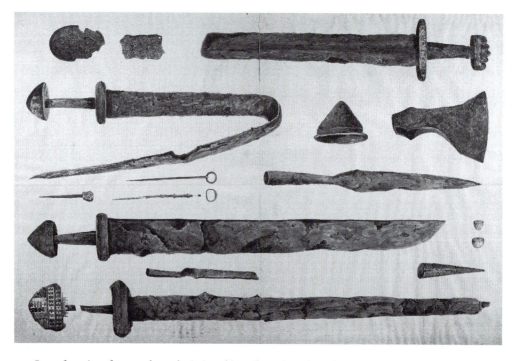

37. One of a series of watercolours depicting objects from the Kilmainham/Islandbridge burials, Dublin, by James Plunket, 1847

graves were identifiable by the presence of weapons, including swords, shield bosses and axes of Scandinavian types, although a lesser number of Frankish and Anglo-Saxon swords was also present.[13] A distinctive conical type of shield boss has been identified by Stephen Harrison as an 'Irish Sea' type (*37,* centre right) and is represented elsewhere in the region, such as at Balladoole and Woodstown. Some of the weapons had been ritually 'killed' by breaking or bending out of shape. The burials were accompanied by personal ornaments and items including equal-armed and oval brooches, pins and beads. The burials also produced knives, gaming pieces and lead weights. Ringed pins are depicted on several of the 'Plunket Tables'. These objects are not of Scandinavian origin, but instead reflect convergence and reinvention of material culture types within the Viking settlements of Ireland. This shows that from an early stage the Dublin Vikings were adapting their cultural and technical *repertoire* to encompass and reformulate new influences from the host country (below, Chapter 8).

The Dublin area accounts for the overwhelming majority of Viking graves in Ireland, reflecting its dominance as the location of Viking settlement prior to the mid-tenth century when furnished burial largely ceased. Bøe recorded a possible male burial at Dollymount, on the north-eastern fringes of Dublin, and a male burial with sword, spearhead and arrowheads, allegedly accompanied by two unfurnished female burials, was found in 1879 in what was described as a 'great sepulchral mound' (actually an existing Irish burial ground) at Aylesbury Road, Donnybrook, south-east of the mouth of the Liffey.[14] In 2004 a furnished adult female inhumation was discovered close to the church at Finglas (the site of an early monastery), on the northern outskirts of the city. The woman was aged between twenty-five and thirty-five, and she was found with a complete oval brooch on her shoulder with a fragmented second brooch, a bone comb, and surviving scraps of textile from garments. This was initially reported as a burial of the ninth century, although a calibrated radiocarbon date has yet to appear in print.[15]

Elsewhere in Ireland, the distribution of Viking graves is predominantly coastal, isolated, and not of recent discovery, meaning that few of the burial sites are fully understood archaeologically. Inland, but possibly related to the extended influence of Dublin in the central and eastern midlands, are finds of human bones with a battle-axe and 'other iron weapons' from Barnhall, Co. Kildare (1788), and a skeleton with horse-bit, harness mounts and 'buttons' (possibly weights) from Navan. Co. Meath (1848).[16] On the Leinster coast south of Dublin at Three-Mile Water, between Wicklow and Arklow (Co. Wicklow), a female grave with two oval brooches and a silver chain was discovered close to the shoreline in 1900.[17] Oval brooches of Petersen Type 51 (see also Claughton Hall and Cumwhitton, below) are most often dated to the late ninth to early tenth century, and hence this burial is unlikely to be connected to the earliest Viking presence, but more probably a post-917 settlement in the locality. A nearby find of a fragmentary sword with a fine silver-plated guard and gold filigree, from a coastal peat deposit at the Morragh, across the river from Wicklow town, may be more comparable in date to the Kilmainham burials.[18]

Another Viking cemetery exists at Church Bay, Rathlin Island (Co. Antrim), the island that is a leading candidate for identification as the *Rechru* of the 795 raid. A splendid silver penannular brooch of Irish manufacture, known as the Rathlin or 'University' Brooch (given to Trinity College but now in the National Museum, Dublin), was disinterred from amongst bones within stone cists in a group of 'small tumuli' on the flat coastal strand here prior to 1784. A later account from the 1850s described a 'great number' of skeletons, at least one of which had an iron sword, and a brass vessel, ladle or patera; rings and beads are also mentioned, along with pottery of Bronze-Age date.[19] Viking-period inhumations here, the precise number of which is unclear, were evidently buried above or alongside an existing prehistoric cemetery. Nearby on the same bayside strand is the site of an early Christian monastery – the obvious target for the raid, if it took place here and not on Lambay. Are these grave finds, therefore, connected to the 795 raid? Based on present information, this link cannot be substantiated. Sustained burial practice requires at least a semi-permanent presence, which here, in all probability, is later in date than the raid. There is evidence of probable later Viking activity on Rathlin: there is a Hiberno-Norse coin hoard from the island dated to the mid-eleventh century, and there are annalistic references to the Dublin Vikings defeating the Ulaid on *Rechru* in 1045. Archaeological surveys have been carried out on sites in other areas of Rathlin by the universities of Ulster and Queens, Belfast, in recent years, but have yet to offer further illumination on the site of the burials.

Other Viking burials in Ulster are also coastal, and seemingly isolated, although further land-scape research in their vicinity may yet reveal evidence of related occupation. At Ballyholme, Co. Down, in what was probably a mound on a sandy foreshore (a situation not unlike Rathlin), a female burial with a pair of ninth-century Petersen Type 37 oval brooches (see e.g. **37** upper left) and a bronze bowl was found in 1903. This may have been a boat burial, as a contemporary description refers to it being found in a V-shaped cutting.[20] Ó Floinn suggested that its location within 2km of the monastery of Bangor indicated a localised Viking settlement and perhaps even a temporary takeover of the monastery in the ninth century. At nearby Larne (Co. Antrim), a burial on the shore with a sword, spearhead, comb and ringed pin was found in 1840 south of the modern town. Like Ballyholme (ON *holm*, 'island'), the site is associated with a Norse place-name. The small inlet of Larne Lough was named *Ulfreksfjord* in Snorri Sturlason's *Heimskringla* in reference to a defeat by the Irish of Earl Einar of Orkney in 1018, possibly implying another small coastal settlement at a strategic natural harbour. A possible boat burial from Ballywillin, Co. Antrim[21] – together with isolated finds, including a sword from Cah (Co. Derry) and a ringed pin from Kinnegar Strand on Lough Swilly (Co. Donegal),[22] all of which were once seen as evidence of further burials – have more recently been dismissed.[23]

The Ulster distribution of Viking burials, therefore, remains sparse and entirely coastal. On the more remote and exposed west coast of Ireland, a male weapon burial was found in eroding sand dunes at Eyrephort, Co. Galway, in 1947.[24] This, like the northern Irish burials, and indeed those at Benllech and Talacre on the north coast of Wales (see below), was seen at the time of its discovery as the result of an isolated landfall by seaborne Vikings. This has since been reinter-preted as indicative of probable localised settlement,[25] and indeed archaeological evidence of a sunken-featured building and middens, with a find of a Hiberno-Norse antler comb, associated with two unfurnished burials, has been found in sand dunes four miles south of Eyrephort at False Bay, Truska townland.[26] The type of building echoes the structure discovered many years ago at Beginish Island, Co. Kerry, which had a complete steatite bowl.[27] Also in Co. Kerry is the cave site of Cloghermore, where twenty-four burials – some with Viking-type objects such as amber beads, combs, a whetstone and a single spearhead, along with animal burials – were discovered in 1999–2000. A silver hoard of armlets and ingots was found nearby. The excavators were confident that this site reflects a settlement of Scandinavians (who they argued came from Sweden) in the south-western Irish landscape.[28] However, we now know that silver and other generally smaller Scandinavian-style objects were in widespread circulation amongst the Irish population, so, as with many of the other burials, the biological and cultural identities of the inhumations continue to be a matter of debate.

Regional surveys 2: The Isle of Man

Excavations of Viking burials in the Isle of Man were pioneered by two scholars, one a Manxman and one a German refugee. P. M. C. (Philip) Kermode (1855–1932) was a lawyer and later Curator of the Manx Museum, whose massive publication of the Manx Crosses (1907) is still a standard work of reference.[29] Kermode's excavation of a mound at Knock-y-Doonee in autumn 1927, on the sandy northern coastal plain of the island, foreshadowed further investigations of mound buri-als in the 1940s. Knock-y-Doonee was excavated poorly in Wilson's opinion,[30] but was promptly, if briefly, published in 1930.[31] The mound has subsequently been reconstructed. Approximately 17m in diameter (reduced somewhat by ploughing on its northern side) and 2.3m high, it was built up with layers of reddish sand packed around a core of stone boulders that surrounded and protected the central burial. Over 260 iron rivets or clench-nails, some with decayed wood still attached, were found. Their position was not closely recorded but their elongated distribution pattern in an area measuring 10m by 2m led Kermode to suggest that they represented the remains of a boat within which the burial had been placed. Only a scrap of human cranium remained, but a better-preserved group of horse bones was found at its eastern end. The inhumation was accompanied by a weapon group including an axe, a hemispherical shield boss, a broken sword with a wooden scabbard and silver wire on the guard (identified by Wilson as Petersen Type U – a type interestingly not found in Ireland),[32] a spear with parts of the wooden haft still attached, together with an enamelled copper-alloy pin, a buckle, leather fragments, iron tools suggesting smithing, fishing gear, and the metal attachments and mounts of a bridle. The weapons were of original Scandinavian types, whereas the personal and equestrian ornaments showed a more hybrid mixture of Hiberno-Norse and Frankish objects.

The Isle of Man was designated by the British Government during the Second World War as an internment camp for German nationals. Many of those incarcerated on the island were opposed to Hitler, but nevertheless spent the war in enforced exile. One such was Professor Gerhard Bersu (1889–1964), an established academic who fled from Frankfurt to England in 1935. Bersu excavated major Neolithic sites on Salisbury Plain in the late 1930s, and went on after the war to hold distinguished chairs in Ireland and West Germany. Between 1944 and 1946, with local volunteer labour, he excavated three burial mounds, at Balladoole in Arbory Parish in the south of the island, and Ballateare and Cronk Moar in Jurby Parish. Bersu also excavated trenches at several other sites on the island, including St Patrick's Isle, Peel, and at Vowlan, Ramsey (above, Chapter 4). The finds from the 'three Viking graves' were lodged in the Manx Museum, but Bersu did not live to see final publication of the excavations, which came about under the editorship and co-authorship of Wilson as the first monograph of the Society for Medieval Archaeology in 1966.[33]

Two of Bersu's Viking grave sites, Ballateare and Cronk Moar, were prominent barrow burials overlooking the north-west coast of the island, with central furnished inhumations in lined sunken pits. Cronk Moar, a degraded sandy mound of approximately 10m diameter, had been largely cleared as an upstanding mound in the late summer of 1939 for the construction of Jurby RAF airfield. The removal of the mound (which took place under the archaeological supervision of two Manchester geography students) left the central burial pit unexcavated – a job that was completed by Bersu after the end of hostilities, in October 1945. The rectangular burial pit was lined with the remains of oak planks, and inside it was a fragmentary male skeleton with the remains of a pile-weave cloak fastened by a plain-ringed polyhedral-headed ringed pin of probable early tenth-century date.[34] A sword with an ornamented leather-covered scabbard was associated with a series of zoomorphic copper-alloy strap distributors, mounts and buckles forming a baldric/belt arrangement for a sword sling, a conical iron shield boss, a spear-head, an iron knife and a number of rivets found in both 1939 and 1945, which gave rise to the mistaken initial impression between these interventions that a boat burial lay within the mound.

Ballateare was also what might be termed a 'rescue' excavation, as the burial mound was obstructive to farmyard traffic and Bersu was allowed to examine it in 1946 prior to its removal by the landowner. The mound, which measured 12m in diameter by 3m high, was excavated in 20cm spits in quadrants (*38*). Just below its upper surface, which was marked by a post-hole and sealed by a layer of cremated animal bone, was discovered the horizontal and poorly-preserved skeleton (with upraised arms suggesting rigor mortis), of an adolescent or young adult female, the back of whose skull had been sliced off in a violent blow by a very sharp slashing weapon (*39*). No grave-goods were associated with this dramatic and unexpected discovery, but much lower down, below the original ground-level under the turf-constructed mound, was found the rectangular burial pit (*40*) of a male skeleton aged between eighteen and thirty, accompanied by a suite of weapons and personal ornaments, including a Petersen Type V sword with a copper and silver inlaid hilt, a leather-covered wooden scabbard, a copper-inlaid spearhead (both of Scandinavian type, probably from Norway), and a hemispherical shield boss with apparently deliberate slashed damage representing 'ritual killing', associated with gesso-decorated wood fragments in alternate white and black bands with red dots.[35] A copper-alloy strap distributor, probably from a sword sling on a belt much like the Cronk Moar example, two spearheads of Irish style and a polyhedral-headed ringed

38. Ballateare: Bersu's excavation

39. Ballateare: the female skull

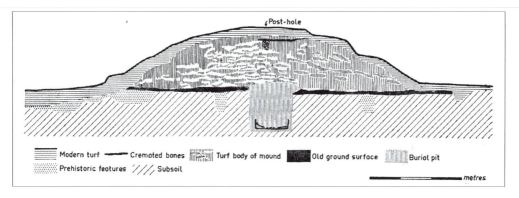

40. Ballateare: half section of the mound showing central burial pit and overlying features

pin, completed the hybrid Irish Sea references, and a somewhat 'late' (early to mid-tenth century) deposition date for the burial seems likely.

A male inhumation with weapons, well away from a church or consecrated burial site, was perhaps enough in itself to justify an interpretation of a truly unchristian burial, but the visions of horror prompted by the presence of the semi-decapitated female in the upper layers of the mound have perhaps given undue prominence to this single, unusual example, and have come to epitomise the heathendom of the early Viking presence on the island. The presence of the female body is apparently easily explained: surviving accounts of Viking funerary practice such as that of the Arabic commentator Ibn Fadlan – whose description of a Viking funeral in the early 920s on the River Volga in Russia is one of the most colourful and oft-quoted – point towards the rape and sacrifice of young female slaves as part of extended ritual performances at the highest-status funerals.[36] The Hindu term 'Suttee' has also been invoked. So conclusive seem these allusions that few commentators on Ballateare have sought to question whether the female was indeed sacrificed at, or for, the funeral of the male buried beneath. Nevertheless the dry and cautious words of the 1966 pathologist's report stated that 'It was impossible to say whether this injury [i.e. the slashing of the skull] had occurred in life or death',[37] although the time of injury was judged to be within forty-eight hours at most of death, as the particular effect of the cut required the brain to be fully intact supporting the inside of the skull. It could therefore just possibly have been a post-mortem act, with the real cause of death being illness, or injury to soft tissue, the effects of which are no longer detectible. Did the woman die elsewhere, to be prepared for burial here – not as a sacrifice, but as a melancholy and respectful addendum to the 'main event' of the male inhumation? Opening a person's skull in this way could be seen as an act of trepanation, as a means of liberating evil spirits, madness or internal pressure from within the head, perhaps allowing the soul to depart or otherwise find peace. None of these alternative theories can be proved, any more than that of ritual sacrifice, but they at least serve to show how common assumptions may be challenged.

Although different in its landscape context, the mound excavated by Bersu at Balladoole was similar to Knock-y-Doonee in that it was also a boat burial with an equestrian theme. The Volga funeral described by Ibn Fadlan also involved boats, fire, and the slaughter of domesticated animals including dogs and horses. The horse/boat combination found by Kermode at Knock-y-Doonee is an unusual feature in Irish Sea burials, but is paralleled very closely by a grave found in sand dunes at Kiloran Bay, Colonsay (Inner Hebrides) in 1882.[38] The burial site at Balladoole is located within a small earthwork enclosure of prehistoric date overlooking Bay ny Carrickey, on the island's sheltered southern shore (*41*). At the west end of the enclosure, known as 'Camp Keeill Vael', is the site of a small chapel of later Medieval date. Bersu had begun his excavation work here only with the intention of investigating the prehistoric earthwork, but just to the south-west of the eastern entrance was surprised to discover the Viking burial cairn, which was not visible on the surface at that time (it has now been reconstructed) (*42*). It lay below an eroded sandy

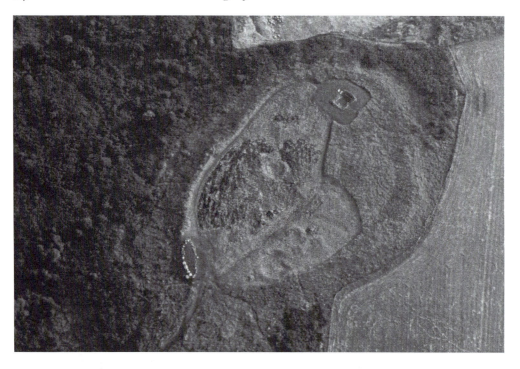

41. Camp Keeill Vael,
Balladoole, Isle of
Man: Viking burial on
boundary towards lower
left

42. Balladoole: the
reconstructed stone
ship-setting

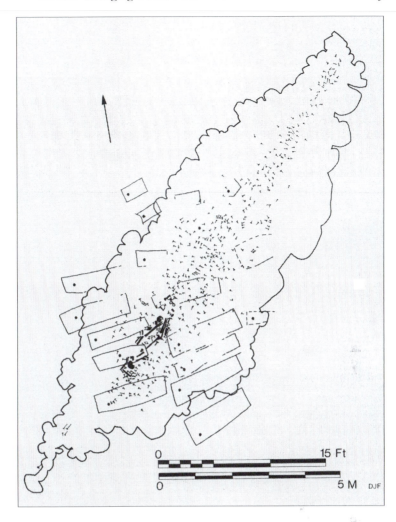

43. Balladoole: plan of burial (with clench-nails); lintel graves beneath

mound 0.7m high which is now gone. The burial was placed within a boat marked by at least 268 iron clench-nails in an elongated hollow, lined by large boulders and banked with smaller stones along its outside, measuring 11m by 3m, suggesting that the boat inside was 9m or 10m long and about 2.5m–3m wide. A line of heavier clench-nails was found at the centre of the distribution, suggesting these held together the joints of the keel and lower strakes; traces of the edges of oak planks clinging to some of the nails suggested it may have been a clinker-constructed boat (**43**). In a recent study, Howard Williams suggested that the boat could have been buried with mast and rigging showing above the mound – an attractive proposition for which there is sadly no surviving evidence.[39] Cremated horse bones were found with those of dog, cat, ox, pig and sheep in the upper layers of the mound. Iron stirrups emphasise the equestrian theme, and iron loops may have been part of a leather saddle. Amongst the grave-goods, perhaps the most impressive is a group of copper-alloy bridle mounts bearing roundels and incised panels, with a silver-gilt buckle and copper-alloy strap ends bearing Frankish/Carolingian-style vegetal ornament. Unusually there were few weapons – no sword, but a conical shield boss and handle of a type paralleled at Kiloran Bay, but unlike contemporary examples in Scandinavia. Knives, an iron bucket, a strike-a-light, a pierced whetstone, a fragment of linen cloth and a ringed pin of ninth- or early tenth-century type completed the personal apparel and equipment of a male skeleton in the southern end of the boat – undoubtedly the focus of the burial.

Two further skulls were thought at the time to be associated with the main Balladoole inhuma-tion, perhaps representing female or slave burials, but these now seem more likely to be displaced from what lay underneath the boat burial. The stone boat-shaped cairn had been raised on top of an existing lintel-grave cemetery of early Christian date (*44*). At least seventeen east–west ori-ented graves in shale long-cists, without grave-goods, were arranged in three north–south rows beneath the boat burial cairn. The kerb and stones surrounding the boat had breached a number of the lintel graves, leading to the possibility that the skulls were derived from them – possibly they had been deliberately reburied along with the contents of the boat burial. The juxtaposi-tion of the boat burial and the lintel graves has given rise to conflicting interpretations. Wilson, possibly reflecting Bersu's view, suggested in the 1966 monograph that the boat burial had 'delib-erately slighted' the Christian graves in order to demonstrate that the Vikings 'were now masters in the island'.[40] The 'desecration' theme (a word also used in the 1966 monograph) was picked up even more fiercely by Sarah Tarlow in a 1997 article, who interpreted the evidence as a 'violent rejection' of Christian ideology in a 'struggle for symbolic and actual possession for the most prominent position in the landscape'.[41] Wilson rowed back somewhat on the confrontation theme in his 2008 version, only partly agreeing with Tarlow and pointing to an 'acceptance of the sacred nature of the site'.

The four mound burial excavations briefly summarised above add to a fragmentary picture of earlier and other, less well documented discoveries. Mid-nineteenth-century finds of Viking weapons thought to be from possible mound burials are known from Ballelby, Patrick Parish, and Ballaugh. A mound at Ballachrink, Jurby Parish, was opened in 1880 revealing a 'sword, spearhead

44. Balladoole: Bersu's
excavation, the Viking burial
cairn with lintel graves beneath

45. St Patrick's Isle/Peel Castle, Isle of Man, from west. The tenth-century burials were immediately north of the roofless cathedral at the east perimeter

and perforated stone disc', and another known as Cronk yn How, in Lezayre Parish, was partially excavated in the 1920s revealing clench-nails, a glass bead and a spindle whorl – like Balladoole, this mound was raised over a pre-existing lintel-grave cemetery.[42] Not all furnished burials in the Isle of Man were in obvious mounds. Viking objects, including weapons, have been found in a cluster of flat lintel graves in the vicinity of Tynwald Hill (above, Chapter 4). A group of Scandinavian weapons was found in the 1970s at Claghbane, near Ramsey, apparently without an obvious association with a body, which led A.M. Cubbon to suggest that this site may have been a cenotaph,[43] or empty burial – an interpretation only very cautiously aired by Wilson.

A further series of finds of Viking weapons, predominantly swords, has come from Christian contexts in Manx churchyards, at Kirk Braddan, Malew, Maughold, West Nappin, Jurby and Kirk Michael. The close juxtaposition of furnished burial and churchyards is a widespread one, as some of the Dublin examples have shown, and other examples exist in south-west Scotland and Cumbria.[44] Nevertheless, a number of keeills (chapels) with extensive burial grounds came into use as Norse chapels after the Christian conversion took hold on the island, and the presence of a large burial mound within Jurby churchyard reminds us that Christian burials occur on sites before *and* after furnished Viking burials. The most extensively documented group of burials was excavated in 1982–87,[45] just to the north of the roofless shell of the Medieval St German's Cathedral, on St Patrick's Isle, the castellated islet (**45**) forming the outer rim of Peel Harbour. St Patrick's Isle (also known as Peel Castle), although probably not the *Inis Phátraic* raided in 798, has been a centre of Christianity on the Isle of Man since the sixth century. Numerous cross-inscribed slabs have been found during these and previous excavations, and its stone round tower has traditionally been compared with Irish examples, such as those at Glendalough and Clonmacnoise. The site has a tradition of burial from pre-Viking lintel-grave cemeteries, through the Viking period and onwards into the Medieval period and beyond.

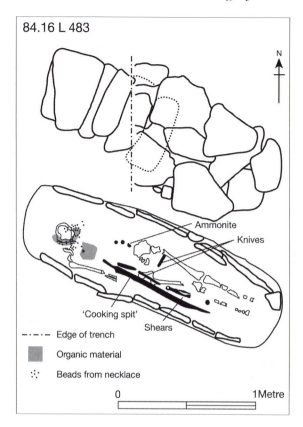

46. Peel Castle, Isle of Man, the 'Pagan Lady' burial

Amidst 327 individual burials identified at Peel Castle (mostly later Medieval), there were seven of tenth-century date, identified as such by artefacts and coins.[46] Two of these were of infants, one (uncoffined) of which had an Anglo-Saxon silver penny of Eadred (946–55) in its mouth, and the other (coffined) was buried with a quartz pebble, six glass beads and one of amber, a suspension ring and a small pyramidal copper-alloy bell of a type found elsewhere in the Irish Sea region and beyond (Chapter 8). A coin of Edmund (939–46) was found on the floor of the grave under an adult inhumation, which had been wrapped in shroud made of a reused garment, decorated with eighteen woven silver-wire balls, a polyhedral-headed ringed pin, and a small copper-alloy buckle with an interlace-decorated plate. Two further adult coffin burials (identified as such by the iron nails and fittings found in the graves) were each accompanied by groups of objects; the more extensive one included an iron knife with the remains of a scabbard decorated with a round glass ornament, a roundel-decorated copper-alloy buckle, a strap end embedded in decayed woven fabric with a particularly fine gilt interlace panel attached, and a blue glass bead; the other had a square buckle, a strap end, a loop-headed ringed pin, the iron rivets from a comb, and an iron awl. A further (uncoffined) adult burial had four silver-wire balls similar to those in the grave with the Eadred coin, probably coming from a cloak or shroud.

By far the most impressive grave in the tenth-century cluster (no. 84.16/L.483) was found within a robustly built stone cist, built elaborately, but still within the existing Manx lintel-grave tradition, and which had, to a great extent, protected the burial from later disturbance (**46**). It was the only one of the seven where the skeleton survived sufficiently for its sex and approximate age to be clearly determined – a middle-aged woman, showing evidence of rickets (a symptom of Vitamin D deficiency caused by diet and low exposure to sunlight). The skeleton was supine and extended, with the skull laid on the remains of a feather pillow. With the body was a collection of ten objects, carefully laid within the cist. These included two iron knives, one with a silver-wire decorated handle, an antler comb, two needles in a bag of organic material, a pair of iron shears, a decayed mass comprising a copper-alloy rod and fragments with three glass beads, an iron ring, a stone cube, an ammonite fossil, a goose wing, and a curious small stone cup-shaped object interpreted as a pestle and mortar. Some of these objects are so unusual and impractical that they have been seen as symbolic or magic objects, implying pagan rituals in life or at death. Most impressive of all was a collection of seventy-one amber, glass and jet beads that had formed a single, splendidly coloured necklace. A further object, a tapering iron rod, 83.7cm long, with the impressions of feathers in decayed textile in its corrosion products, was interpreted by James Graham-Campbell, who wrote the published report, as a cooking spit.[47] However, an alternative theory has been advanced by a leading commentator on Viking religion and ritual, Neil Price.[48] He suggested that the rod or spit indicates that the dead woman had been a vólva or sorceress. Price pointed towards a small number of seeds sieved from the grave deposits as possible evidence for hallucinogenic herbs, but disappointingly, subsequent botanical identification has not supported this suggestion, indicating that they are merely charred cereal grains.[49]

Peel's 'Pagan Lady', as this burial quickly became known following its discovery, presents in microcosm almost all of the interpretative issues and problems surrounding the spread of Viking culture in the Irish Sea region. The dead woman's biological ancestry and geographical origin is unknown, as no DNA or stable isotope analysis has yet been carried out on her remains. She was buried with an elaborate display of objects (some of which hint at magic and pagan practice), almost certainly in the early decades of the tenth century. Although located in proximity to six roughly contemporary graves, each with some grave-goods, hers was by far the most elaborate, and therefore stands out as a special burial within this group. Yet the structure and location of her burial were embedded in the indigenous tradition of the long-lived Christian cemetery on St Patrick's Isle – east-west oriented, and within a stone cist or lintel grave. Although parallels exist in Scandinavia for high-status and even 'magical' female burials, apart from the iron staff, none of the objects buried with Peel's lady is of unambiguously Scandinavian type. How representative was she of contemporary culture and society? One mitigating factor in our lack of certainty about this point is that the cemetery was not fully excavated: other burials remain *in situ* outside the 1980s excavation trenches, and amongst these may lie the answer as to whether the 'Pagan Lady' was partnered by other, similarly spectacular, burials.

The tenth-century Peel burials represented an unusual but temporary phenomenon amidst the more long-lived tradition of unfurnished lintel graves. By the end of the second quarter of the tenth century, as far as we can tell on present evidence, mound burial had ceased in the Isle of Man and burial practice reverted to lintel graves concentrated within detached cemeteries (*rhullicks*) and around keeills and churches. Almost contemporaneously with the end phase of furnished burial came the emergence of a newly invigorated tradition of stone sculpture, accompanied in some cases by runic inscriptions to add to the revived use of Ogham. A reinvention of a long-lived indigenous tradition of stone memorials, it brought the language and symbolism of the Old Norse world into a vibrant encounter with the re-emergent twin themes of Gaelic culture and Christianity (below, Chapter 8).

Regional surveys 3: From the Solway Firth to Wales

The Manx mound burials are unique in their concentration and visibility in the landscape. There were, however, as we have seen, also possible mound burials in the Dublin area. The evidence from the British side of the Irish Sea is more diffuse, with fewer obvious traces grouped so clearly together, suggesting patchier and more localised patterns of Viking influence.[50] At Aspatria, (Cumbria), on fertile land facing the Solway, a burial mound was discovered and removed in 1789. About 30m in circumference, it stood 2m in height upon a slight rise known as Beacon Hill. The mound was 'levelled', during which a stone kerb or cist was exposed beneath the cairn, inside which was a poorly preserved skeleton. A report of the discovery with an engraving of the finds (**47**) was published in the journal *Archaeologia*.[51] The burial was accompanied by grave-goods (now lost) including a sword of Viking type, with a straight guard decorated with 'inlaid silver flowers' but missing its handle, a dagger (or possible a spearhead) 'studded with silver', a spearhead, a gold or gilt strap end of Frankish/Carolingian type, a gold buckle, and iron objects including a spur, a horse bit, an axe and possibly the remains of a shield. Also illustrated were two curious carved boulders bearing circular and linear marks – these may have been Bronze or Iron Age in origin and have been re-used as part of the stone cairn of the Viking burial, although no other prehistoric material was apparently discovered. The site was re-investigated in 1997 in advance of the construction of a mobile telephone antenna on Beacon Hill.[52] Nothing of the mound remained visible, so an area of topsoil covering its probable location was stripped, within which two test-trenches were dug. An elliptical pit was discovered in one of the test-trenches, which contained pieces of disarticulated human bone and several finds, including a copper-alloy ringed pin of the plain-ringed, loop-headed type (of late ninth to early tenth-century date), a tin-plated buckle, a folding knife, part of an axehead and fifteen further corroded iron fragments. The objects are consistent in date with those illustrated in 1792, suggesting that, as a group, they were probably interred some time in the early tenth century. The 1997 excavators suggested that the pit they exposed was in fact the very burial that had been disturbed in 1789, although, if this were the case, the lack of any obvious trace of the stone cist visible in 1997 was a puzzling factor.

Two similar examples of antiquarian discovery resulted from separate road realignment works in 1822. The more northerly of the two was at the inland location of Hesket-in-the-Forest, Cumbria,

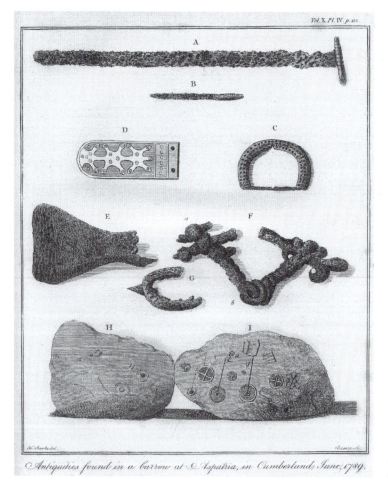

47. Aspatria, Cumbria, finds from burial mound

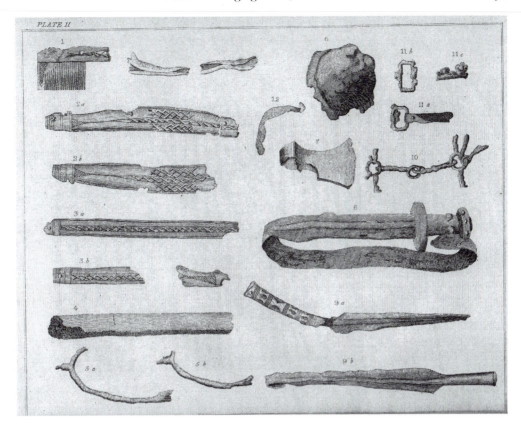

PLATE II

48. Hesket-in the-Forest, Cumbria, finds from burial mound

next to the north–south Roman road near the west bank of the River Eden. A mound that for-merly caused a slight deviation of the Carlisle-Penrith road was removed and charred fragments of a burial were discovered beneath it (as reported in the Newcastle journal *Archaeologia Aeliana*). It appeared not to be inside a cist, but to lie on a bed of ashes and charcoal, which led to suggestions that it had been exposed to 'considerable heat',[53] although this could not have been a crema-tion *in-situ* because an unburnt bone comb and case were included in the deposit together with another twenty or so items (**48**), some of which survive in the Tullie House Museum, Carlisle. A sword, probably of Petersen Type O, was found deliberately bent, with silver decoration on the pommel somewhat melted, as if fired. The other metal finds were all of iron, including an axe of Petersen Type E, with two spearheads (one with a deliberately bent point), a conical or domed shield boss, a horse-bit, spurs, and two small iron buckles; there was also a small hone or whetstone.

South-east of Morecambe Bay, near the banks of the River Wyre (Lancashire), stands Claughton Hall, an eighteenth-century manor house with a park. A new road, being built to take passing traffic further away from the house, necessitated the levelling of a small sandy mound. It revealed a grave assemblage, including two gilt copper-alloy oval brooches of Petersen Type 51 (**49**) arrayed back to back with traces of cloth, two beads, and a human molar between them. A sword, spearhead, axehead, hammer head, and a brooch converted from a gilt copper-alloy Frankish/Carolingian style baldric mount were also discovered.[54] The whereabouts of the iron objects are unknown, as are those of a pot (possibly of Bronze Age date, suggesting that the mound itself was a re-used prehistoric barrow) which contained burnt bones, but the brooches and beads survive in the ownership of the Fitzherbert-Brockholes family and are on long-term loan to the Harris Museum and Art Gallery, Preston.

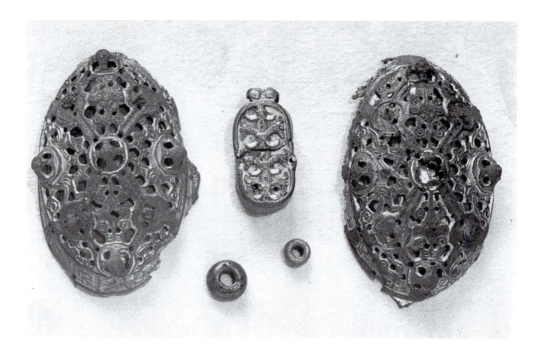

49. Claughton Hall, Lancashire, oval brooches, beads and belt fitting

Despite idiosyncrasies of size, content and preservation, the similarities between some of the Manx mound burials and the few known from north-west England are clear: upstanding sandy or stony monuments overlay the burials, which were mostly inserted below ground level and in one case (Aspatria) in a rough stone cist. Iron weapons of Scandinavian type and Carolingian-style ornamented belt fittings are found amongst both the Manx and Cumbrian burials, although these are not characteristic of all. Mound burial seems to have been much rarer on the British mainland. Only a single antiquarian reference to a possible Viking mound burial exists for south-west Scotland, where in 1756 a 'parcel of burnt human bones, amongst which are several teeth [were] found in the heart of a cairn in the lands of Blackerne in the parish of Crossmichael' (Kirkcudbrightshire, Dumfries and Galloway) together with part of a silver arm ring and an amber bead.[55] To the south of Claughton Hall, possible cairn burials have been noted at Blackrod, near Wigan, and at Billington, on the Ribble (both Lancashire).[56] References to a 'British burial mound' in the sandhills at Meols (Wirral) may be linked to the discovery in the winter of 1877–78 of a series of finds of iron weapons, including a spearhead, a deliberately-bent arrowhead, a shield boss and an axe (50), which suggest a furnished burial was exposed by the sea at this time.[57]

This possible Meols burial was in a highly marginal coastal location, in sand dunes only slightly above the beach, a location that is paralleled by some of the Irish grave sites such as Eyrephort (above). Two such coastally sited graves are known from North Wales. In 1931 a charabanc party from a local field club saw a single substantial stone cist grave that had recently been exposed under dune sand by workmen at Talacre, Flintshire, across the mouth of the Dee Estuary from Meols. Inside it was a skeleton with an iron spearhead and a knife, both now lost.[58] Parts of the skeleton have recently been rediscovered in a London Museum collection and an (as yet unpublished) radiocarbon date taken from it appears to suggest the burial could have occurred in the Viking period. It is hard to interpret the context of this burial, although the massive stone cist seems to belie the view of its reporter that it could have been the result of a temporary landfall to bury an individual who had died onboard a vessel at sea. In 1940 a probable female burial inside an iron-riveted coffin with a fragment of antler comb was found on a ridge overlooking the sea at Benllech, north of Red Wharf Bay on the eastern shore of Anglesey. Both the Talacre and Benllech burials were within localised areas of some Viking influence (Chapters 4, 6), but the site of neither discovery is known to be immediately associated with other burials or settlement remains. Less than a mile from Benllech is the ninth- to tenth-century trading site of Llanbedrgoch, which itself in 1998 produced a strange group of five skeletons, apparently related, as they share certain physiognomic features, which had been thrown casually into the enclosure ditch and buried under rubble. These may have been the victims of raiding (discussed further below, Chapter 6). Their random placement is reminiscent of a 1920s description by H.C. Lawlor of 'heaped' burials found at the monastery of Nendrum overlooking Strangford Lough (Co. Down), which he associated, on the flimsiest of historical grounds, with a Viking attack in 974.[59]

Further antiquarian observations of finds suggestive of burials on the British side of the Irish Sea come from rural sites apparently associated neither with settlements, mounds nor churches. A pair of iron stirrups from St Mary's Hill, Glamorgan may simply be a stray find. Other objects in this uncertain category may possibly belong to more extensive and elaborate deposits. These are mostly isolated finds, such as a Petersen Type L sword (a ninth-century Anglo-Saxon type) and a spearhead, which were found some time prior to 1788 during road construction near Bolton, north-west of Manchester.[60] Quarrying has produced some chance discoveries, such as another Petersen Type L sword, a 'dagger' and pot found at Crossmoor, near Inskip, on the Fylde Peninsula (Lancashire) in 1889. Another single find of a ninth-century Anglo-Saxon sword

50. Meols: weapons from probable Viking grave found in 1877–78

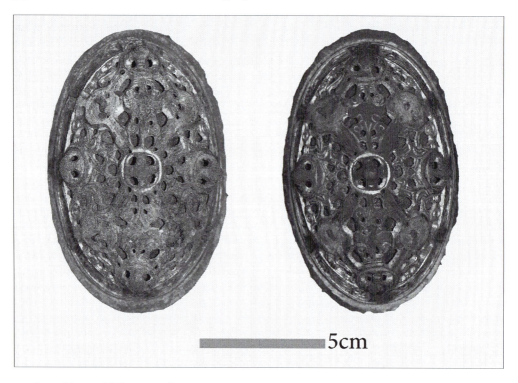

5cm

51. Cumwhitton: gilded copper-alloy composite oval brooches

occurred at Ecclefechan, near Dumfries (the significance of Anglo-Saxon sword types in Viking burials is discussed below, Chapter 8).[61] A sword with a skeleton, a 'halberd' (possibly an axe) and a 'fibula' (a brooch) were discovered in 1814 at Tendley Hill, Eaglesfield, and a deliberately-bent sword in a gravel bank in 1902–3 at West Seaton (both locations being near the River Derwent on the Solway-facing plain of north-west Cumbria). A sword from Witherslack, near Kendal (Cumbria), was found on a flooded gravel bed, leading to suggestions that it may not have been from a grave but a ritual deposit in a 'watery place' of a type well known in Iron Age, Anglo-Saxon and Viking contexts.

The spread of metal detecting by amateur hobbyists has been the spur to discovery of new sites across the UK in recent decades. The Portable Antiquities Scheme (PAS) in England and Wales was set up to provide a mechanism for the reporting and recording of finds. Peter Adams of the Kendal Metal-Detecting Club reported to the PAS in spring 2004 the discovery of first one, then another, Viking-style composite copper-alloy oval brooch of Petersen's Type P51 (dated to the ninth or early tenth centuries and of the same type as the Claughton Hall pair). These finds (**51**) occurred in open agricultural land on a ridge above a small beck at Townfoot Farm, Cumwhitton, in the Eden Valley (Cumbria). Finds of oval brooches, especially in pairs, are normally an indication of furnished burial; this implication led to further investigation and then full excavation by English Heritage and Oxford Archaeology North during the summer of 2004 (**52**).[62]

The initial two oval brooches came from a grave (Grave 85) that turned out to be part of a small unenclosed cemetery (**53**). Six burials in all were exposed; Grave 85 was set 10.25m apart from the other five. These five formed a tight cluster in an area measuring 8m by 7m, orientated south-west to north-east with their heads to the west, apparently without an external boundary. Apart from a fragment of badly decayed cranium found within Grave 85, no human bone was retrieved due to acidic soil conditions, but traces of wooden linings survived in two of the graves. However, a rich and varied assemblage of artefacts was recovered, as both iron and non-ferrous metals had survived reasonably well (**54**). Analysis of the finds continues, and a final publication has yet to appear, but a summary may be given as follows. Based on the types of object and the presence or absence of weaponry, the occupants of four of the graves were interpreted as having been male, and two as female (including the initial discovery, Grave 85, with the two oval brooches). There were no coins but later objects in the graves help to give a provisional date of the early to mid-tenth century for the group. Apart from the oval brooches, these included D-shaped and square, scallop-edged belt buckles, ring-and-dot decorated strap ends, and ringed pins of types found generally in tenth-century contexts elsewhere around the Irish Sea (see also below, Chapter 8).

Glass beads, combs, small shears, chain links and more utilitarian objects such as flint strike-a-lights, small whetstones and plain iron knife blades were found in varying quantities in the six graves. All were flat rectangular cuts; the central one of the cluster of five (Grave 25) had a semi-circular ditch surrounding one end, which the excavators have suggested may signify the presence of a now ploughed out mound. This was the richest of the graves, including a sword (type as yet unclear), a ringed pin, a drinking-horn mount, a silver-inlaid knife, a spearhead and spurs. Some of the weapons from the four 'male' graves were of recognisably Scandinavian types, such as a sword with ornate hilt of Petersen's *Saertype* 1 or 2 and an inlaid hilt (**55**) in the form of a circular cross and diagonal design (which has an eighth-century parallel from Stensvik, Norway), a domed shield boss, a Petersen Type E axehead with wooden haft (both of which have numerous

52. Cumwhitton, Cumbria: OA North photographers record the burials inside temporary excavation shelter, 2004

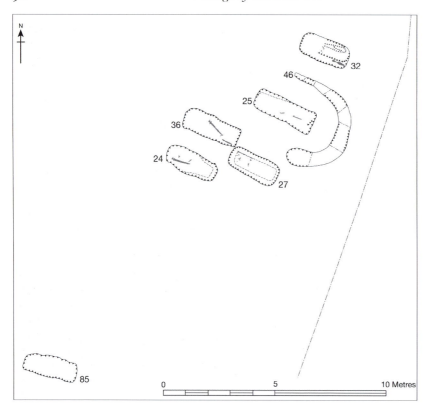

53.
Cumwhitton
Viking
cemetery,
Cumbria,
plan of the six
graves

Norwegian parallels), and two spearheads, probably of Petersen's type K of the ninth to tenth century. Not all of the weapons were of Scandinavian types, however, Grave 36 produced a Petersen Type L 'Anglo-Saxon' sword hilt. Of the two 'female' graves, one (Grave 27) had a bead, an antler comb, a copper-alloy pendant, a possible drinking-horn mount and a jet finger-ring. The other female grave (Grave 85) had produced the initial pair of oval brooches, which on examination turned out to have traces of mineralised textile attached. Grave 85 also included a glass bead, and the remains of a wooden box probably placed at the feet of the body, containing a lignite or jet bracelet, beads, needles, shears, a lock, a hinge, a glass linen smoother and a lead spindle whorl. In addition, seven fragments of another oval brooch of the earlier 'Berdal' type, commonly dated to the eighth century, were found in soil surrounding the graves and this may suggest that another (female?) grave had possibly once existed here, but had been dispersed by ploughing.

Viking-period finds and burial in churchyards

Cumwhitton is the only certain example in the Irish Sea region, outside Ireland, of a cemetery consisting exclusively of furnished Viking burials. A mixed picture of burials with Viking-style objects from within detached burial grounds largely consisting of unfurnished lintel graves is common in the Isle of Man. There may be a parallel for these amongst shadowy antiquarian records from Cumbria, where a stone cist cemetery, found in 1785 at the hill known as Fluskew or Flusco Pike at Newbiggin, near Penrith, apparently occurred near to the find-spots of silver penannular brooches and two more recent silver hoards found in 1989 and 2005 (below, Chapter 6).[63] Across the Solway Firth in south-west Scotland, a sword, a ringed pin of the plain-ringed loop-headed type (a ninth- to early tenth-century type) and a bead, together indicating a probable furnished grave, were found in proximity to St Cuthbert's Church, Kirkcudbright, some time

54. Cumwhitton: artistic reconstruction of Grave 25 by Dominic Andrews

55. Cumwhitton: X-ray of inlaid sword pommel

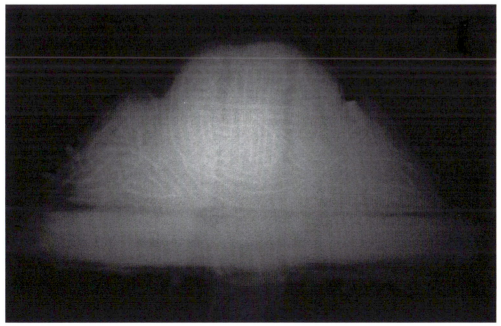

before 1888, although they seem to have come from just outside the original churchyard, having been found in an area being prepared for extension.[64]

The proximity of furnished graves in Dublin and the Isle of Man to churches, chapels and monasteries has already been referred to above. Finds of Viking-age material have occurred in churchyards in north-west England and Wales. B.J.N. Edwards collated a series of observations of antiquarian finds from churchyards in Cumbria, including a ringed pin from underneath the church tower at Brigham, south of Aspatria, and a sword from Rampside on the Furness Peninsula. A burial found in the churchyard at Ormside in the upper Eden valley in 1898 had a sword of Petersen Type M, a shield and a small knife. This discovery occurred in the same churchyard as the earlier find (*c.* 1823) of the 'Ormside Bowl' – a splendid Anglo-Saxon silver cup with a copper-alloy lining, decorated in *repoussé* with four panels bearing animals entwined with plant-tendrils, divided by protruding metal bosses.[65] It was originally made in the eighth century, but had been repaired in the ninth, so was far from new when deposited. Edwards, following the earlier comments of W.G. Collingwood, described the object as 'Viking loot' and listed it amongst stray finds of precious metals. However, its churchyard context suggests that it more probably came from a burial, the rest of which was not recognised at the time of discovery. In his survey of Vikings in Wales, Mark Redknap suggested possible graves on the basis of finds of a polyhedral-headed ringed pin shank from the churchyard at Llanfairpwllgwyngyll (Anglesey), and a spear and axe from the burial ground of an early Medieval church sited within the walls of the Roman town of Caerwent (Monmouthshire).[66]

To these older chance discoveries from churchyards can be added three 'transitional' groups of multiple burials with Viking-period objects from unambiguously ecclesiastical sites, excavated under modern conditions. St Patrick's Chapel, Heysham (Lancashire), a Northumbrian minster dating to the eighth century, stands as a roofless ruin on a headland overlooking Morecambe Bay. It is well known for the presence of eight spectacular rock-cut graves in two separate rows of six and two, which are situated outside the south side of the building. The rock-cut graves were emptied and denuded long ago, but excavations in 1977–78 revealed a further ninety burials, some of which were stone lined, and which had been cut into gullies between ridges of bedrock.[67] One skeleton had a complete decorated iron-riveted bone comb of tenth-century Viking-type placed by its pelvis, another re-used as a pillow a carved stone in the from of a stylised bird. Another unstratified carved stone, once re-used as a crude water basin, was found on the surface nearby. Unusually, this ancient ecclesiastical building is located very close to another, St Peter's Church, which may also be pre-Viking in origin. St Peter's houses a major group of eighth- to eleventh-century stone sculptures, including a hogback grave monument, found on the northern side of the church, allegedly in association with a (now lost) iron spearhead, in 1800.

Another 'transitional' cemetery was discovered in 1988 during excavations prior to the construction of a new diocesan treasury at the west end of Carlisle Cathedral (Cumbria),[68] within which some of the finds are presently housed. The earliest parts of the present cathedral building date to 1120, but it almost certainly stands on an earlier ecclesiastical site. Evidence of post-Roman occupation in the form of post-holes next to a cobbled road surface had been covered by a deep layer of 'dark earth' into which forty-one inter-cut graves had been placed. One was lined with sandstone slabs, and only three more were coffined. Grave 251 had a particularly impressive group of grave-goods, including a decorated buckle, a knife, a copper-alloy ingot, a pan fragment from a balance scale, and a silver-capped pendant whetstone. An array of other largely tenth-century objects was found in the cemetery, including four more buckles, six strap ends, a gold-wire ball comparable with the silver ones from Peel Castle, a gold toggle, beads, pins, knives and what Graham Keevill, the excavator, described as 'a bone object which resembles a comb but is toothless' (likely to be an antler comb case plate).

A further group of graves with Viking-period objects was discovered at the fire-gutted church of St Michael, Workington (Cumbria), which was partly excavated, prior to renovation, in 1994–97.[69] The damaged church is largely late Victorian, but stands on the site of a Norman predecessor. An even earlier church at the site was already suspected from finds of pre-Norman stone sculpture that had been displayed in the tower for many years prior to the excavations. Conclusive traces of a pre-Norman building proved elusive, but amongst over 100 burials (mostly Medieval and later) were discovered two copper-alloy belt fittings of Viking-age date, including a Borre-style strap end, one of which was associated with an inhumation; three more pieces of stone sculpture were discovered in secondary contexts. Despite the long intervals since they took place, the Carlisle and Workington excavations have yet to be fully published, so we are left with only interim reports at present. Nevertheless, it is clear from these, as at Heysham, that a reduced form of 'accompanied' burial was being practised at these sites in the later tenth century. This included combs and personal dress ornaments such as belt-fittings, but lacked the more elaborate displays of weapons and other objects seen in the mound burials and at Cumwhitton. Six of the seven Peel Castle burials also conform to this 'transitional' group, the exception being the curious and dramatic anomaly of the 'Pagan Lady'. At Whithorn, in Phase 1 of Period III (coin dated to 845–65), a single infant burial was discovered with amber and shale beads on its chest, near a 'bundle of bones' from two individuals – one of whom was identifiably female – that had been buried in a hollow with a cow bone.[70] Although the Kirkcudbright and Rampside examples imply that weapon burial took place in or close to churchyards, in neither case is the church itself known to be a pre-Viking foundation, so it is not entirely clear whether the burials might in fact pre-date the churches.

Even if radiocarbon data is available (and its implications tend to be less clear-cut than many might hope), the date of deposition of individual furnished graves containing a group of objects, all deposited at the same time, still can have occurred only after the date of manufacture of the *latest* object present. These, in most cases, were not the largest or most prominent objects in the grave, such as weapons or oval brooches, but small, rather ordinary, pieces of 'hybrid' metalwork (see below). Many of the objects buried in the graves are not Scandinavian in origin. We may therefore ask the question: how genuinely 'Viking' were these burials? There is no absolute 'Viking' standard, of course, with which to compare them, and, indeed, ninth- and tenth-century burials in Scandinavia are also characterized by imported objects (including ringed pins and other 'Irish Sea' style, Anglo-Saxon and Frankish objects). In some cases, the first hints of Christianity appear amongst grave-goods. On present dating evidence, it seems that pagan or furnished burial practice did not continue beyond the middle decades of the tenth century in the Irish Sea region, which coincides with other evidence for the end of paganism and the spread of Christianity. Strikingly, the *floruit* of stone sculpture in the Isle of Man and Cumbria, much of which bears scenes from pagan Norse mythology, also dates to the mid-tenth century. Few of the sculptured stones can be directly linked with burials, but their association with religious change and landed patronage is clear (below, Chapter 8).

Despite the attention given to it here, furnished burial with grave-goods is much rarer in the Irish Sea region than unaccompanied burial in contemporary unfurnished Christian cemeteries. Furnished burial therefore cannot account for all the Viking settlers or their immediate descendants, so must be seen as a specialised rite with social, political and religious significance. It is no longer acceptable merely to divide the practice of furnished and unfurnished burial along simplistic ethnic lines, with the latter being seen as an exclusively 'native' phenomenon. Just as people of non-Scandinavian origin may have been accorded pagan rites at their interment or cremation, others who did have direct or familial Scandinavian backgrounds were probably buried in unfurnished graves, almost indistinguishably from those of the people they had settled amongst. Science, particularly stable isotope analysis, promises to illuminate this question further. Nevertheless, the evidence from burials adds greatly to the picture of developing cultural hybridity around the Irish Sea, which is addressed again below (Chapter 8).

CHAPTER 6

TRADE, SILVER AND MARKET SITES

As early as 798, the *Annals of Ulster* recorded that the 'heathens took cattle tribute of the territories', indicating that raiding had very quickly diversified from simple and destructive thefts of precious objects towards the expropriation of larger and more elaborate resources. This would have required communication with members of the local population, and with it would have come the beginnings of an understanding of their landscape and economy. There is also evidence that newcomers were exploiting natural resources in ways which were traditional in Scandinavia, but remarkable in Ireland: in 828 there was 'a great slaughter of porpoises on the coast of Brega by the foreigners'.[1] Full-scale territorial conquest was not necessary merely for Vikings to establish an armed camp and to secure enough supplies to last through a winter. There were other straightforward, if brutal, ways of achieving at least temporary mastery of landscape and resources, by bribing or blackmailing individuals into committing acts of treachery against their compatriots, by the holding of hostages to intimidate local rulers into compliance, by the recruitment of local mercenaries, or by dividing political and territorial factions against each other. With each growing level of complexity, the stark cultural divide between foreigner and native was broken down a little further and the potential for mutual entanglement increased. The fragmented nature of Irish, Welsh and Cumbrian political loyalties can only have helped the incomers to gain a foothold. Apart from the slaves they took and the mercenaries they paid or blackmailed, Vikings also attracted opportunist or alienated fellow travellers, as the incomers' contributions to ancient feuds and rivalries began to serve existing political vested interests.

As discussed above in Chapter 2, raiding and trading were not mutually exclusive activities. Raided goods frequently found their way into wider circulation, through buying and selling locally, or after export back to Scandinavia or elsewhere. The most valuable and portable items tended to travel the furthest. Cattle were prestigious possessions in Ireland, with large herds signifying political authority – it is probably this factor that provided the early temptation for the invaders. It is hardly conceivable at this time that hundreds of live cattle could have been herded to the coast, loaded onboard ship and ferried to Viking settlements in Scotland or Scandinavia, so the mention of cattle tribute implies further entanglements of negotiation and deals, perhaps involving extortion and ransom demands for precious metalwork, prisoners, women, or rights and securities to free passage on land. Tribute flowed towards the invaders when they enjoyed the military advantage, and was avenged at other times. Slavery has been seen as a primary motivation for Viking incursions into Ireland. References in Irish sources to the capturing of hostages for ransom need not necessarily imply that all those incarcerated were destined for export as chattels and a life of servitude, but it seems many were. St Fintan, an Irish hermit about whom a life was written, was captured, as was his sister. Dalkey Island, off the south Co. Dublin coast, functioned as a slave market, and the *Fragmentary Annals* (above, Chapter 3) refer to Arabic slaves (possibly from Islamic Spain).[2]

As with slave trading in more recent centuries, it is inconceivable that it could have happened without local participation.[3] Indigenous political and economic interests had almost as much to profit from trading in humans as did the 'foreigners'. Vikings engaged in economic dealings with populations in the Irish Sea region brought with them their own accumulated cultural traditions, albeit perhaps salted with a greater measure of ruthlessness and duplicity than was normal amongst settled societies at home. However, Viking activity here quickly became conditioned by existing Irish, Welsh and other conventions of exchange and value. Far from simply collapsing in the face of the foreigners' demands, indigenous forms of economic behaviour were resilient and rapidly drew in the newcomers by making them party to deals, debts and internecine feuds. Only the general spread of commerce (freely entered transactions at a mutually agreed price), with the take-off of urban markets in the tenth century, began to dilute the earlier social basis of exchange. Prior to this, economic life in Ireland and western Britain was largely pre-commercial in that it was dominated by elaborate social bonds and obligations, through which productive surpluses of agriculture and craft manufacture circulated on an annual and seasonal basis. Hospitality dues, land rents and seasonal food gifts consolidated the wealth and authority of local and regional dynasties. Imports of fine objects, such as Mediterranean and Gaulish ceramics and glassware, had been sought by ruling elites in the pre-Viking centuries. These were principally needed in order to supplement the ability of rulers to demonstrate and symbolise their own prestige and wealth in the form of portable possessions, to furnish ceremonies and feasts with lavish exotica including wine, and to confer reminders of their abundance upon their followers, vassals and rivals.

Ireland and Wales (and presumably also contemporary Cumbria and the Isle of Man, although we know less about these) had highly developed and widely accepted conventions of value. Standard expressions for the values of slaves, weight, head of livestock, and areas of land have all left traces in contemporary sources, the most extensive and detailed of which are the Irish law tracts.[4] *Míach* was a sack of malted barley, *sét* a unit of livestock and *cumal* a female slave. In the law tract known as *Cáin Aicillne, bó* (a cow) was worth one *uinge* (ounce), but came in variations depending on its state of calving. A *cumal* seems also to have become a recognized measurement of silver. Gold remained a rare and largely decorative metal throughout the period.[5] However, the arrival of Vikings, with their trading contacts in England, Frankia, and eastwards across Europe to Russia and central Asia, brought about an increase in the circulation of imported silver in the far west of Europe. The silver they introduced seems to have come from a variety of sources, including English and Frankish coins, together with distinctive 'Kufic' coins from western Asia bearing the Arabic signature of the Islamic caliphate. Finds of Frankish and Kufic coins in particular seem to be indicative of early Viking trading activity. Silver quickly took on a widespread role as a currency medium, acting by weight and purity alone as broken-up pieces of bullion (hack-silver), by mixtures of foreign coin and in recognisably 'pre-coinage' forms of currency such as standard-weight ingots and arm-rings. Coins, even if used merely as bullion, mostly have an identifiable mint signature, although they may have changed hands many times prior to their deposition.

Northumbrian *styca* coins – debased silver-copper alloy issues dating to the ninth century, probably produced in York – apparently did not cross the Irish Sea to Ireland or the Isle of Man. This is surprising in view of their relatively widespread occurrence in hoards on the Irish Sea coasts of north-west England and south-west Scotland, including at Meols, Whithorn and Luce Sands (see below).[6] Coins and a trefoil brooch with garnets were discovered at Kirkoswald (Cumbria) in 1808, to which a deposition date of *c.* 865 has been assigned.[7] A mixed silver hoard dating from the 870s was found in 1912 in peat cuttings at Talnotrie, near Kirkcudbright (Dumfries and Galloway), containing Anglo-Saxon ornaments of the pre-Viking Trewhiddle style, a gold finger-ring, and Anglo-Saxon and Frankish coins, together with a decorated lead weight, a jet object and three stone spindle whorls. The Talnotrie Hoard has been described by James Graham-Campbell as a

56. Hiberno-Norse silver pennies of Dublin of Phases I, II and III, (*c.* 995–*c.* 1050)

'Northumbrian metalworker's hoard', and is not usually attributed to Viking activity, although had it been found in Ireland, it almost certainly would have been.[8]

The early tenth century, especially the three decades after 917, saw the rapidly growing commercial influence of trade with English markets, particularly at Chester and York, and English-minted coins spread out to Ireland, the Isle of Man, Wales and Cumbria, gradually ousting Frankish coin from use. However, not all coin circulating in this area or further west was York- or Chester-minted, as coin from other mints filtered in from the south and east.[9] Outside the English kingdom, Anglo-Saxon silver coins could simply be used as another form of hack-silver for their bullion value alone. However, particularly amongst traders habituated to dealing with English markets, they could also be acceptable for their 'face value' as pennies, thus foreshadowing a truly monetary currency. Coin production was heavily policed and regulated within the Anglo-Saxon *burhs* because it provided such profitable revenue for the crown. Moneyers were wealthy and privileged with freedoms denied to many ordinary townspeople, but could expect violent punishment if they minted false coin or let official coin dies pass into the wrong hands.

Coin production started at Chester as soon as, if not actually before, the *burh* was created in 907. The Chester mint became, for a brief period under Æthelstan (924–39), the most productive coin-producing centre in England, reflecting the upsurge in trade at Anglo-Saxon England's 'window' on the Irish Sea, together with the tribute and booty brought in from victories in Wales and against the Vikings. As the only fully-fledged English burghal port on the Irish Sea coastline at this time (below, Chapter 7), Chester's mint covered a huge area of political and economic influence, from Gwynedd to Cumbria. Of the twenty-eight moneyers whose names are recorded on Chester-minted coins from the period 924–39, up to six had Scandinavian names and one had the Gaelic name Maeldomen, with the remainder consisting largely of English, with two possible Welsh and two possible Frankish names.[10] One of the first Chester moneyers, from the reign of Edward the Elder, has the Scandinavian name *Irfara* ('Ireland Journeyer'). No clearer evidence could exist for the cosmopolitan nature of the growing trading community in the Irish Sea ports.

Viking-ruled kingdoms in Northumbria and the Danelaw produced their own coinages at this time, but their counterparts further west did not initially follow suit, partly because of the cessation of Scandinavian rule in Dublin between 902–17 and also presumably because, unlike in York and the Danelaw *burhs*, they were trading principally in Irish, Scottish and Manx areas which had no indigenous tradition of coin use. A silver-bullion economy operated in areas beyond English rule until at least the mid-tenth century, into which Anglo-Saxon coin was initially drawn along with other non-English coinages, primarily for its weight value alone. Its 'face value' was nevertheless gradually accepted in these areas, and the use of Anglo-Saxon silver coinage eventually became so pervasive across the Irish Sea region that, in the period 995–1020, rulers in Dublin, the Isle of Man and even possibly Gwynedd (see below), were tempted to begin production of their own coinages to try to cash in on the (real or perceived) prestige and revenue-raising opportunities which they brought. Thus arose the 'Hiberno-Norse' coinages, which began as cheaper imitations of English coin, starting in Dublin around 995–7 during the reign of Sigtryggr 'Silk-Beard' with the (mis) use of an English die of Æthelred II taken from Watchet in Somerset. Michael Dolley identified Phase I as exclusively imitative of English coinage, whereas Phases II and III of the early eleventh century became identified with local rulers (**56**). Some numismatists have contended that the production of Hiberno-Norse coinage spread to Limerick later in the eleventh century, although, perhaps surprisingly, there is no evidence of any such minting at Waterford prior to the Anglo-Norman takeover.[11]

Hoards and currency

Hoards of silver and gold are unparalleled reservoirs of information on the trading economy of the Irish Sea. Hoarding acted as a primitive means of banking, in that wealth could be concealed in a measure of safety, and high levels of hoarding have traditionally been associated with periods of political upheaval and warfare. More recently (somewhat to the distaste of traditionalist scholars), hoarding has been interpreted as a form of ceremonial concealment to imbue a place or landscape with hidden and mythical wealth, or to remove certain objects from circulation. What is unarguable is that we have a sample biased by the fact that we only know about hoards which were never retrieved by whoever buried them, but which were subsequently discovered and reported upon many centuries later. What proportion these are to the original whole, discovered and as yet undiscovered, is unknowable, making some of the statistics bandied about them at least subject to some provisional caution.

Numerous silver hoards and a handful of gold hoards 'of general Scandinavian character'[12] have been found in Ireland, a total now exceeding 130 for the period 800–1000. These consist of three general types which in very broad terms follow on from each other chronologically: coinless hoards of silver objects only, mixed hoards including some coin, and the rest being coin-only hoards. Ninth-century hoards from Ireland are predominantly coinless, with only three coin-only hoards containing Anglo-Saxon (Mercian) or Frankish coins, all of which were found in the eastern coastal districts of Ireland.[13] Coinless hoards are much harder to pin a specific date of deposition upon than ones which contain coins, but it does seem there was an upsurge in silver hoard deposition in Ireland in the mid-ninth century, probably reflecting the influence of the newly founded *longphuirt*. The first Irish mixed hoards containing both coin and other objects date from the early tenth century, when English silver pennies and coins of the Viking kingdoms of York and East Anglia start to appear. The pattern of deposition of early Viking silver hoards in Ireland is striking (**57**). These extend well beyond the immediate environs of the coastal and riverine *longphuirt* well into the Irish interior. Coinless hoards are spread most widely across Ireland, including examples from Ulster, Connacht and Munster, but their distribution is most heavily concentrated on the central midlands in the Shannon Basin and Co. Westmeath, perhaps reflecting the relationship between the Dublin Vikings and the southern Uí Néill. There is a particular cluster centred on Lough Ennel (Co. Westmeath). These include the Carrick and Dysart Island hoards, where massive ingots were found on Irish crannóg sites. Coin hoards are more regionally focused, with a distribution much more obviously within a 50km radius of Dublin and northwards along the coast. Coin use was concentrated in tenth-century Dublin, but, as a result, much of it ended up in Irish hands, having 'leaked out' beyond Dublin's immediate hinterland to areas in which its economic influence was most strongly felt. The old view that possession of silver was exclusively a Viking phenomenon has been comprehensively refuted in recent studies. The broad distribution of coinless hoards in particular led John Sheehan to state:

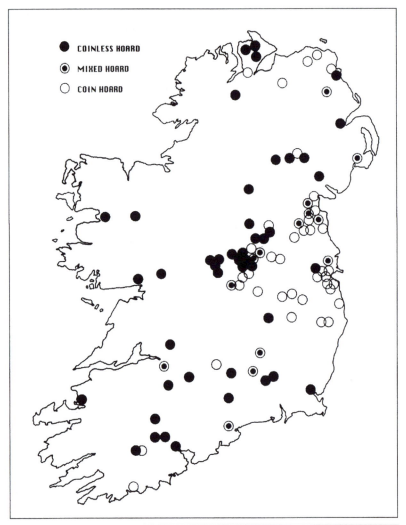

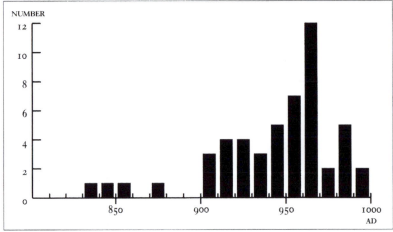

57. 'Early Viking Age hoards' in Ireland and (below) histogram showing dates of deposition of coin hoards

The inescapable conclusion to be derived from this particular distribution pattern, as well as from the overall distribution trends of the coinless hoards, is that a very considerable proportion of Ireland's Viking Age silver wealth ended up in Irish ownership.[14]

The types of non-numismatic object represented in hoards around the Irish Sea have been studied in great detail by Viking-period silver specialists. Ingots were made by pouring melted silver into rectangular or cigar-shaped reservoirs on stone ingot moulds, and were frequently cut into sections, as silver was required for payment or further manufacture. They are largely undecorated, and are the most functional and therefore the least culturally diagnostic of the non-numismatic hoard objects. Most Viking silver ingots are generally small and weigh well under 1kg, hence the anomalously large size of two of the ingots from the Dysart Island Hoard – weighing over 3kg – has been taken to imply that these were made by Irish silversmiths. Noticeable on some is the practice of 'pecking', marked by little impact-points on the surface, and 'nicking' which consists of small sliced grooves in sides and corners. These techniques allowed silversmiths and merchants to make sure the object was not just surface-plated with silver, and to test the malleability and hence the quality of the metal. Silver was susceptible to debasement with other metals such as copper and tin, and there was keen awareness of this danger amongst contemporary traders. Anglo-Saxon, Frankish and Kufic silver coins have been analysed to test their metal content; only general trends have been observed, but European and Arabic types do show distinctive combinations of pure silver, gold, copper, lead and bismuth. However, hopes of being able to identify in more extensive detail the geographic origins of the metals used in Viking silver made in the west have so far remained largely unfulfilled: so much of it was melted together and re-used that geological source elements have become difficult to trace in metallurgical analyses.[15]

Many of the objects in Irish Sea hoards are of more recognisable cultural form, even if dating their manufacture and deposition is still inexact. Fragments, and in some cases whole objects, of recognisably imported Scandinavian types, such as twisted 'Permian' rings, are known from the Cuerdale Hoard (Lancashire) and several Irish hoards, but are outnumbered by arm-rings and ingots which are likely to have been manufactured in more immediate locations by the melting and hammering of coins, hack-silver and ornaments by Viking silversmiths in the *longphuirt*. 'Hiberno-Viking' silver arm-rings are the most common type in Ireland. There are a number of sub-classes of these, some of which have closed, twisted terminals, but the most common are the broad-band penannular type which consists of a thick tapering strip with unclosed ends, usually decorated with characteristic bar or dot-like punches, often with diagonal lines of punching on the expanded central area. Sheehan's research shows that the majority were manufactured to conform to multiples of a weight standard of 26.15g, which differs by only 0.45g from the standard of 26.6g which is characteristic of tenth-century lead weights from Dublin.[16] He has identified over a hundred examples of 'Hiberno-Viking' arm-rings from twenty-nine hoards in Ireland, many of which are dated to the late ninth or early tenth centuries. They are also found in lesser numbers in hoards in Wales, such as the Dinorben Hoard from Red Wharf Bay, Anglesey (*58*), in England at Cuerdale and the twenty examples from a hoard found by a metal-detectorist in 2004 at Huxley, near Chester (*59*).[17] Two hoards in the York area and another nine from Norway have them, leaving little doubt about the claim for a provenance in Ireland. A different style of ring usually known as 'ring money' has a smooth, plain penannular tapering arm-ring type of rounded or square cross-section. This so-called 'Scoto-Viking' ring money is more characteristic of Scottish hoards of the tenth and eleventh centuries, but is also found in the Isle of Man; it only occurs in small numbers in Ireland.[18] It generally conforms to around a 24g standard (a weight standard more characteristic of Scandinavia, but different from the Irish examples). Both types of arm-ring represent a simple, recognisable form into which ingots could be hammered rapidly and in large numbers.

Not all such silverware was utilitarian and plain. Viking Irish Sea origins have been attributed to elegant silver penannular brooches with long pins, which, like the more mundane copper-alloy ringed pins, were a Viking development of Irish metalworking tradition (below, Chapter 8). These have either ball-type terminals (some decorated with dense cross-hatching known as 'brambling',

58. Dinorben Hoard of silver arm-rings, Anglesey

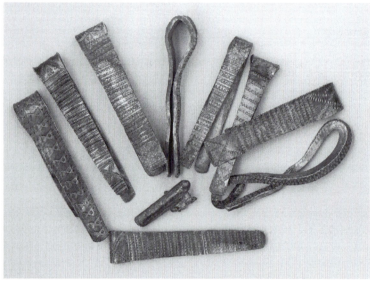

59. Part of the Huxley Hoard of flattened silver arm-rings, Cheshire, found in 2004

creating a thistle-type appearance), or flat decorated terminals with one or more small upstanding hemispherical bosses.[19] Two such large silver thistle or ball-brooches were found at Fluskew or Flusco Pike, Newbiggin (Cumbria) in 1785. In what came to be known as the 'silver field', six more penannular brooches were found by metal-detectorists in 1989. A further, apparently separate, hoard of 120 Anglo-Saxon and Viking coins and thirty-three pieces of hack-silver, dating to around 925, was found during archaeological rescue work in 2005.[20] Silver penannular brooches occur in the Cuerdale Hoard (see below), and in hoards in Chester (Castle Esplanade), at Orton Scar, Cumbria (**60**), and Ballaquayle in the Isle of Man. Their distribution as complete objects or hack-silver extends well beyond the Irish Sea region, to three hoards near York, at Goldsborough, 'Vale of York' and Bossall/Flaxton, and a large hoard from the Bay of Skaill, Orkney.

The presence of hack-silver, melted silver and weights in the finds from the Viking camp at Woodstown has been noted above (Chapter 2). Sheehan has argued on the basis of these, and gold and silver hoards from Lough Ree, at Ballaghkeeran and nearby Hare Island, that concentrations of finds of precious metals may be characteristic of the *longphuirt*.[21] Little such material, however, has so far been found in Dublin, although arguments have been advanced that the Cuerdale

Hoard (Lancashire) of *c.* 905–10 represented the portable wealth of the recently exiled dynasty. Another apparently vast, but now lost, hoard found in 1846 near Drogheda (Co. Louth) has been suggested as war-booty resulting from the surrounding kingdom of Brega's leading role in the expulsion of Vikings from Dublin in 902.[22] Cuerdale is indeed a massive treasure, and even though it was found as long ago as May 1840 (by workmen repairing the south bank of the River Ribble), it remains the most extensive, if not quite the heaviest, Viking silver hoard known from anywhere in the world. Its contents, apart from those stolen at the time of its discovery, were subsequently split into several groups, meaning that it is now housed in separate collections, the largest of which are in the British Museum, National Museums Liverpool and the Ashmolean Museum (**61**).

Due to the manner in which the hoard was dispersed after discovery, it is impossible to put an exact figure on the hoard's contents, but James Graham-Campbell has stated that it contained 'some 7500 coins, together with over 1000 ingots, rings and hack-silver pieces'.[23] The silver was already spread into separate barrow-loads of soil and various people's pockets almost as soon as it was noticed, but fragmentary remains of a lead container and five bone pins were also retrieved, suggesting it had been buried together in moneybags within a box or chest.[24] The hoard may be dated to 905–10 by the latest coin issues to appear in it. The majority of the coins, around 5000, were recently minted Viking issues of York and East Anglia, together with about 1000 Anglo-Saxon coins of Alfred and Edward the Elder, and a similar number of Frankish coins from the Rhineland and Loire areas, together with Italian and Byzantine issues. A minority of the coins came from further afield, demonstrating the extent of Viking trading links. Four have been identified as from the trading town of Hedeby in southern Denmark, and around fifty Kufic coins range in mintage from Al-Andalus in Arabic Spain to the Abbasid Caliphate at Baghdad, three mints around the Caspian Sea, Andarabah in Afghanistan and Al Banjhir in the Himalayan foothills.[25] The Kufic coins all date to before 895, but the very recent mintage of the York and East Anglian coins suggests that the hoard was not brought over in its entirety from Dublin but was at least in part assembled in northern England. A parcel of coins from east of the Pennines could have been added to it in Lancashire, and it may have been intended as a payment for land, or for an attempt to re-capture Dublin. Graham-Campbell estimated in 1992 that the hoard was probably worth about £300,000 in modern terms (a figure which would have to be increased substantially nearly

Left 60. Orton Scar, Cumbria, silver bossed penannular brooch
Right 61. Cuerdale Hoard, Lancashire, some of the silver including ingots, arm-rings, 'ring-money' and coins

62. Chester, Castle Esplanade Hoard, found in Chester Ware vessel in 1950

two decades on).[26] We cannot know the reason why it was never retrieved, but it is less surprising that an exiled dynasty should possess such wealth, than that it should have been left forgotten in the ground for 930 years, with the worldly potential power and authority it represented lost to its original owners.

Cuerdale is the most spectacular of a series of silver hoards deposited on the Irish Sea margins of western Britain in the early decades of the tenth century. The distant mint of Andarabah is represented in another coin hoard find, which occurred in the mid-eighteenth century at Dean, near Cockermouth (Cumbria).[27] An even less recent find occurred in April 1611 at the Harkirke, a recusant burial ground near Little Crosby (south-west Lancashire). A hoard of up to 300 coins, the deposition of which probably occurred in about 910, was discovered in the enclosing ditch, and described and illustrated by the landowner, William Blundell. His notes and a copper engraving of thirty-five of the coins survive, although the silver itself is now lost.[28] A mixed hoard containing ingots, hack-silver and around 100 Anglo-Saxon coins deposited in around 935–40 was found at Scotby, east of Carlisle, in 1855. The spread of metal-detecting activity in recent years has added several new examples to those found in earlier decades and centuries. The hoard of Hiberno-Viking arm-rings found at Huxley near Chester has already been referred to; its date of deposition is virtually contemporary with Cuerdale, and it was also found with the remains of a lead container. A hoard of hack-silver, bent bars, a section of an ingot and three Kufic coins was found in 1997 at Tewitfield, Warton, near Carnforth, on the north-eastern margins of Morecambe Bay, and in 2002 a small hoard containing an ingot, a bar, a polyhedral blob of silver and a pierced stone were discovered beside the River Dee at Eccleston, south of Chester.

Chester has produced four hoards, the earliest of which is a coin-only hoard found at St John's Church in 1862 and dated to 917–20.[29] A large mixed hoard dating to *c.* 965–970, with twenty-seven ingots, 120 pieces of hack-silver and 547 coins, in a broken Chester-ware pot, was found at the Castle Esplanade, Chester, in November 1950 (**62**). This is an unusual hoard with a very long age-structure (meaning it contained much obsolete coin, going back to Alfred's reign, as well as the most recent issues which determined its date of deposition). In this respect it is less like mid- and later tenth-century hoards in England and more like contemporary hoards in Ireland, such as those from Killyon Manor, Co. Meath (*c.* 958), Ballitore, Co. Kildare (*c.* 965), Smarmore, Co. Louth (*c.* 970), Dalkey, Co, Dublin (*c.* 975). The hack-silver from the hoard includes 'ring money' and ball-type brooch fragments, and these types most closely resemble hack-silver in the hoard from Ballaquayle, Isle of Man (*c.* 975), although the latter has only one ingot and includes a gold arm-ring. A stone ingot mould was found near the Castle Esplanade at Cuppin Street in 1986, which suggests that the hoard may have been associated with a silver-working area or even the Chester Mint itself, and that it was possibly a silver-worker's or moneyer's private reserve of scrap silver, which would have been intended for the melting pot had it been retrieved. Two more hoards from the city, from Eastgate Row and Pemberton's Parlour (found in 1857 and 1914 respectively), date from the 970s, and their coin-only content reflects a move away from the use of bullion at this time.[30]

Hoards in Wales, particularly north Wales, are closely reflective of the picture around Chester. The deposition of the Dinorben Hoard of five Hiberno-Viking arm-rings may, like Cuerdale and Huxley, be related to the upheavals surrounding the outpouring of people and wealth from Ireland in the first years of the tenth century. Ingimund's attempt to wrest land in eastern Anglesey (above, Chapter 3) is an enticing, if perhaps all-too convenient, historical context for it. Two silver hoards, the earlier including hack-silver and Kufic coins, were deposited across the Menai Straits in the monastic settlement of Bangor in around 925 and 970. The only known coin bearing the name of a Welsh ruler in the tenth century, a silver penny of Hywel Dda, was struck by the Chester moneyer Gillys in the 940s. Later hoards from Wales, such as the Bryn Maelgwyn and Pant-yr-Eglwys hoards from near the Great Orme, deposited in the 1020s,[31] show the continued dominance of the Chester Mint, although a short-lived non-English series, imitative of the Cnut Quatrefoil issue of the later second and third decades of the eleventh century, are represented. Mark Blackburn suggested that the Norse settlements in Wirral were producing an imitative Hiberno-Norse coinage at this time,[32] but the present author argues instead that Rhuddlan – Edward the Elder's *Cledemutha*, which is recorded in Domesday Book as having a mint, and which was temporarily under the rule of Gwynedd between 1015–1063 – was the more probable origin of the imitative coinage. Thus, if correct, this shows that production of 'Hiberno-Norse' coinages was not restricted to Viking-dominated areas.

The tenth and eleventh centuries bring a patchy picture of hoarding and coin use in the other areas around the Irish Sea, which lay outside the borders of the English kingdom at this time. Excavations at Whithorn (Galloway), which produced over sixty *sceattas* and *stycas* of the eighth and ninth centuries, produced only one of the tenth century (a penny of Edgar) and one of the eleventh (a Dublin Hiberno-Norse penny), before coin finds of the twelfth century onwards became more numerous again, with mostly Scottish issues. A small amount of silver-working evidence, including a fragment of 'ring money', is more convincingly dated to the trading settlement which developed there in the eleventh century (Period IV).[33] Although Anglo-Saxon pennies have been found in burials at Peel Castle (above, Chapter 5), the Isle of Man seems to have been something of a backwater in terms of silver use until the mid-tenth century, with only one possible hoard pre-dating the 960s.[34] It was only after the introduction of Hiberno-Norse coinages in the early eleventh century that the number of hoards started to increase.

Single finds and market sites

Hoards are tremendous stores of information, but as a rather specific and secretive activity, hoarding cannot tell us everything we need to know about patterns of exchange and payment. Single finds of silver objects and coinage, such as may be dropped by mistake during a transaction, perhaps convey more readily the actual patterns of use of silver and coin. In the pre-Viking period, as we have seen, coin was not unknown but very rare in Ireland, and almost non-existent as single finds betokening market activity. Two coins of Offa from near Dundalk (Co. Louth) may have been part of a hoard,[35] but tell us little about contemporary uses for coinage. That 'ordinary' people possessed coinage in the ninth century appears to be confirmed by finds of four low-value Northumbrian *stycas* of the 850s at the upland farmstead of Gauber High Pasture, Ribblehead (above, Chapter 4).[36]

Occasionally, individual pieces of Viking metalwork are found in coastal locations, such as a tapering rod with twisted ends found on the edge of the Solway Firth on the English-Scottish border near Gretna in the 1970s, and a copper-alloy ball-type brooch from Culver Hole Cave on the Gower Peninsula (Glamorgan).[37] A 'magnificent' gold finger-ring was also found at Tundergarth, near Dumfries.[38] Metal-detecting activity has contributed considerable new information to our understanding of the spread of Viking-period finds. In the Irish Republic it was prevalent in the 1970s and 1980s but is now illegal. In England and Wales, the Portable Antiquities Scheme has brought enhanced co-operation and reporting, albeit with some cageyness as to precise location in some cases. A spread of new finds in Cumbria, Lancashire and Cheshire is attributable to this, including the Cumwhitton cemetery and the recent silver hoards mentioned above. Recent single finds of Scandinavian objects such as a gold ring of Scandinavian type from 'near Kendal'; a decorated lead weight from near Preston, Lancashire (**63,** *left*), and an openwork copper-alloy scabbard chape from Chatburn, Lancashire enhance the body of evidence hitherto dominated by antiquarian finds.[39] Finds of objects from coastal locations suggesting early Irish Sea Viking activity include two items of Irish-style gilded bronzework, one of which is a human-faced escutcheon (**63,** *right*), from Arnside on the shores of Morecambe Bay.[40] These add to earlier finds of Irish-style metalwork, including an interlace-decorated metal boss (now lost) from Ribchester Roman fort, and a small bronze head found in 'Furness' donated to the British Museum in 1870, which is reminiscent of saints' faces depicted in seventh- and eighth-century Irish illuminated manuscripts.[41] An eighth-century Irish-style gilt pseudo-penannular brooch with chip-carved panels and glass studs, found at Llys Awel, near Abergele (Denbighshire), is similar to examples found at the Viking cemetery at Westness, Rousay, Orkney, and Eidfjord, Norway. Several other finds of small pieces of gilt copper-alloy Irish-style metalwork have occurred in Wales, including a roundel from Din Lligwy (Anglesey), and two cruciform harness mounts from Sker Point (Glamorgan), which are paralleled in a probable Viking grave at Navan, Co. Meath.[42]

Our chances of detecting market activity are, however, greatly enhanced when numerous discoveries of coins or other finds occur at a single location. The sand dune site and probable beach market on Luce Sands, at the head of Luce Bay in Galloway, has produced large amounts of

2cm

63. Recent finds: *Left:* Preston, Lancashire: decorated lead weight; *Right:* Arnside, Cumbria: hanging bowl mount with human face

64. Meols, from the East

metalwork and coinage from the Roman to Later Medieval periods, including a series of *sceattas* and *stycas* from the pre-Viking period, but there is a hiatus here in coin and metalwork finds from the tenth and eleventh centuries. Similar topographically to Luce Sands in many ways, but more revealing of Viking influence, is Meols (Wirral).

Meols (the place-name is from ON *Melr*, 'sand-hills') was discovered in the nineteenth century when the sea began to erode a sandy promontory known as Dove Point, which formerly protruded about 500m into the Irish Sea from the present north coast of the Wirral Peninsula (**64**). As the sea gradually removed the overlying sand dunes, complex archaeological layers were exposed dating to between the Mesolithic and post-Medieval periods. Thousands of finds, including metalwork, pottery, stone, glass, leather, bone, coins and clay pipes, were picked up by local people from the mass of eroding sand and occupation layers, which became known as the 'Ancient Forest' as they overlay the stumps and peaty remains of a post-glacial forest. We would know little today about Meols but for the devoted attentions of a group of antiquarians in the period 1846–1905, foremost amongst whom was the Revd Abraham Hume (1814–84), an Irishman from Co. Down and a graduate of Trinity College, Dublin, who was an Anglican vicar in Liverpool. Hume's 1863 monograph, *Ancient Meols*, is a classic of Victorian erudition,[43] but came too early to tell the whole story of the Meols landscape which continued, and indeed continues, to reveal archaeological evidence. Thanks to Hume and others, notably Henry Ecroyd Smith (Liverpool Museum's first curator), Joseph Mayer and Charles Potter, much of the material discovered at Meols was collected and saved, ultimately to enter museums in Liverpool, Chester, Warrington and London. Bomb damage to Liverpool Museum during the Second World War caused much disruption to its Meols collection, and it took until 2007 for a comprehensive study of the site and collections to be published.[44]

Finds at Meols of imported metalwork, ceramics and coinage of the Iron Age, Roman and pre-Viking periods, including a small group of primary *sceattas* and *stycas* of the eighth and ninth centuries, indicate that sporadic trade had been carried out there on the sandy foreshore for many centuries before the Vikings appeared. Coincident with the time of the Norse settlement in Wirral

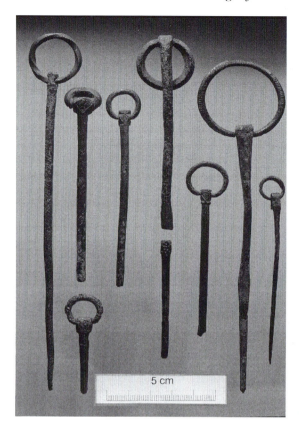

65. Meols: ringed pins

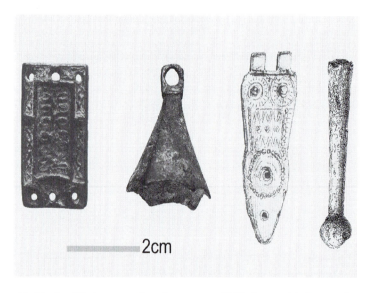

66. Meols: gilded copper-alloy plaque, pyramidal bell; roundel-decorated buckle plate and drinking horn terminal

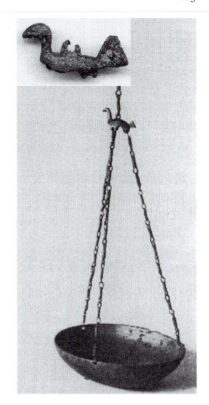

67. Meols: copper-alloy bird from merchant's balance scale (inset), with part of a complete example from Jåtten, Rogaland, Norway

and the rise of nearby Chester as a trading port, Meols experienced an upsurge in activity. Thirty-six single coin finds are known from Meols, from the reign of Edgar (959–75) to the beginning of the reign of Henry I (1100–35). This total may not look large in comparison with some of the hoards, but is far greater in terms of single finds than the number known from Chester, and is comparable with the total known from excavations in Dublin. Even after three or more decades of metal detecting to swell the total, the number of single finds of coins of this period in north-west England is otherwise very low, suggesting that Meols had a specialised role as a market site.

Amongst the other finds from Meols are several objects suggestive of Viking raiding and trading activity in the ninth or tenth centuries. Nineteen complete and incomplete parts of copper-alloy ringed pins of later ninth- to early twelfth-century types (below, Chapters 7 and 9) are identifiable amongst the collections (**65**), a total greater than that of York, and only outnumbered by the finds from Dublin (the only place where they are known to have been manufactured). A small gilded copper-alloy plaque, re-used as a strap end, is probably an Irish-made object of the eighth century (perhaps a book mount), which had probably circulated amongst Viking traders. A drinking-horn terminal (now lost), and a small six-sided pyramidal bell (**66**), together with a stirrup mount and a small buckle decorated in derivative versions of the early eleventh-century Ringerike style, are further evidence of contacts with Dublin and the Danelaw. A small copper-alloy bird with suspension loops above and below (**67**) was thought to be a Roman object until Viking artefact specialist Colleen Batey pointed out in 2006 that it resembled a similar decorative metal bird from a Viking balance scale found on the island of Gigha (Argyll). Similar examples are also known in Scandinavia, and its discovery at Meols adds to the evidence for trade at the site. However, with the possible exceptions of this and the drinking-horn terminal, few of the Meols objects imply intensive or direct trading contacts with Scandinavia. Like many of the finds from graves and settlements elsewhere around the Irish Sea, they tell the story predominantly of new styles and fashions which evolved more locally, in Ireland and England, as Viking influences became embedded and enriched by those of existing populations in the region (below, Chapter 8).

Left: 68. Ness, Wirral, silver ingot

Below: 69. Llanbedrgoch: plan of excavated settlement; buildings marked 1–5

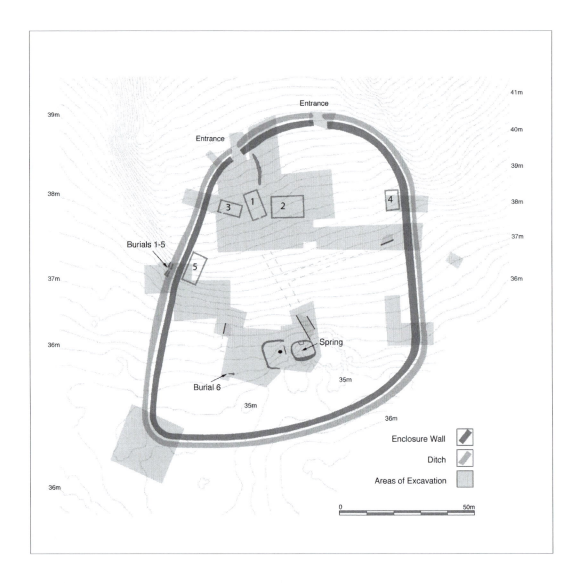

Meols probably acted as a seasonal beach-market, where Cheshire salt, slaves, livestock and portable dress items were traded and exchanged. The position of Meols on the outermost coast, nearest to deep water, is central to the network of routeways that came together at the eastern end of what became a regular Viking trade route between Dublin, Anglesey, Chester, and the Mersey and Ribble estuaries. It may have had an illicit role in evading taxes and dues, as it stood just outside the fiscal remit of the port of Chester as defined in later Medieval documents, which make it clear that 'Arnald's Eye', a sandstone reef at the mouth of the Dee, near Hilbre Island off the north-west tip of Wirral, was the outer limit of the port. Inland connections by boat via the two estuaries are suggested by the remains of several logboats dredged from the bed of the Mersey near Warrington between the 1890s and 1930s, five of which have been radiocarbon dated to the ninth, tenth and eleventh centuries.[45] Perhaps Meols was protected as a separate trading site by the semi-independence of the Viking settlements in the 'Hundred of Caldy' (above, Chapter 4). There was also a permanent settlement here, given that antiquarian records of the 1870s to 1890s make it clear that buildings were being eroded from under the sand dunes. Extensive evidence of later Medieval structures and of circular round-houses can probably be discounted as relevant to the Viking period, but descriptions of 'lines of wattle' forming 'cattle sheds', and nearby stone- and clay-walled buildings (approximately 10m by 4m in size), are strikingly reminiscent of Viking longhouse-style buildings excavated elsewhere (Chapters 4 and 8). There are also references in antiquarian accounts to a 'British burial mound' found in the sand dunes behind the high-tide mark. A group of iron Viking-period weapons (**50**), including a hemispherical shield boss, an axehead and a deliberately-bent spearhead, were found close together in the winter of 1877–78 suggesting a possible furnished weapon grave was exposed at this time (above, Chapter 5).[46]

The local influence of Meols is marked by finds of coinage and other traded items in its hinterland. Excavations in 1987–88 at Hoylake Road, Moreton, less than 3km inland from Meols, produced a mudstone hone and a silver penny of the Circumscription Cross type of Eadwig (955–9), minted in south-west England, possibly at Barnstaple.[47] At Irby, 6.5km south of Meols, excavations in 1990 produced rare evidence of bow-sided rural buildings (above, Chapter 4), together with an amber bead. Further south on the Wirral Peninsula, three finds were discovered by metal-detectorists in the 1990s. A small silver ingot of Viking type (**68**) and an offcut of hacksilver were found in a field at Ness. Nearby on the edge of the Dee Estuary was found a silver halfpenny bearing a raven, which was minted at York in the name of one of the two principal losers at *Brunanburh*, Óláfr Guðrøðrsson (OE Anlaf Guthfrithson), King of York 939–41. Sadly for advocates of Bromborough as the location of the battle (above, Chapter 3), the coin post-dates the event. At the neighbouring village of Puddington, a Frankish denier of Charles the Bald (840–77), minted at Melle in Aquitaine, was discovered in 1993.[48]

The south Wirral find-spots described above have yet to be investigated further, but they may well hold further evidence for rural settlement. What were initially very similar indications in an Anglesey field at around the same time, were, however, followed up by field investigation, with considerable success. A report in 1992 to the National Museum of Wales, by metal-detectorists Archie Gillespie and Peter Corbett, of a group of Frankish and Anglo-Saxon coins, together with hacksilver, silver ingots and decorated lead weights, started a research and excavation project which has become one of the most informative yet for Viking-period studies in the Irish Sea region (**69**).

The metal-detected finds occurred on Glyn Farm, Llanbedrgoch, near Red Wharf Bay on Anglesey's eastern coast (**70**), just inland from the site of an apparently isolated Viking grave at Benllech (above, Chapter 5). An earlier coin find from 1989 of a silver penny of Cynethryth, wife of Offa, was subsequently reported. Mark Redknap of the National Museum of Wales responded by investigating the area around the find-spots using aerial photography and geophysical survey. A gently sloping field with a spring at its centre produced geophysical evidence of a sub-oval enclosure, which was excavated in a series of short summer seasons between 1994 and 2001, throughout which controlled metal-detecting activity continued.[49] The enclosure is 1.2 hectares in interior extent and is marked by a combination of a ditch and an impressive 2.3m wide stone wall which was probably constructed in the ninth century. The ditch pre-dates the wall, indeed, the remains

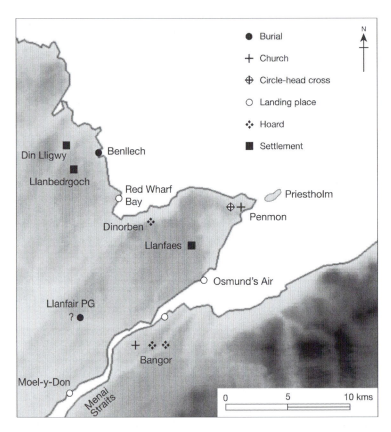

70. South-eastern Anglesey and the Menai Straits: sites mentioned in text

71. Hacksilver from Llanbedrgoch, Anglesey

72. Decorated
lead weights from
Llanbedrgoch, Anglesey

of earlier circular structures show the site was occupied well before the Viking period, but the wall represents a major defensive re-working and reoccupation in the later ninth century.

Just over a third of the enclosed area has since been excavated, revealing the remains of five buildings (two of which were particularly clearly preserved), middens, metalworking hearths, stone-lined pits, a paved path or road, and an impressively wide range of artefacts that strongly suggest Irish Sea Viking trading contacts in the ninth and tenth centuries. The hack-silver (**71**), much of which is of Irish Viking origin, is accompanied by other trading items, notably nineteen lead weights, including decorated, discoid, conical and square forms (**72**). Three of the weights conform to the 'Dublin Standard' of 26.6g (below, Chapter 7), but the others are more diverse. A Kufic coin and two Anglo-Saxon silver pennies of 939–75 were found, but here (unlike Meols) the tenth-century coins are outnumbered by ninth-century issues. The finds include no obvious Scandinavian-style weapons, but an iron bridle with an enamelled stud, with a red and yellow stepped equal-armed cross-motif, and a fragment of a Petersen Type 51 oval brooch, have since been paralleled by some of the Cumwhitton finds. Coloured and polychrome glass beads, personal ornaments such as hooked tags, ringed pins, a decorated buckle and two small pyramidal bells, provide a very similar group of 'hybrid' tenth-century material to that found at Meols and in the Peel Castle burials on the Isle of Man. A sherd of tenth-century Chester Ware pottery from a midden layer confirms the link east to the Dee and west to Dublin, where such pottery has been found in abundance (below, Chapter 7). Over 2000 iron objects include clench-bolts, which may be boat fastenings, together with buckles, strap ends and more utilitarian items such as knives, door fastenings and ordinary nails.

The metalwork and glass finds from Llanbedrgoch broadly favour the tenth century in date, offering a slight contrast to the earlier emphasis in the coin finds. The two best-preserved buildings (Nos 1 and 2) from the Viking-period phase were rectangular longhouses with sunken floors. Building 1 measured 10.5m by 5m internally, and had raised side benches around internal roof supports and a central longitudinal hearth. The well-preserved hearth layers have been dated using archaeomagnetic techniques to AD 890–970 at a 95 per cent confidence level. A flagged area in the lower, southern, end of the building was probably a byre where animals were kept (**27**). Building 2 was wider, measuring 11m by 7.5m and on a different (east–west) alignment; two radiocarbon dates from it give a combined range of AD 705–1035. Refinements to the dating range of these buildings are expected in the final publication, which is in prospect.

Other evidence from the site implies that it may have fallen out of use by the end of the tenth century. Five skeletons were buried without ceremony under rubble in the enclosure ditch (above, Chapter 5); these may be the victims of raiding, which Redknap has suggested led to the demise of the site's trading role in favour of Llanfaes. The latter lies 10km to the south-east, and has produced metal-detected finds of Viking hack-silver and a sword pommel, and, as coin finds show, continued as a market site into the Medieval period. There is an impressive group of stone sculptures in the church of St Seiriol at Penmon, on the eastern tip of Anglesey, which contains elements of Scandinavian artistic influence, such as the Borre ring-chain (below, Chapter 8). These, and a scatter of local Norse topographic place-names such as 'Osmund's Air' (a coastal shingle bank near Beaumaris) may reflect the presence of local Viking lordship in the eastern portion of the Cantref of Rhosyr, which borders the Menai Straits. Traversing this swirling and dangerous east-west tidal corridor can save hours of arduous sailing around the exposed north coast of Anglesey on the route from Dublin to Chester. Menai seems to have grown in strategic significance around 1000, when, according to the *History of Gruffudd ap Cynan,* Gruffudd's grandfather Óláfr Sigtryggsson of Dublin built a castle at a place called 'Bon y Dom' (above, Chapter 3). Some commentators have suggested this was at or near the site of the Moel-y-Don ferry, on the Anglesey shore about half way through the straits,[50] although the site remains archaeologically unidentified.

With its small cluster of buildings, the fortified settlement at Llanbedrgoch was never a major, densely populated settlement approaching urban status, but its position above a sheltered tidal anchorage at Red Wharf Bay (to which it is still linked by an ancient lane) was significant. It has long been suspected that small Viking manufacturing and trading enclaves existed along the north Wales coast in the tenth century, allowing ships travelling between Dublin and Chester to anchor, re-provision, and engage in local trade.[51] Despite its similarities in material culture to other more obviously Viking-dominated sites, there is no easy way of knowing whether Llanbedrgoch was an expression of independent Viking political authority, or whether it remained subject to the rule of Gwynedd throughout. The defensive wall and ditch, and the territorial ambitions implied by the short-lived Ingimund episode in Anglesey, and the Haraldsson brothers' short-lived lordship over the island later in the tenth century (above, Chapter 3), suggest that the site could have been established as a defended enclave of Viking traders in the Welsh landscape, but which at times could have been accompanied by some measure of overall political authority. Viking traders would, however, still have had good reason to be there irrespective of whoever ruled the locality, and the rulers of Gwynedd had every incentive to foster a connection with external trade on the Irish Sea.

Small market enclaves and 'beach-market' sites on islands and at anchorages have a long history in the Irish Sea region.[52] Llanbedrgoch's relationship with the nearby landing-place at Red Wharf Bay merits further archaeological investigation. There must surely have been more Viking-period coastal landing-places and harbours around the Irish Sea than those that are currently identified. Some settlements near sheltered inlets with more limited ranges of finds, such as Ronaldsway on the south-eastern tip of the Isle of Man (which produced a merchant's balance-scale during excavations in 1940), may have played some sort of minor role as trading sites.[53] Disappointingly, a recent survey of Strangford Lough (Co. Down), revealed little new evidence for Viking-period settlement, although some ninth- and tenth-century radiocarbon dates were obtained from wooden fish traps.[54] Ireland's east coast south and north of Dublin Bay, Cumbria, Lancashire and the Isle of Man all as yet lack significant coastal or near-coastal concentrations of traded material (coins, weights, silver, imported metalwork or pottery) such as that found at Meols and Llanbedrgoch. Peel probably had a trading zone near the cemetery. Wicklow, Arklow, Annagassan, the Isle of Whithorn, Kirkcudbright, Bowness-on-Solway near Carlisle, Ravenglass, Barrow-in-Furness, Arnside, the lower Lune near Lancaster, and the Ribble west of Preston, all suggest themselves strongly on topographic grounds as possible locations of Viking-period landing-places or harbours, although little evidence has yet been found in these locations. New and more technically advanced investigations are needed on land and under water, but for yet greater evidence of the Viking-period trading economy in the Irish Sea region, we must now turn to those sites which grew well beyond beach markets or small defended settlements, to take on the status of towns.

CHAPTER 7

TOWNS AND URBANISATION

Previous generations of scholars tended to assume that the Vikings who raided Britain and Ireland in the later eighth and early ninth centuries, like most of the Scots, Welsh and Irish at the same time, were not from urbanised cultures. The inspiration for the growth of towns in the Irish Sea region has generally been sought elsewhere, in England or Frankia. Yet Vikings were no strangers to markets and towns. Trade in foreign goods and fine metalwork, serving powerful tribal chiefdoms, had existed throughout the pre-Viking Iron Age in Scandinavia. By the beginning of the Viking period, major pagan estate centres such as Uppåkra, in southern Sweden, were acting as regional trading centres. The northern Norwegian merchant Ottar, who met King Alfred (above, Chapter 1), mentioned a place called *Sciringes Heal* in southern Norway. This has been convincingly identified as Skiringssal, the location of a major trading settlement known as Kaupang, in Vestfold, south-east Norway (*8*).[1] Kaupang (ON *kaup*, 'trade', comes from the same origin as the English 'shop') acted partly as a redistributive market for material that had been taken from Ireland and Britain. Excavations began there on the impressive mound cemeteries in the 1860s. In the 1950s and 1960s, a substantial area of waterfront revetments and occupation deposits was exposed, resulting in hundreds of finds of insular and Viking artefacts.[2] The full structural implications of these discoveries, and many more, were revealed during new excavations in 1999–2003. A densely constructed, but apparently undefended, trading and manufacturing settlement grew up in the early decades of the ninth century. Around 5.4 hectares in extent, it had an estimated population of between 400 and 1000. Planning and organisation of the site began in around 800–803, and numerous coin and silver finds show its international trading connections.[3] Houses constructed using lines of posts and stakes, with internal roof supports, were placed within an estimated 90–100 plots (six of which have now been fully excavated). These surrounded the harbour, which was revetted and stabilised with stone. Kaupang was probably under Danish rule when it began, and archaeological evidence suggests its growth dissipated coincident to political changes in the later ninth and early tenth centuries, with the site probably becoming derelict by the mid-tenth century.

At the opposite end of the early Medieval Danish realm, on an inlet from the Baltic Sea at Hedeby (now within the German state of Schleswig-Holstein), a much larger trading town within a 27 hectare waterfront enclosure was created at around the same time as Kaupang.[4] Ribe in western Jutland (Denmark) was already trading with the *emporia* of the North Sea basin by the end of the eighth century.[5] Over the course of the eighth to tenth centuries, Viking trading enclaves were established at Birka, near modern Stockholm in central Sweden, and along the river systems leading south-eastwards from the Baltic Sea through Ukraine and Russia to the Black Sea and the Caspian Sea, at Novgorod, Kiev, Smolensk and Gnezdovo. Located at central convergences of routeways and rivers, these places benefited from tribute, trade, and the profits from war. They gathered together people and resources to such an extent as to dominate contemporary rural settlements. Amongst their mixed populations arose new hybrid forms of group identity (such as the *Rūs* of Russia) and they provided a fertile opportunity for the growth of new religions (such as Christianity).

In their fully developed phases, Hedeby, Birka and probably also Kaupang, were sufficiently large and complex to qualify under most archaeological and historical definitions as a 'town'. Nevertheless, another wave of urbanism around 1000 saw the focus of trade and population shift away from some of these sites.[6] Such focal settlements did not, however, exist everywhere in the Viking world. The north Atlantic settlements of the Faeroes and northern and western Scotland, and the Isle of Man, all lacked any significant trace of incipient urbanism in the ninth, tenth or even the eleventh centuries. It is possible that the resource-base of Viking activity in these areas was not concentrated enough yet to support the rise of permanent markets and towns. Patterns of exchange with surrounding indigenous or non-Scandinavian populations seem also to be crucial in assisting the rise of towns, and where these relationships were sparse or non-existent, there was less impetus for people and resources to concentrate in one place.

Tenth- and eleventh-century Dublin

The extent of Scandinavian-led urbanisation in the Irish Sea region remains less clearly demonstrated for the ninth century than for the tenth. Conclusive evidence for ninth-century settlement at Dublin and Woodstown has only recently come to light, and these exposures so far have been piecemeal and partial. Until recent excavations by Linzi Simpson and others (above, Chapter 2), settlement in ninth-century Dublin had not been clearly identified. The precise location and extent of the (probably) defended *longphort* itself remains open to debate. Nevertheless, the ninth-century buildings discovered at Temple Bar West show evidence for continuity into the tenth century. The excavated structures survived in enough detail to enable Simpson to describe them as conforming to 'Type 1' as defined by Patrick Wallace in his publication of buildings from Wood Quay (description below). Type 1 can now be shown also to resemble strongly in plan and constructional form a number of the ninth-century buildings from Kaupang, thanks to the recent excavations there.[7]

The evidence for Dublin's rise as a trading town in the tenth century is more wide-ranging and conclusive. The discoveries at Temple Bar West showed that some of the resident population almost certainly stayed on after the *longphort* was breached in 902. Little is yet known of what actually happened here between 902 and 917, although it is likely that whatever remained of portable value was quickly removed into the Irish interior. In the years following the end of the political hiatus in 917, increasingly large numbers of people, engaged in more and more diverse ways of making a living, were accommodated on the banks of the River Liffey. The post-917 period was also the time when Dublin's rural territories were recast and expanded. This was probably intended to consolidate enough land to provide a reliable supply of basic foodstuffs and raw materials for the urban population, meaning the town did not have to depend wholly on its fractious relationships with surrounding Irish kingdoms for these necessities. Dublin's rural hinterland (**73**) became known as the Dyflinarskíri, and the Fine Gall, the territory of the foreigners. The Thingmote near College Green is also likely to have been established or restored at this time (above, Chapter 4).

Nineteenth-century antiquarians such as Sir William Wilde (above, Chapter 5) collected and published Viking finds from the heart of tenth- and eleventh-century Dublin, but the topography of the Viking town was little known at that time. Numerous excavations have occurred all over the core of the city since the early 1960s; a very useful detailed summary dating to 2000 is available,[8]

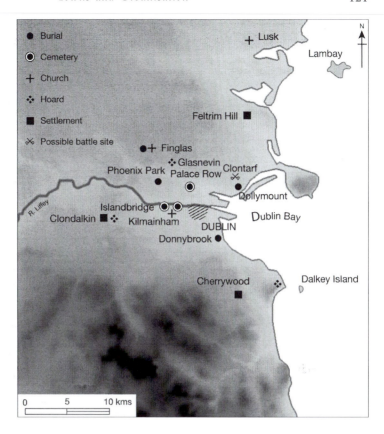

73. Dublin Area: sites mentioned in text

but with the private-sector boom of recent years, much more evidence has surfaced and an update is needed. These investigations began in 1961–2 within Dublin Castle, a prominent site overlooking the Pool (above, Chapter 2). Planked pathways and wattle screens were found, together with Viking-period artefacts. This was an early indication of the generally excellent state of organic preservation, particularly of wood, wattle, textile, leather and bone, which came to be a celebrated feature of subsequent excavations. Dublin Castle produced further evidence of tenth-century defences and structures in 1984–86, as have a rash of small-scale development sites within and outside the Medieval walls of the city.[9]

The largest-scale excavations so far took place in the period 1962–81, immediately west of Dublin Castle and Temple Bar, in the streets surrounding the Medieval Christ Church Cathedral (**74**). These were prompted by redevelopment in what was, in the 1960s, an extremely run-down area, and were undertaken by the National Museum of Ireland. South of the cathedral and away from the river, excavations took place at High Street and Christchurch Place, directed by A. B. Ó Ríordáin in the periods 1962–3 and 1967–76. The largest concentration of evidence for Viking-period urbanism in Dublin comes from a cluster of adjacent excavation sites north of Christ Church Cathedral, located on ground sloping down towards the river, known as the Wood Quay area. Ó Ríordáin excavated at Winetavern Street on the western side of this zone in 1969–72. The most extensive discoveries occurred in a 1.8-hectare excavation on the block of land between Fishamble Street and Wood Quay in 1974–81 (**75**), which was directed by Patrick F. Wallace. The latter seasons, particularly 1977–81, were surrounded by controversy as a public and direct-action campaign was waged to 'Save Viking Dublin', to prevent a development of concrete office blocks ('The Civic Offices') on the site.[10] Thanks to public pressure, some extra time was provided for the excavations, but the office blocks eventually went up nonetheless. The subsequent decades have seen a massive ongoing post-excavation analysis and publication project at the National Museum

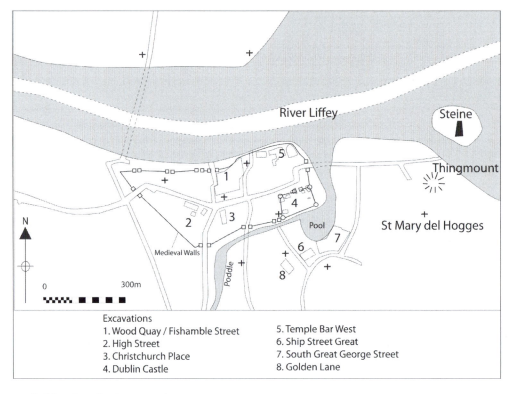

Excavations
1. Wood Quay / Fishamble Street
2. High Street
3. Christchurch Place
4. Dublin Castle

5. Temple Bar West
6. Ship Street Great
7. South Great George Street
8. Golden Lane

74. Dublin: plan of major excavations

under Wallace's direction, producing a wealth of information in the form of monographs, exhibitions, catalogues, popular books and media programmes, for which it is possible to provide only a very limited and selective summary here.

The Liffey was a much wider and shallower river in the Viking period than it appears today. Before industrial dock and quay construction in recent centuries, the sea came in much closer to the centre of the city, and the effects of tides would also have been more pronounced. The natural river margins were soft and shallow, requiring construction to provide flood protection and harbourage. The northern, riverfront, half of the Wood Quay area was characterised by the remains of nine successive waterfronts built successively out into the river between the tenth and fourteenth centuries. Two low flood banks were constructed above the high-water line in the tenth century, which were later replaced by defences. Wallace has described the earliest, and southernmost, of these as a 'palisaded earthen bank which […] probably encircled the settlement',[11] noting that a very similar structural sequence was exposed on the town's south (inland) side at Ross Road.[12] The defences were renewed in about 1000, with a cobbled lane inside the circuit, and a breakwater on the river side, and were replaced by a stone enclosure wall around 1100. Inside the defensive banks, up to three metres' depth of complex stratigraphy was encountered, comprising building remains, streets and walkways, occupation debris, middens and industrial deposits.

Most of the excavated areas in Dublin had been damp and easily waterlogged during the Viking period, and, fortunately for their archaeological preservation, had largely remained so. Floors and walls had needed to be regularly renewed as the old ones merged into the soggy ground, providing a treasure-store of well-preserved organic material to be excavated. Occupation levels were often 20cm or more in depth; instead of clearing out and dumping their trodden-in domestic refuse, the occupants had tended instead to re-surface their living areas and build over the top

75. Dublin, Type 1 building, Fishamble Street Excavations

76. Dublin: Fishamble Street Excavations in progress

of them. Sawdust and woodchips were used to cover up and refresh interior surfaces. Dating the occupation levels was a complex process involving relational dating, using artefacts (great reliance was placed here upon coin finds) and cross-referencing sequential events. The approach of excavations in the 1970s and early 1980s differed somewhat from those carried out in Dublin in the 1990s and 2000s, which have relied more upon radiocarbon dating, raising some interesting chronological conundrums (above, Chapter 2).

A wide cross-section of building plots or tenements was exposed in the Wood Quay complex of sites, revealing a densely packed commercial and industrial district. Tenement boundaries consisted of wood and wattle fences, which had been repeatedly renewed *in situ*. These had been established early in the period of occupation, perhaps before the mid-tenth century, leading Wallace to propose that part of the settlement had been planned.[13] A row of fourteen long, narrow, plots fronted at their narrow ends onto the north-south curve of Fishamble Street, which remains a city street

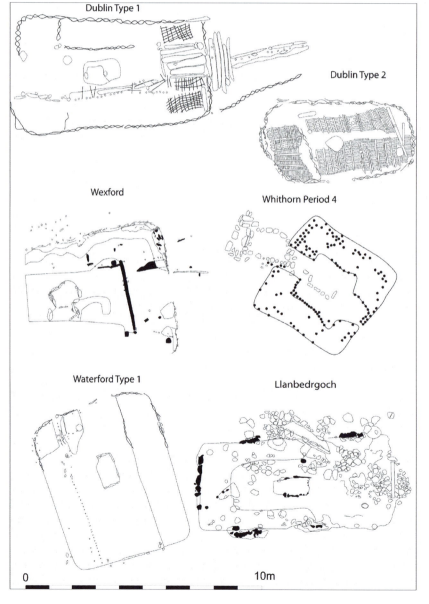

77.
Comparison of buildings from urban sites with Llanbedrgoch as comparison (see **27**)

on more-or-less the same line today. The longest plot was 24m in length, but not all the plots were of the same size, and the fact that no individual plot was completely excavated makes any conclusion on their average size somewhat speculative. Up to thirteen superimposed occupation levels with house remains were recorded in some of the plots, with at least six or seven in most of them. Houses were sited longitudinally on the tenement plots (**76**), with their narrow ends towards the street. Several plots had two or even three buildings of different types, encompassing domestic occupation, storage and craft production. Spaces outside the buildings were divided by plot boundaries and walkways constructed of wattle, planks, and half-sectioned logs.

The completeness of the street scene, which can be almost miraculously reconstructed from the Fishamble Street evidence, was not matched quite so consistently elsewhere. Wallace has pointed out that the Fishamble Street building sequence is 'not typical of Viking and Hiberno-Norse Dublin',[14] and evidence from his predecessor Ó Ríordáin's excavations shows greater diversity, including some larger buildings at Christchurch Place, and a less obviously planned layout with a more congested placement of smaller buildings at High Street and Winetavern Street. The broad conclusion drawn from the material found on these sites suggests that the areas away from the riverfront and further towards the southern line of defences were characterised by less obvious evidence for planning (perhaps indicating that land further from the waterfront was less at a premium) and a greater concentration of industrial and craft workshops.

The buildings from Ó Ríordáin's excavations were published in 1983, and Wallace published a monograph in 1992 that reviewed the evidence known thus far.[15] Wallace produced a typology of buildings from Dublin which has been applied subsequently at Waterford, Wexford and Cork, and also at Whithorn (**77**). Type 1 accounts for the majority of the buildings excavated in Dublin (amounting to about sixty-seven per cent of those reported upon by Wallace in 1992), and is the main dwelling-house type. Type 1 was an urban building without the internal byre, which characterised the rural longhouses of Norse Scotland, and also of Building 1 at Llanbedrgoch. Thirty-four were exposed completely, averaging 7.52m by 5.38m in plan, and tended to become slightly smaller in the eleventh century. Sub-rectangular with rounded corners and a central hearth, constructed with lines of post and wattle walls (in some cases double walls with bracken insulation between), they were represented throughout the excavated Fishamble Street sequence of thirteen levels. The interior of the Type 1 house was divided into three longitudinal spaces, with the hearth flanked by benches on the two longer sides, and the entrances were in one or both of the ends, often with planked thresholds. The roof, which was thatched with straw fixed to a turf underlay, was supported by four internal posts in two pairs. In a recent publication, Wallace described the Type 1 building as:

> An Irish urban variant (built in local materials and indigenous building methods to the dictates of the local climate) of the more widespread north-west European rectangular three-sided building, characteristic of the Norse in their western expansion.[16]

Type 2 has a smaller, less elongated plan (measuring on average 5m by 3.1m), with more rounded corners. Type 2 formed less than six per cent of the buildings and was not found at all levels; it was not subdivided into three units and lacked a hearth, although the floors were often covered in wattle mats, leading to Wallace's suggestion that these buildings were used for storage or for sleeping. Type 3 buildings, which were only slightly more numerous than Type 2, were described as a small version of Type 1, and were found 'almost exclusively' on Plots 5 and 6 at Fishamble Street. Averaging 4.9m by 2.96m, these rather flimsy buildings were a later introduction than Type 2, and probably served a similar ancillary purpose. Type 4 was a very different style of building altogether. It was small, measuring around 4.4m by 1.9m, had a sunken floor (somewhat more like contemporary Anglo-Saxon buildings) and only four were recorded in Wallace's corpus, three from Winetavern Street, and one from 'a comparatively early level' at Fishamble Street. No hearths were found in these, which led to some uncertainty as to their function, but this might not be such a surprise if the floor had in fact been suspended over the sunken 'cellar'. A comparison of Type 4

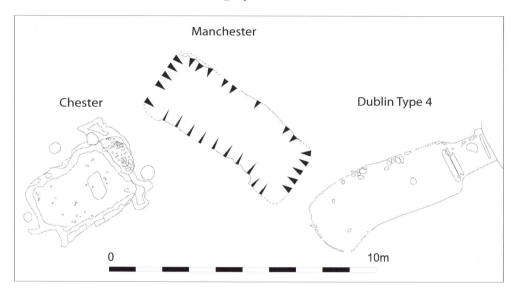

Manchester

Chester

Dublin Type 4

0   10m

78. Comparison of sunken-featured buildings

with early tenth-century sunken-floored buildings from the Cheshire *burhs* (**78**) reveals a striking similarity, which may support Wallace's contention (discussed further below) that Dublin's early topography was to some extent influenced by Anglo-Saxon examples. Some of the buildings from Ó Ríordáin's excavations displayed evidence for buttressing and stave construction. Type 5, which formed less than five per cent of the buildings, was the least complicated of the Dublin buildings, a small hut on average 3.3m by 1.9m, which probably functioned as an outhouse. Other buildings were fragmentary, so were described as 'unclassifiable'.

Trade and industry in Dublin is evident in the vast number of finds from within and around the buildings. No single type or occupation amongst these appeared to be predominant, indicating that the town had a mixed and multifarious economy encompassing international, regional and local trade. The excavations produced evidence of production of metal and organic materials and objects, crafts, woodworking, textile-making, butchery, and all the secondary redistributive, defensive and administrative services which are required to prevent chaos in a small, densely populated area largely dependent on imported food. Dublin's physical defences and gateways can only have been intended as a short-term security or even a traffic-control measure, as its need for regular imported supplies from its hinterland made it vulnerable. It is possible in post-917 Dublin, with the benefit of twenty or more years of experience of land purchase and political deals in north-west England (above, Chapter 4), that negotiation with neighbouring Irish kingdoms over relatively humdrum matters of mutual benefit was a more regular occurrence than in the pre-902 period. This did not prevent Dublin from being attacked on numerous occasions during the tenth and eleventh centuries, but it may have provided enough political intelligence and security of supply to prevent it once again being wiped out by its enemies.

The supply of food to Dublin is shown by the animal bone and archaeobotanical finds from the excavations. Soil samples analysed by Siobhán Geraghty have provided an insight into the range of cereals, herbs, nuts, seeds and plant fibres, which were used for food, for domestic comfort and insulation, for making textiles and clothing, and for treating ailments.[17] These included six-row hulled barley, oats, flax, hazelnuts, and pips from blackberry, apples, sloes and wild strawberry. Fibrous mosses were found in cesspits, suggesting they may have been used as a form of 'toilet paper'. The remains of acid-loving plants such as heather and bilberry allowed Geraghty to postulate that extensive gathering had taken place in upland areas, probably in the Wicklow Hills to the south of Dublin. Henbane, a medicinal or magical plant was found, but may have grown in the town as a weed. Small domestic fowl, dogs and cats were probably kept in the tenements, but larger livestock was driven into the town from the countryside when it had reached maturity.[18] Fish and eels could be caught in the Poddle, the Liffey, and the outer estuary, but these alone were probably not enough to sustain the town's requirements without venturing further out to sea and upriver.

Finds of fishing weights and equipment suggest the presence of a fish market (a 'fish-shamble'),[19] which was probably operated by specialist fishing families. Meat consumption was dominated by cattle, with smaller amounts of pig, goat, sheep and horsemeat also being eaten. These proportions may well reflect the emphasis placed on cattle in the Irish kingdoms, suggesting that not all Dublin's supply was farmed in its own hinterland, but was in part traded with local rulers in return for the sorts of things Dublin was renowned for supplying – silver, imports, fine woodwork and manufactured objects. These have been found, not just in hoards, but in some abundance in indigenous centres of power, such as the large royal crannóg sites at Ballinderry and Lagore.[20] Mary Valante has mapped finds of material such as amber, jet and bone (antler) combs which probably came through the Dublin market or possibly its smaller counterparts at Waterford, Cork or Wexford.[21] The distribution of this material is similar to that of coinless silver hoards (discussed above in Chapter 6), and is spread widely across Munster, Leinster and Ulster. Less archaeologically detectible valuables also circulated: the possibility that Dublin acted as the major slave market for Ireland has been referred to in the context of the *longphort* (above, Chapter 6). An iron neck-ring with a chain has been quoted as an example of rare archaeological evidence for slavery,[22] but this could just as easily be related to ordinary criminal punishment. Later on, further evidence for trade links within the interior comes in the form of 'Souterrain Ware', a relatively utilitarian pottery type characteristic of Irish rural sites, and found in Dublin.

Wood, wattle, turf, clay, stone, moss and reeds for thatching, which went into the construction of the Dublin buildings, must largely have come from outside the town. Consumption of timber was vast. Apart from firewood, and the various domestic crafts, rebuilding after frequent fires would have necessitated large quantities being brought into the city overland or downriver. Some fresh timber may have been imported and some was certainly re-used from broken up ships, harbourage or buildings. Securing a regular timber supply from the surrounding countryside would have required land, as well as a managed and productive foresting and coppicing regime. Domestic blacksmithing, amber working, textile working, woodcarving and the manufacture of large numbers of distinctive small dress items were also evident in the archaeological finds from Dublin. The practice of art and decoration is evident in the many 'motif pieces' (formerly referred to as 'trial pieces' of bone, metal and stone that were discovered (**79**). Antler combs, small copper-alloy strap ends with distinctive zoomorphic forms, stick pins and ringed pins, are all characteristic of the material culture of the tenth- and eleventh-century town. Ringed pins form a particularly distinctive group, and Dublin is the only place that has produced manufacturing evidence (below, Chapter 8). These have already been referred to (above, Chapter 6), as they occur at Meols (**65**), Llanbedrgoch, and in many of the pagan burials of Ireland, the Isle of Man and Cumbria. They also spread out to the Scottish isles, Northumbria, Scandinavia, Iceland and as far as L'Anse aux Meadows in Newfoundland, Canada. Most are made of copper-alloy, although silver examples are known, and they are perhaps the most striking indications of Dublin's contacts across the Viking world.

Historical evidence (above, Chapter 2) is unequivocal in its emphasis on the fleets which were at the disposal of Dublin's Viking rulers. Evidence for Viking shipbuilding has for many years been sought in Dublin. Large numbers of iron finds including clench-bolts from the excavations gave rise to the near-certainty that somewhere, or perhaps in several places along the Liffey, ships were being built or repaired. Dramatic confirmation of Dublin's prowess as a shipbuilding centre came, not from excavations in the city, nor even elsewhere in Ireland, but amongst a group of well-used and worn-out wooden vessels that had been deliberately sunk to form an underwater barrier in Roskilde Fjord, Denmark, and which were rediscovered in 1957. The five 'Skuldelev' ships were subsequently excavated inside a drained cofferdam in 1962 and formed the centrepiece of the Roskilde Viking Ship Museum. They included a very large warship, *Skuldelev 2*, which, although badly damaged *in situ*, was found to be around 25–30m in length and 3.8m wide. It was built

79. Dublin: bone trial or motif piece
bearing Ringerike-style designs

around 1042, and was repaired in the 1060s. Tree ring samples taken from the vessel's oak planks did not match the known Scandinavian dendro-sequence, but were a close match for the Irish sequence from the mid-eleventh century. A full-sized reconstruction of the ship, named the *Sea Stallion from Glendalough* (**back cover**), made a highly-publicised, if somewhat hard-fought passage, from Denmark, via Orkney, to Dublin in 2007, before returning to Denmark in 2008 (below, Chapter 9).

It is not the Irish-built warship but another of the Roskilde ships, *Skuldelev 1*, a slow, tubby but capacious and seaworthy ship or *knarr,* which perhaps best symbolises the ability of Viking-period merchants to cross stormy seas with considerable cargoes. Inevitably, objects brought from the furthest and most exotic locations have received the greatest attention. Dublin was certainly known in the Islamic world as a trading city.[23] Eastern Mediterranean links are evident in some of the imported textiles, including Byzantine silk,[24] but most Kufic coins were probably melted down on arrival. Green porphyry came in as a pilgrim souvenir item, or as part of the relic trade that was a feature of early Medieval towns. Scandinavian trading links have been particularly celebrated. Amber from the Baltic, whale and walrus-bone from Norway or perhaps from Greenland, together with steatite (soapstone) vessel fragments, probably from Shetland, show Dublin's northern links.

The majority of the coins and imports found in Dublin favour trading locations nearer at hand than the Mediterranean or Scandinavia. Over a hundred lead weights have been studied by Wallace to produce the standard 26.6g figure for the 'Dublin ounce' (above, Chapter 6). Numerous small metal pans and fittings from merchants' balance-scales were found in the excavations, showing there was a culture of precision when it came to the buying and selling even of small-scale materials, with which the evidence from other Irish Sea sites such as Meols and Llanbedrgoch can be compared. Amongst the coin finds from the Dublin excavations, those from the tenth century are dominated by Anglo-Saxon issues. No single mint is predominant, with coins from London, Canterbury, Chester, East Anglia and south-west England being represented on a roughly equal basis.[25] In such a small total number, this assortment may be statistically meaningless and be simply due to factors affecting their loss and preservation, but it contrasts somewhat with tenth-century hoards in central and eastern Ireland, which are more obviously dominated by coins from Chester and York. Dublin did not start producing a 'Hiberno-Norse coinage' of its own until 995–997, but thereafter the locally-produced coins dominate the finds and the Anglo-Saxon coins tail off after the reign of Cnut.

A group of Anglo-Saxon disc brooches were interpreted by Wallace as evidence of the import of English dress items. Further evidence of trade with England, more particularly with Cheshire and northern Mercia, is found in the large number of sherds of Chester Ware pottery (see also Llanbedrgoch, Chapter 6). These utilitarian grey or orange-brown vessels (**62**), often shoulder-decorated with roller-stamped dots or chevrons, were made and exported during the tenth and early eleventh century (see below). Their circulation within England is largely restricted to Mercia, but they evidently found a ready market in Dublin, along with lesser amounts of Stamford Ware and some continental pottery. These wares were presumably valuable products in a city that produced no indigenous pottery. An Irish source, *Aislinge Meic Conglinne,* refers to *Salann Saxannach* ('Saxon salt'), indicating that it was imported from England.[26] It is possible that such relatively small vessels as the Chester Ware pots were used to transport Cheshire salt, if a particularly refined table salt was available. Quantities of broken glass or cullet, and a sherd of Roman *terra sigillata* possibly also came in from Chester; the latter was probably mixed up in stony ships' ballast loaded on the banks of the Dee.

Anglo-Saxon urbanisation and tenth-century Chester

In the years after the Wood Quay excavations ended, Wallace published a number of insightful papers considering the impact of Anglo-Saxon and Anglo-Scandinavian urbanism on the growing town at Dublin. During this time he noted the most obvious difference, in that the two most influential comparisons for Dublin in the tenth century – York and Chester (together with many other contemporary Anglo-Saxon and Anglo-Scandinavian towns) – were former Roman settlements.[27] Carlisle, with its rich cemetery excavated at the west end of the cathedral in 1988 (above, Chapter 5), might have taken on some urban characteristics in the early to mid-tenth century (a time when it remained under British rule), but so far little evidence of these has been found. Excavations by the York Archaeological Trust at 16–22 Coppergate, which went on for several years at the same time as the Fishamble Street excavations, provided an inevitable and much-quoted comparison with Dublin, especially given the Viking dynastic connections between the two cities.[28]

Organic preservation was similarly good in York to that in Dublin, with extensive wooden, archaeobotanical, leather and bone deposits surviving. Regular publicity at the time pointed to much the same story of Viking influence on the two cities. There are indeed numerous similarities in material culture, although the direct Scandinavian influence in each case has turned out to be less overwhelming than once thought. As the long post-excavation projects have progressed, and the detail of the discoveries interrogated, numerous differences have emerged, and the popular belief that York and Dublin were virtually twin Viking cities has undergone some revision in favour of emphasising more specific local influences on each. For example, Wallace was unable, on the strength of the information available in 1992, to point to significant similarities in building forms between the early tenth-century wattle-constructed houses excavated at Coppergate and those from Dublin,[29] and the change towards plank and stave-built sunken-featured structures observed in York from the mid-tenth century onwards made the architectural differences even more marked.

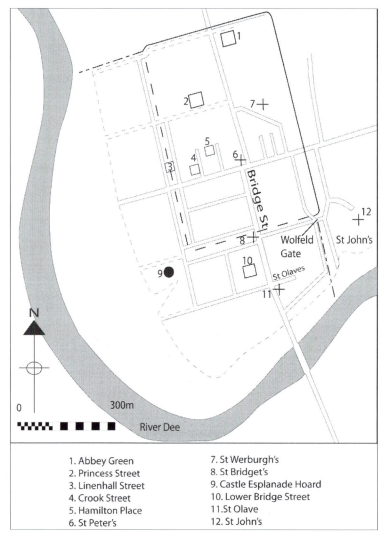

1. Abbey Green
2. Princess Street
3. Linenhall Street
4. Crook Street
5. Hamilton Place
6. St Peter's
7. St Werburgh's
8. St Bridget's
9. Castle Esplanade Hoard
10. Lower Bridge Street
11. St Olave
12. St John's

80. Chester: plan of churches and major excavations

Chester (*80*), which although never dynastically linked to Dublin, actually faces the Irish Sea, was in economic terms the most important town connected to Ireland in the tenth and early eleventh centuries. Its status as a royal *burh* meant that it was part of widespread development of shire towns with defensive and trading privileges, which were set up across Wessex and Mercia during the later ninth and early tenth centuries. The geopolitical background to the establishment of *burhs* in the Dee and Mersey basin has been outlined above (Chapter 3). Chester is situated upon a dry red sandstone rise above the River Dee (*81*), so organic preservation in waterlogged layers was much less common than at York and Dublin, but the relative softness of its geology had invited the creation of rock-cut features which, where not damaged by later cellaring, survive very well. Occupation in the Anglo-Saxon and Viking period took place amidst swathes of derelict Roman masonry. Much of the archaeological challenge of excavating in Chester lies in disentangling robbed and re-used phases of Roman buildings and defences. Many older archaeological excavations occurred in Chester, with the Roman military enthusiast Robert Newstead being particularly active in the early twentieth century. In those days, post-Roman archaeological layers tended to be little regarded or recorded in comparison with the remains left by the Roman army. The curatorships of Graham Webster and Hugh Thompson at the Grosvenor Museum in the

81. Chester: a reconstruction of the tenth-century town from the south-west, by D.P. Astley and A.M. Beckett

1950s and 1960s saw greater attention paid to the broader chronology of the city's past, which was consolidated with the formation of the Grosvenor Museum Excavations Section (later Chester Archaeology) in 1973.

The Mercian defences of Chester were adapted from the derelict walls of Roman Deva. A palisade trench excavated at Linenhall Street on the west side of the Roman fortress in 1961–2 suggests that there may have been an early and superseded Mercian scheme simply to refortify the full Roman circuit of walls. Instead of pursuing this to its full extent, it is more likely that the walls were subsequently extended by new constructions to the river from the north-west and south-east corners, creating a larger enclosure than the Roman one. This had the effect of including within the *burh* a substantial stretch of river frontage, which developed harbourage functions in the tenth century. The extra-mural church of St John, which stands just to the east of the city walls beside the former Roman amphitheatre, was a significant and powerful religious house, and it is likely that some important extra-mural residences existed around it. Within the area of the former Roman fortress, apart from a poorly dated stone structure constructed at its centre some time between the fourth and ninth centuries, little else but minor agricultural remains are demonstrable from before the later ninth century. Occupation began in the very late ninth or early tenth century with the construction of rectilinear sunken-featured huts, the partial remains of which have been found at Hamilton Place, Hunter Street School and at 26–42 Lower Bridge Street.[30] Sunken-featured structures have also been found at Rhuddlan, the 921 *burh* of Cledemutha, in north-east Wales, and also at Manchester (*78*), suggesting that these rapidly-constructed buildings were characteristic of the early occupation of the north-west Mercian *burhs*.[31] As discussed above, these are possibly an overlooked comparison for Dublin's Type 4 buildings.

The 26–42 Lower Bridge Street excavation of 1974–76, outside the southern Roman walls but within the larger post-907 enclosure near the harbour and bridge, produced the most complete and informative series of building remains so far revealed from the tenth or eleventh centuries in

82. Chester: cellared buildings, Lower Bridge Street Excavation

Chester. This site was excavated in advance of redevelopment by the Grosvenor Museum, and was directed by David Mason.[32] Phase IV of the site, which Mason dated to the early to mid-tenth century, produced evidence of three sub-rectangular timber buildings built over rock-cut cellars, with sloping entrance-ways, measuring 5.10m by 4.5m and 1.8m in depth (*82*). These were found arranged in an apparent 'courtyard' plan, together with the remains of two more buildings that were ground-based or only semi-sunken.

The cellared buildings (*83*), which probably had separate ground-level entrances as well as the sloping steps to their lower levels, may have been warehouses or workshops, of two or perhaps even three storeys including attics. Their occupation might also have lasted somewhat longer than Mason suggested, because the buildings may have been modified for further occupation towards the end of the tenth century, continuing into the eleventh century, after which they were re-used as tanning pits. These buildings are similar to contemporary Anglo-Saxon urban buildings from London, Canterbury and Oxford, together with later tenth-century plank-constructed buildings from Coppergate, York, and Thetford. They bear only a distant resemblance to the Dublin Type 4, but they do, however, resemble a group of four sunken-featured buildings of later eleventh-century date excavated at Peter Street, Waterford in 1987–88 (*84*), a building excavated in 1994 at Werburgh, Street, Dublin, and somewhat later structures from Limerick.[33] In Chester, the cellared buildings were apparently restricted to the newly built-up area between the Roman walls and the river. Contemporary structures within the Roman walls were revealed in excavations in the 1970s and 1980s, at Crook Street and Hunter's Walk in the north-west quadrant of the Roman fortress, which show partial survivals of simpler, ground-based, post-built hall-type structures of widths between 5.06m and 5.6m. In the north-eastern quadrant, an open-sided shed, a gravel path, a corn-drying kiln and an antler-soaking pit were found at Abbey Green, in 1975–8.[34]

Dating the later Anglo-Saxon and Viking-period phase of Chester's development has been a challenge. Much emphasis has been laid on stratified finds of Chester Ware, which circulated between the second quarter of the tenth and the early eleventh century. Ironically, no kiln site has been discovered in the city; the only known production site is in Stafford, and it is also known as North Midlands Ware. Other site finds of the period from Chester include utilitarian iron tools and Anglo-Saxon objects, such as a ninth-century silver brooch (which occurred as a residual deposit in a later phase of activity at Lower Bridge Street), small everyday personal items such as small dress pins, pierced whetstones and metal-hooked tags, decorated metal and bone strap ends, and a sparse collection (fewer than ten) of Anglo-Saxon coins. Four copper-alloy ringed pins are known from the city, including a very fine complete one from Crook Street (below, Chapter 8). Comb fragments, spindle whorls, a small silver ring fragment and a stray find of a plaited gold finger-ring also emphasise Viking connections. Three decorated stick pins with expanded shanks and small, round decorated heads, have been found in the city. These are eleventh- to twelfth-century types that are known in much greater numbers from Dublin. The most recent of these (a silver-gilded example) was found during excavations at the Roman amphitheatre in 2005, but was not accompanied by a significant structural context. The most impressive artefact of Viking type as yet known from Chester is a copper-alloy disc brooch found in excavations at Hunter Street School in 1981. Measuring 3.2cm in diameter, it consists of two separately cast discs (the rear, plain one bore the pin). On its convex openwork faceplate it has a double-contoured ribbon animal, decorated with transverse billets and spiral hips, coiled upon itself within a circular border. The design encompasses elements of the Viking Borre and Jellinge styles of the late ninth to mid-tenth centuries, and thus is probably an early tenth-century piece. It is paralleled by a brooch from High Street, Dublin (**85**), together with other examples from Cottam, near York, 'the vicinity of the Wash' in eastern England and the trading town of Birka, Sweden.[35]

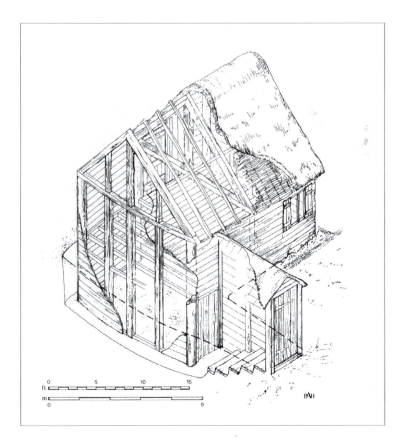

83. Chester: Lower Bridge Street, reconstruction of Type IV cellared buildings

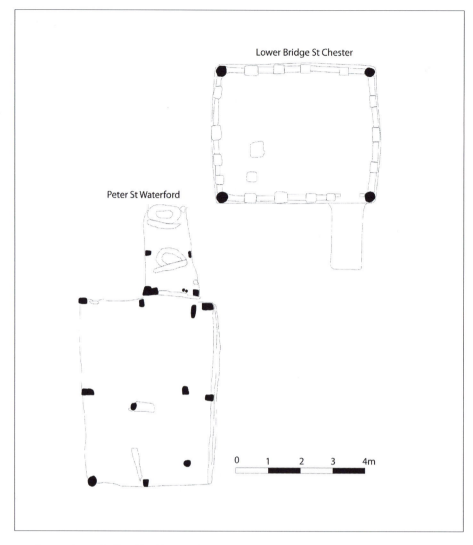

Lower Bridge St Chester

Peter St Waterford

0   1   2   3   4m

84. Comparison of cellared buildings: Chester and Waterford

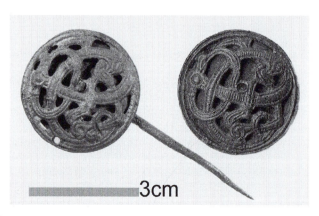

3cm

85. Identical Borre/Jellinge-style
disc-brooches from High Street
Dublin (with secondary pin attached)
and Hunter Street, Chester

The walls of the Lower Bridge Street Phase IV buildings displayed a slight tendency towards bow-sidedness, which led their excavator initially to suggest this might have been a Scandinavian-inspired trait.[36] However, it must have been barely noticeable in practice. The rest of the Chester buildings are utilitarian, and their ground plans do not betray strong cultural affiliations; their superstructure might have been more distinctively decorated, but on the basis of the evidence we cannot know this. How influential were Viking settlers in Chester? Following the rebellion of 924, in which they may have had a hand, they seem to have become loyal, integrated citizens, whilst remaining to some extent an identifiable group within the townspeople. The Scandinavian names of a minority of the Chester moneyers have been referred to (above, Chapter 6). St John's Church has a collection of red sandstone tenth- and eleventh-century sculpture including two circle-headed crosses (below, Chapter 8). Minor names in the city, such as the now-superseded 'Clippe Gate' and 'Wolfield Gate' (from the ON personal names *Klyppr* and *Ulfhildr*) also betray the presence of Scandinavians. Alan Thacker drew attention to the fact that Handbridge, a suburb across the river from the southern edge of the city, was assessed in Domesday Book in the Anglo-Scandinavian style of carucates rather than in English hides, and a reference to the city having twelve justices is a feature more commonly found in the Danelaw.[37] Although seemingly fairly late (possibly twelfth century) in foundation, two of Chester's historic church dedications to St Bridget and St Olave (ON *Óláfr*) suggest that these two small city parishes were once inhabited by people of Scandinavian descent, and serve to remind the visitor today of the city's Scandinavian and Irish connections.

The ceremonial rowing by the northern *subreguli* of Edgar on the Dee in 973 (above, Chapter 3) was the high-water mark of Chester's political and economic status in Anglo-Saxon England, and shows the extent to which the Irish Sea and its neighbouring kingdoms had become a vital strategic concern to the English monarchy during the tenth century. The fortunes of the Chester Mint seem to have gone into relative decline over the following decades, but instead of resulting from the attack in 980, this may ironically have been due to Edgar's other major achievement of 973, a coinage reform which limited the independence of regional mints. Chester's port and mint continued in business, as shown by a particularly extensive record of the city's shipping tolls in Domesday Book,[38] but it gradually lost its tenth-century pre-eminence as the principal English commercial window on the Irish Sea to ports and trading networks located further south.

Trade in the Bristol Channel, and the later Hiberno-Norse towns

A Viking presence on the Bristol Channel is noted in the *Anglo-Saxon Chronicle* for 893 and also for 914, when an unusually detailed account describes the activities of a fleet under jarls Ottar and Hroald arrived from Brittany. They captured Cyfeiliog, Bishop of Archenfield, who was ransomed by the king for forty pounds of silver, and then ravaged along the Welsh and Somerset coasts and on the lower Severn and Wye, reaching inland as far as Hereford. Having been successfully resisted by a coalition of English and Welsh forces, they took refuge on the small island of Steepholm, in the centre of the Bristol Channel, where many of them died of hunger, before the remainder escaped first to Dyfed and then on to Ireland.[39] Raids continued in sporadic phases, including a concentrated series of raids on monasteries in south-west Wales, particularly on St David's in the 980s and 990s.[40] These attacks may have preceded small instances of land-take, and some Welsh rulers made use of Viking mercenaries. Settlement, marked by names in *–bý* along the Glamorgan coast such as at Womanby, Hornby and Lamby near Cardiff, and a cluster in *–garðr* ('enclosure'), such as Fishguard, in Pembrokeshire, may in part pre-date the Norman Conquest, but place-name scholars have generally, and rather cautiously, attributed them to the Anglo-Norman period.[41] There is no doubt, however, that the long maritime corridor represented by the Bristol Channel and the Severn Estuary formed a highly vulnerable entry-point into the heart of Wessex and Mercia.

Chester's refortification by Æthelfæd in 907 was closely paralleled on the River Severn at Gloucester.[42] As at Chester, this strengthening of the border helped to extend Mercian influence

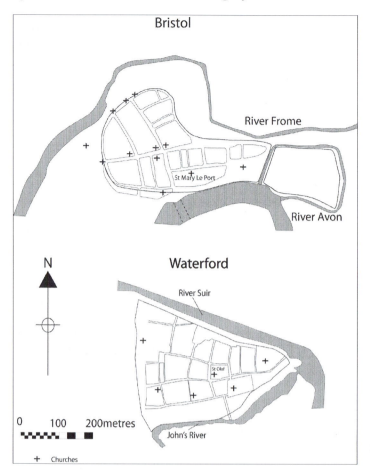

86. Bristol and Waterford, plans of the eleventh-/twelfth-century towns

far into Wales, where the sacking and burning of Llan-gors Crannog in 916 was a related event. Gloucester's mint produced coins which have been found in Irish hoards and site finds in Dublin, indicating that trading contacts were spreading along the south coast of Wales and across to Ireland in the tenth century. Gloucester, which is located on treacherous tidal channels far up the Severn Estuary, seems, however, to have lost out commercially in the early eleventh century to the rising trading centre of Bristol, which is located on a sheltered tidal harbour connected by the Avon Gorge to the sea. Bristol was not a royal *burh*, and only rated a minor mention in Domesday, where it was included in the entry for Barton Regis, a local manor.[43] Its mint began issuing coins during the reign of Æthelred II around the turn of the tenth to eleventh centuries, but so far only a tiny amount of structural archaeological evidence has been revealed for the pre-Norman period in Bristol – mostly a series of disconnected features producing metalworking evidence, pottery and bone dress pins in excavations at the church of St Mary le Port (**86**).

Bristol became a trading powerhouse from the mid-eleventh century onwards, and finds of Medieval pottery from excavations in Ireland indicate extensive contact with south-west England in the twelfth and thirteenth centuries. It also participated in the Irish Sea slave trade. We have an unusual reference to this in William of Malmesbury's *Life of St Wulfstan* (Archbishop Wulfstan II of Worcester, who died in 1098). William describes Wulfstan's visits to the port of Bristol in the later eleventh century, probably while staying at his demesne manor at Westbury-on-Trym. During these visits he preached against the slave trade, to the extent that it was temporarily abandoned by the townspeople.[44]

The Hiberno-Norse towns of Wexford, Waterford, Cork and Limerick have produced varying amounts of archaeological evidence, which in all cases has so far been extremely limited for the tenth and early eleventh century, in comparison to the later eleventh century onwards. Their defences and layouts, on islands and points of land between rivers, echo the situation of Dublin (and indeed that of Chester, Bristol and York), as do several church dedications (**87**), but morphological traits suggesting common elements of planning are less obvious.

Waterford has produced the most extensive archaeological evidence so far, having undergone a total of about 6000m² of excavation in the later 1980s and early 1990s.[45] Historians have tried to date its foundation, on a triangle of land between the River Suir and the minor John's River, to annalistic mentions of Vikings in Port Láirge in the early tenth century,[46] but structural archaeological evidence for occupation at this early date has not yet been found within the city. Instead, the settlement at Woodstown (above, Chapter 2), further upstream on the Suir, may have continued for several decades in the early tenth century. Maurice Hurley, who directed a number of the city excavations, postulated a plausible scheme whereby the area of the town had gradually expanded away from the point of the triangle (now marked by the Medieval Reginald's Tower), beginning with a tiny enclave or camp in the early tenth century (**86**). Defences are only archaeologically demonstrable from the later eleventh century and Hurley was forced to admit that 'there is no excavated evidence for the tenth or early eleventh century Viking town, and its exact location remains speculative'.[47] Nevertheless, the 1986–92 excavations showed that significant urban growth had occurred from the mid-eleventh century. Type 1 post-and-wattle buildings (forty-three in all) bearing very close resemblance to the Dublin examples, together with lesser numbers of ancillary Type 2 buildings, lined Waterford's new streets by the third quarter of the eleventh century. Excavations at Peter Street, so far the largest in the city, produced evidence of fourteen plots along a 90m street frontage, upon which 16m of the street surface had survived.

87. *Left:* St Olave's Church, Chester; *Right:* St Olaf's Church, Waterford with medieval masonry exposed at street level

88. Whithorn: Reconstruction of Type 1 house

Later in the eleventh century, a new type of sunken-featured building was introduced with sloping entrances, some of which still had stone steps *in situ*, in a form and size very similar to the Chester Lower Bridge Street Phase IV buildings. Four of these were excavated (three from Peter Street and one from Olaf Street), and one was dated by dendrochronology to AD 1083±9. None of the 496 pits catalogued in the excavation report could be dated to any earlier than the mid-eleventh century, giving a good indication for the beginning of urban occupation. Churches, streets, and the growth of an urban material culture with extensive craft working, all seem to have had their beginnings in the mid-eleventh century, but by the twelfth century were extensive and established. No tenth- or eleventh-century coins were found in the 1986–92 excavations, the earliest coin being a silver halfpenny of King John (1190–98), but pottery and other finds show Waterford's growing external trading links were predominantly with south-west England and north-west France.

Wexford has also produced evidence of urban occupation in a small excavation at Bride Street in 1988. Ten levels of occupation were detected, which the excavator, Edward Bourke, provisionally dated to between 1000 and 1300.[48] A final report following full post-excavation analysis and scientific dating has yet to be published, so the provisionally early date of 1000 may be treated with some wariness, given the more established mid-eleventh-century date of comparable occupation in neighbouring Waterford. The earliest levels at Bride Street consisted of post-and-wattle Type 1 buildings, averaging 7.6m by 6.5m (**77**). Finds included combs, pins and a bone mount, which are reminiscent of eleventh-century finds from Dublin and Waterford.

Limerick and Cork, despite extensive excavations in the latter, have so far produced almost no urban evidence dating to before 1100. In both cases, the location of the ninth-century Viking camps mentioned in the annals (above, Chapter 2) remains unidentified. At Cork, archaeological work has concentrated on the roughly oval-shaped conjunction of two islands, composed of low-lying and formerly marshy ground surrounded by channels of the River Lee, which was gradually stabilised and fortified to form the core of the Anglo-Norman trading city. The spine of the north and south islands is formed by Main Street, off which, at right angles, lead narrow lanes and streets, with narrow east-west tenements on the plots between. Excavations took place at a piecemeal collection of redevelopments in and around these streets and lanes. Partial exposures of Type 1 post-and-wattle structures, of comparable dimensions with the buildings in Dublin and Waterford, occurred at the South Main Street and Washington Street sites, the earliest of which was dated by dendrochronology to AD 1124±9; these buildings were replaced in the twelfth century by a sill-beam type, with walls using upright earth-fast staves, later mounted on stone foundations.[49] There are a few dendro-dates from fencing and other non-domestic timbers straying into the later eleventh century, but these could simply be from old or re-used wood. Excavation in the undercrofts of Limerick's St John's Castle has produced three cellared timber structures not unlike the four Waterford structures, but these are of a 'slightly later period'.[50]

The astonishing longevity and influence of post-and-wattle constructed buildings with internal roof supports can now be seen to span ninth-century Dublin to twelfth-century Cork. These buildings are distinctive and would have been recognised as a familiar feature of these towns in the tenth to twelfth centuries. Generations of people lived out their entire lifespans in them, and their success is evident in that, despite their regular need for repair and reconstruction, there was little change in their basic form for nearly two centuries. Post-and-wattle urban building forms are similar in many constructional details and materials, if not in size and plan, to indigenous Irish buildings, such as the large circular round-house of roughly the same date at Deer Park Farms, Co. Antrim.[51] Nor were these buildings entirely restricted to Ireland in their later periods of use. Buildings that closely resemble the Dublin Types 1 and 2 were found in excavations in 1984–87 at the monastic settlement of Whithorn (Galloway).[52] After something of a hiatus following the disastrous fire of the mid-ninth century (above, Chapter 3), activity resumed at Whithorn and a series of new buildings was constructed on the silted rubble of the Northumbrian outer monastic enclosure. This was the beginning of 'Period IV', which was very broadly dated by pottery, metalwork and radiocarbon dates to between the early eleventh century and the later thirteenth centuries. Around ten small, sub-rectangular post-and-wattle dwellings and workshops were constructed on the lower slopes of the site south of the restored church. The most complete of these, Building 7 (**88**), had a double line of stakes forming a 'sub-square' plan with internal benches and a central hearth (**77**), and, on the basis of finds from the surrounding exterior, was interpreted as a cobbler's workshop. Finds included copper-alloy stick pins, buckles, spindle whorls, horn, leather and bone objects, together with a Chester coin of Cnut and a Dublin Type III Hiberno-Norse coin of 1035–55. These confirm that eleventh-century Whithorn had a similar (if much more limited) repertoire of portable and manufactured material culture to contemporary Dublin.

Peter Hill, the excavator of Whithorn, initially published a very strong argument for affinity with the Dublin buildings, describing these unambiguously as 'Hiberno-Norse' and suggesting a Dublin-based community of artisans and traders had settled in the vicinity of the monastery in the eleventh and twelfth centuries.[53] In the final site report in 1997, Hill adopted a more cautious tone, suggesting that Period IV buildings could be seen as 'revealing marked Hiberno-Norse, although potentially Gaelic, characteristics'. Hill quoted buildings from Irish rural sites at Whitefort (Co. Down), Ballywee and Craig Hill (Co. Antrim) as potential architectural parallels, in addition to Dublin, and suggested the Whithorn community could have had links to one or more monasteries in Ireland or Argyll.[54] Until the Kaupang excavations of 1999–2003, it was thought that the Dublin buildings were essentially a local, domestic adaptation of indigenous Irish forms, lacking the standard features of Norse longhouses such as thick, heavily constructed turf walls and internal byres. However, the Kaupang discoveries, which are earlier than most of the Dublin buildings, have re-ignited the debate about the Scandinavian origins of these buildings, and an increasing realisation is beginning to dawn that 'urban' is as strong a formative factor in shaping cultural identity and environment as conventional nationally-based ethnicities, such as Scandinavian, English or Irish (below, Chapter 9).

CHAPTER 8

ASSIMILATION AND CULTURAL CHANGE

From their first landfall on the shores of the Irish Sea, the roles of Vikings in trade, settlement and urbanisation were conditioned and shaped by biological, cultural, linguistic, political and religious interaction with the peoples already inhabiting these lands and islands. Within the first generation of Viking settlement, social, religious and material cultures had begun to display a convergent or 'hybrid' character. This was a far from uniform series of developments, indeed the story of the Irish Sea Vikings is very much one of local situations and adaptations to a variety of different contexts. The *Gallgoídil* of mid-ninth century Ireland were a different group in a different time and place from the settlers who carefully buried their dead in a field near Cumwhitton, Cumbria two or three generations later, but they were both products, and indeed agents, of cultural change. Such change was, of course, not new either in the Scandinavian homelands or to the Irish, British or Anglo-Saxons. The arrival of Vikings injected a new and potent ingredient in the Irish Sea region, but the cultures and peoples they settled amongst were themselves neither fixed nor immutable, but subject to continuous change. The Irish Sea region had already seen interaction between Gaelic, British and Anglo-Saxon cultures in the pre-Viking period. Scandinavians arriving in the region had often already been exposed to new influences in Orkney, amongst the Scottish isles, in Frankia, Northumbria, the Danelaw and beyond.

Recruitment of allies and followers from indigenous populations, intermarriage, and the takeover of new lands, required a redefinition of ancestral identities to encompass new realities of life in Ireland, Britain or the Isle of Man. Into this potent brew was injected the religious conversion from paganism to Christianity, a process which above all characterises the tenth century. Artistic patronage, landed power and military prowess afforded local Viking rulers the means of shoring up their distinctive authority by continuing to display 'conservative' traits from their inherited Scandinavian past, whilst subtly and actively reformulating these towards accommodating the symbolism of power, lordship and the majority religion of the new areas in which they settled. We see 'pagan' burial practice taking place near, or at Christian sites, and Viking artistic motifs were applied to stone, wood and bone in ways unfamiliar in Scandinavia itself. Scenes from pagan Norse legend, runic inscriptions, and even depictions of pagan gods appear on stone monuments that are located within or beside churches.

Burial and commemoration

We have seen from the history of the early raids how the committing of sacrilegious acts came easily to some Vikings, but simplistic distinctions between pagan and Christian, and indeed between foreigner and native, are far from clear in the case of most instances of burial practice observed archaeologically. As surveyed above in Chapter 5, the great variety of furnished burials found in the Irish Sea region range from lavishly equipped cemeteries and mound burials, to unobtrusive inhumations with meagre grave-goods. Impressive and distinctive Scandinavian objects were buried in many of the graves, particularly weaponry and oval brooches. It is not certain in most cases, at least without stable oxygen or strontium isotope data (see four recent examples from Dublin discussed above, Chapter 5), whether the individuals buried in 'Viking graves' were themselves migrants from Scandinavia, or local inhabitants who had chosen, or been compelled, to 'become Vikings' in death, if not also in life.

Scandinavian objects may also have been traded onwards, passing through the hands of people unconnected to Scandinavian ancestry or ethnicity. Objects may already be old and invested with particular individual associations with past events or people (often termed 'heirlooms'), when finally deposited or lost. Some of the weapons and oval brooches (such as the 'Berdal'-style oval brooches found at Kilmainham/Islandbridge and Cumwhitton) are considerably older (perhaps as much as two hundred years) than the latest-dated objects in these graves, which mostly consist of smaller items of 'hybrid' metalwork, such as ringed pins (below). Some of the weapons deposited in the graves were themselves not of classic Scandinavian manufacture. Frankish and Anglo-Saxon swords (such as Petersen's Type L), and a conical style of shield boss little known in Scandinavia, are common in the Irish, Manx and Cumbrian graves. Carolingian or Frankish-style ornaments, such as buckles, mounts and strap ends from the Balladoole, Aspatria and Claughton Hall burials, are reminiscent of Viking participation in military campaigns in France during the middle and later decades of the ninth century. In this series of campaigns, the Viking 'Army of the Seine' caused similar disruption to that caused by the Viking 'Great Army' (OE *micel here*) in England. Frankish decorative metalwork was also in traded circulation; a fine example of a silver-gilt strap end with stylised acanthus decoration was found at Hedeby, for instance.[1]

89. Part of the 1815 Halton Moor Hoard, Lancashire

Frankish ornaments were evidently prestigious items and some became heirlooms, as demonstrated by a fine silver cup of eighth- or early ninth-century date, which was found in the Halton Moor Hoard (Lancashire) in 1815 (**89**). The hoard also included a fine woven silver neck ring, two gold pendants and 860 coins, dating its deposition to 1025–30.[2]

Burials are physically marked by their presence in the landscape. They also represented an oral tradition of history and legend, in which the concealed (human bodies, grave-goods) can have as powerful a pull on the imagination as the visible mound or monument. Objects found in pagan graves in the Irish Sea region convey a rich and as yet under-explored store of information on the beliefs and cultural associations of their creators. We cannot know in the fullest sense what the arrangement of objects in graves actually meant to those involved in the funeral. The dead individual's own life story, his or her wealth, beliefs, and ancestry, formed the core components, but these were mediated and perhaps overwritten by those, still living, who created and orchestrated the funeral. Archaeologists have been poor at imagining the scale of subtlety expressed in funerary compositions, and have tended to see each element separately as passively reflective of 'influences' from elsewhere. Pagan burial was a highly visual and symbolic event, which probably attracted many onlookers, and in its more elaborate instances may have lasted several days (**54**). The contents of the grave were deliberately arranged and laid out around the body; these were meant to be 'read' as a tableau of meaning invested with the beliefs, identity and life-story of the dead person, and by proxy their family and community. We are now becoming increasingly aware that objects, as well as people, have biographies. They represent and symbolise connections and events, or imaginary or spiritual associations, within an individual's past or ancestry, and monetary value is no guide to the presence or power of this dimension.

To add a further complication to dating such burials, it is not unknown for human remains themselves to be transported after death in the manner of relics or sacred objects, with the act of their reburial re-conferring their existing prestige onto commemorative practices in new places. The 'bundle of bones' discovered in Phase 1 of Period III (dated to 845–865) at Whithorn (above, Chapter 5) may represent a re-interment in a monastic context some time after initial burial elsewhere. If human remains *were* being transported and reburied in new settlements, this would entirely upset received wisdom that an individual's date of death (confirmed in some cases by radiocarbon dating) is indivisible from the date of final burial. Could the bodies of forebears or fellow-warriors who had died heroically (but probably relatively recently) in Norway or Scotland have been reburied in the Irish Sea region as part of the creation of a new ancestral landscape? Burials recently excavated in Dublin (detailed above in Chapter 5) seem to present something of a dissonance between very early radiocarbon dates, the historical evidence for the Dublin *longphort* beginning only in the 840s, and some of the grave-goods that would normally be dated on typological grounds to the later ninth or tenth centuries. Could some of these inhumations possibly have been disturbed or transferred *after* a period of partial decomposition in the ground elsewhere, to be partially re-equipped for a reburial in Dublin? (There is in fact some limited evidence that at least one of the bodies had been disturbed after death.)[3] Could this potentiality also apply in some way to Cumwhitton, Peel Castle, or other burials elsewhere? Such a proposition, which is admittedly provocative and far from substantiated, is nevertheless worth our consideration. Is it merely posing a hopelessly far-fetched scenario with no parallel in reality? Arguably, it does not: the body of St Cuthbert was moved several times between its original interment on Lindisfarne in 687, from whence the monastic community was forced to migrate after the Viking attack of 793, until it reached its eventual resting place in Durham Cathedral over two centuries later.

A significant proportion of pagan Viking graves were situated in close proximity to existing burial sites associated with churches, chapels or monasteries. As indicated by the dramatic superimposition of the Balladoole boat cairn over an existing Christian cemetery, this was not necessarily a peaceful or consensual process, but nevertheless it physically brought the past and present of native and incomer together under an unambiguous statement of landed authority. By including, or even respecting, elements of existing cultures and religions, the leaders amongst the new Scandinavian settlers could claim legitimacy as successors of previous rulers, and seek to bring their own kin and the local population together as a unified political and religious follow-ing. It is no surprise, therefore, that the symbolism of burial is interlinked with the geography of territorial and political power, most obviously in its association with the 'things' discussed above. Assemblies at Tynwald and the Dublin Thingmote took place in landscapes imbued with the pres-ence of the dead. The role of burial mounds at inauguration and assembly sites (such as Tara) was characteristic of the existing societies around the Irish Sea, and the attached symbolism would have been well understood by the incomers (above, Chapter 4).

The re-use of prehistoric mounds and the recreation of the mound burial ritual is well known elsewhere in Britain, Ireland and Scandinavia during the early Medieval period. In the early sev-enth-century 'princely' burials of Anglo-Saxon England, such as those at Sutton Hoo, Taplow and Prittlewell, a short phase of very elaborate furnished burials immediately preceded conver-sion to Christianity.[4] These burials included grave-goods that were reminiscent of both a pagan Germanic past and the new contemporary influence of Mediterranean Christianity. They seem to offer a possible parallel for Viking mound burial in the Irish Sea region in that they were a short-lived phenomenon marking the cusp of a transition, which was quickly followed by religious conversion and far-reaching political change.

Religious conversion and Viking motifs

Vikings were regularly described as 'heathen' or 'gentiles' by generally antagonistic annalists until the mid-tenth century.[5] This date coincides well with the last vestiges of pagan burial (above, Chapter 5), suggesting that the majority of those of Scandinavian descent had already, or were in the process of, adopting Christianity by this time.[6] Direct evidence for pagan religious practice in the preceding period is, however, surprisingly hard to identify. The 'murdered' woman buried at Ballateare, and the 'Pagan Lady' at Peel (*39, 46*), have been suggested as evidence of pagan ritual, but in neither instance is the case conclusive (above, Chapter 5). Neil Price has drawn attention to a passage in the *Cogadh Gáedhel re Gallaibh,* which mentions Otta, wife of Tuirgéis, who 'gave her answers' upon the altar of a church, perhaps implying she was a seer or sorceress (the reliability of the *Cogadh* has been addressed above, Chapter 2, but if Price is correct, it shows at least an unsym-pathetic awareness of pagan practice by its writer).[7]

Place-names are also little help. Hoff and Hofflunn, near Appleby-in-Westmorland (Cumbria) (ON *Hof*– 'building' or 'temple' with –*lund*, 'grove'), have been seen as indicative of a pagan reli-gious site, based on parallels in Scandinavia and Iceland. This interpretation was aired by A.H. Smith, but its implications were cautiously avoided by Gillian Fellows-Jensen, who stated: 'It is not necessary to assume that any of these names were coined whilst the Vikings were still heathen'.[8] (Nevertheless, these locations certainly merit further investigation.) Explicitly pagan objects, such as silver Thor's hammer amulets are known from elsewhere in England, including York and the Danelaw, and from the Cuerdale Hoard, but single finds are noticeably rarer in the Irish Sea region, even in Dublin.[9] Indeed, Thor himself may not be quite as much of a solely pagan symbol as he seems in this context. As a god he may be seen to have virtuously heroic qualities, in biblical terms analogous to those of St Peter or even Christ himself. Thor's hammer symbols are found on Viking coins which also bear Christian motifs, such as on St Peter Pennies of York,[10] and therefore could be seen in this context as prefiguring the cross.

Recent research confirms that Old Norse paganism was never 'archaic and unchanging' and that many of its 'most distinctively Scandinavian religious features' were construed as a result of contact with the Roman and Christian worlds in the pre-Viking period.[11] Viking paganism was therefore already predisposed to adaptation and change when it entered the Christian world around the Irish Sea. Furnished burial customs preserve elements of pre-Christian practice, but as we have seen, they also suggest that complex dialogues were taking place with Christian elements in the landscape and existing populations. Scenes from Norse legend and mythology and the Germanic pantheon are present on stone sculpture, particularly in the Isle of Man and Cumbria,

90. Gosforth Cross 1 and
drawing of its decorative
schemes

on stone crosses generally dated on artistic and iconographic grounds to the mid to late tenth
century, or perhaps in some cases even later. Oðin appears, with his raven, being swallowed by the
wolf Fenrir on a cross-slab from Andreas (no. 128/102), a stone which has an explicitly biblical
scene of Christ trampling the serpents on the other side.[12]

Another famous example of a graphic combination of Norse legend and Christian symbolism
is on the shaft of the slender and miraculously well preserved sandstone cross still standing in the
churchyard at Gosforth, Cumbria (*90*). Here we see a group of images representing the Viking
doomsday, Ragnarók, interspersed with scenes of the Crucifixion. The Norse gods Viðar and Loki
are depicted. On the east face of the cross shaft, Viðar is shown fighting a terrible monster, which
probably represents Fenrir, the wolf that killed Oðin, whilst on the west face Loki is being pun-
ished for his role in the death of the virtuous god Baldr. Heimdallr, the Norse messenger god,
stands with horn in hand above Loki's punishment, confronting two more monsters.[13] The 'fishing scene' stone, also at Gosforth (*cover*), depicts Thor and his rival, the giant Hymir, in a boat of
recognisably Viking type, as Thor hooks the serpent which encircled the world. Scenes from the
Sigurd Legend – in which the hero killed the dragon Fafnir from below as it passed over the pit
in which he was hiding, and took away its hoard of gold loaded upon the six-legged horse, Grani,
before cooking and eating the dragon's heart – are depicted on four of the Manx crosses (*91*), and
again on the cross-shaft at Halton, Lancashire. (The latter also has a depiction of the dwarf Regin,
who forged Sigurd's sword.)

These scenes do not merely serve as nostalgic reminders of a discarded pagan past, but actively
articulate the Christian message. Struggles with monsters representing evil, drinking from sacred
vessels (horns), and displays of virtuous male heroism, have all been linked to central tenets of the

91. Kirk Andreas Cross 121/95, Isle of Man. Sigurd roasts the dragon Fafnir's heart over flames and licks his burnt thumb

life of Christ, and, indeed, may also have cast oblique credit upon the patrons who commissioned the stones. Sigurd scenes were elaborately carved on the portals of early wooden churches in Norway in the eleventh and twelfth centuries, a fact which reminds us how much comparable material we may have lost in Britain and Ireland – perhaps especially from places such as Dublin, which were rich in woodcarving, but did not have a comparable tradition of stone sculpture with the Isle of Man and north-west England.

In addition to those mythological scenes which the Icelandic sagas have helped us to understand, there is a variety of less easily identifiable images involving horsed warriors, distinctive female figures in profile bearing cups, wearing pigtails, and trailing long dresses (often described as 'valkyries'), and mythical animals. A hunting scene on a cross-shaft from Neston (Wirral) shows beasts of the chase in conjunction with a male hunter facing a cup-bearing female, and a very similar female image exists on Gosforth Cross 1. The standing cross *Maen Achwyfan* in Flintshire (*18*) has, in a panel on its east face, a dancing figure bearing weapons including a Norse-style axe, and an eight-legged beast – perhaps a version of Oðin's horse, Sleipnir – is depicted in a vertical panel on its north side. Human figures, beasts and birds would have each been recognisable and intelligible to those witnessing the sculptural scenes in the tenth century, even if in some cases their meaning has become obscure to us today. Yet there can be no doubt that these were Christian monuments, based ultimately on a pre-Viking tradition of stone sculpture, which were designed explicitly to promote the new faith, whilst also implicitly bolstering the legitimacy and prestige of their landowning patrons. People of mixed Scandinavian, Anglo-Saxon, Manx, Gaelic or British origins would have stood before the stone monuments, witnessing and hearing these stories of heroism and redemption unfold, as their eyes were drawn upwards towards the supreme cross. The meanings of the scenes depicted were presumably articulated in the locally appropriate language and dialect by preachers, themselves no doubt anxious to please their patrons by echoing their world view.

The art and abstract decoration on the stone monuments reveals as much about the cultural repertoire of the landed patrons as do the mythological scenes. Several styles and motifs recur around the Irish Sea region, which demonstrate a complex pattern of contacts and influences, in some cases linking the stones to the artistic fashions prevalent in towns such as Dublin, Chester and York. We have very little evidence for places where stone sculpture was produced; much of it was probably carved *in situ* by specialist masons, but a fragment of unfinished stone sculpture excavated at Coppergate, York, suggests that urban workshops also existed. In towns, stone carvers, metalworkers, bone-carvers and wood-carvers would have worked in close proximity, and would have been exposed and alive to the ideas expressed by their peers. Regional links were consolidated as carvers moved from one commissioning estate to another, and also as finished, or part-finished, products made their way out into the countryside from urban workshops. Hogbacks seem, on the basis of their frequency east of the Pennines, to be a tenth-century innovation closely linked to the kingdom of Northumbria and its lands west of the Pennines in Cumbria and Lancashire.[14] Hogbacks spread to Wirral and south-west Scotland, although Wales and Ireland each have just one rather plain example, and the Isle of Man surprisingly has none at all.[15] Regional variations may be prosaically attributed to geological variation, occurring where the local stone was most suitable (Manx slate being an unsuitable medium for such bulky monoliths), although they could feasibly have been transported by sea. Various sub-types exist in size and decoration; the Cumbrian examples are generally thinner and taller than those found elsewhere. Most distinctive are those of the 'Brompton School' (named after a parish church in North Yorkshire with a particularly splendid group), with gripping beasts or bears at either end of the 'long-house' form. A mini-version of the Brompton type was recently unearthed from the garden of a former vicarage at Bidston, Wirral (*92*),[16] in a parish which perhaps significantly is dedicated to a Northumbrian saint, Oswald. Unlike the crosses, hogbacks rarely exhibit well-understood mythical scenes, but have a more eclectic range of images ranging from battle-scenes to beasts. A battle-scene with helmeted standing warriors arrayed in formation with round shields and spears appears on a Gosforth hogback known as 'The Warrior's Tomb' (*93*), and a ship in full battle formation arrayed with shields appears on a hogback at Lowther (Cumbria).[17] Perhaps this difference indicates that, like the furnished graves, hogbacks were primarily personalised statements, and were perhaps not intended for the same publicly didactic purposes as crosses.

Most common amongst the artistic motifs found on Irish Sea sculpture, and perhaps most easily attributed to Scandinavian influence, is the 'Borre ring chain' (which art historians have argued derives from ninth-century metalwork found at Borre, Norway). This had a particularly widespread use, decorating crosses and slabs from Gosforth (*90*) to the Isle of Man (two of which are attributed by inscriptions to a single carver, Gautr (*94*), and the shaft of a cross at Penmon on Anglesey, where a group of Viking-influenced sculptures suggests the possible presence of local Viking lordship in eastern Anglesey in the tenth or eleventh centuries. The Jellinge and Mammen styles of Scandinavian art, dating to slightly later in the tenth century than the Borre style, are more explicitly zoomorphic in character. There is a Jellinge animal on a hogback from Aspatria (Cumbria) and the Mammen style, showing sinuous animals with pelleted bodies, is represented on crosses from Malew and Kirk Braddan (*95*), on the Isle of Man, and on a cross-shaft from Workington (Cumbria). Spiral scroll ornament is an adaptation of Anglian art of the pre-Viking period and is common in Cumbria, whereas 'stopped plaits' (plait patterns which stop rather than cross under each other) occur in Cumbria and Galloway, extending as far north as Govan in Strathclyde. Other common decorative motifs, such as vertical lines of T-frets, were apparently Viking-period innovations in Cumbria and Cheshire. The form of some of the cross-heads has also been taken to imply contact between areas. Circle-headed crosses (where the circles are complete and overlie the cross arms) are found in subtly different forms in Cheshire, north Wales and Cumbria (*96*), with a smaller cluster along the routeway leading from Morecambe Bay to the

92. Hogback found in 2004 at Bidston, Wirral

93. Gosforth, Cumbria: the 'Warrior's Tomb' hogback with battle scene visible on side facing

94. Kirk Michael Cross 101/74, Isle of Man, carved by Gautr. Decorated with Borre ring-chain, with runic inscriptions upper left and right

95. Kirk Braddan Cross shaft 136/109, Isle of Man. A fine example of animal art of the tenth-century Mammen Style

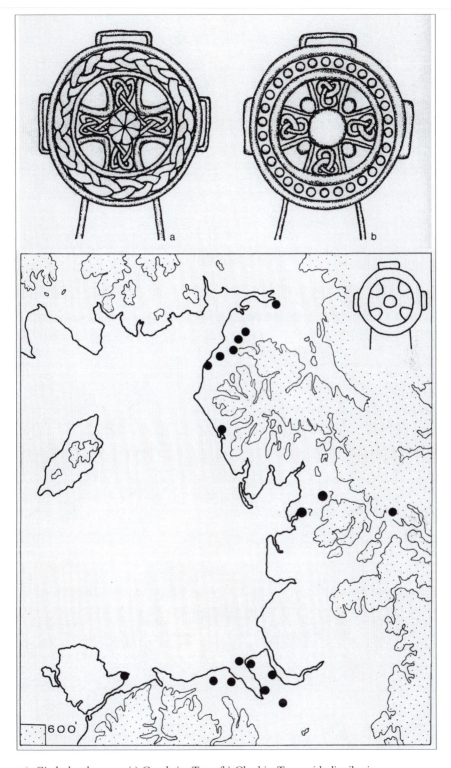

96. Circle-head crosses: (a) Cumbrian Type; (b) Cheshire Type, with distribution map

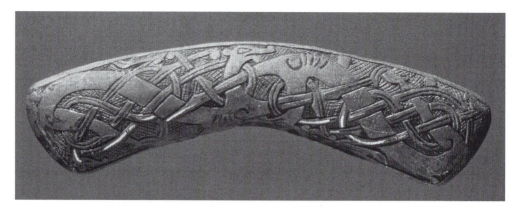

97. The Smalls Reef, Pembrokeshire, Urnes-style sword guard, width 118mm

Pennines.[18] These appear to have been an adaptation in north-west England of the more familiar Irish-style of ring-headed cross (where the cross arms overlie the circle).

Borre ring-chain is also found on wooden objects, including a gaming board from Ballinderry Crannóg (Co. Westmeath), suggesting it arrived via trade with Dublin. The tenth-century Jellinge style of Viking art with complex, abstract, ribbon-like animals is found more often on metalwork than stone, such as the Hunter Street brooch from Chester and the High Street brooch from Dublin (**85**). The Ringerike style of the later tenth century, with elegant vegetal fronds and *fleur-de-lis* motifs, is also rare on stone, but is much more common on a particularly splendid series of wooden and bone objects found in Viking Dublin (**79**).[19] It also occurs on a piece of metalwork from Whithorn and, in its slightly later Anglo-Scandinavian guise as the 'Winchester style', on a stirrup-chape and a strap end from Meols. The eleventh- and twelfth-century Urnes style, often involving sparer and more elongated zoomorphic forms, is the most overtly Christianised of the Viking art-styles. Named after spectacular wooden carvings on the Urnes stave church in Sogn, Norway, it is often found on utilitarian lead and copper-alloy dress accessories from the Danelaw area, but a fine example occurs on a brass sword-guard retrieved by divers from a probable ship-wreck at the Smalls Reef, off the coast of Pembrokeshire (**97**).[20]

Viking influences came into a mixture of artistic traditions around the Irish Sea. These were not fixed or immutable, but reflected a long and vibrant history of innovation and the embracing of external influences.[21] The use of Scandinavian art-styles was widespread within the Irish Sea region, but, as with other forms of art and decoration, this did not simply replicate external influences, but was part of a vibrant mixture of creative activity, within which art and motifs were re-interpreted, reinvented and made meaningful within their own contemporary context.

An Irish Sea metalwork tradition?

It is much easier to attribute regional traditions within a medium such as stone sculpture because, although some pieces have been moved around over the intervening centuries, most of them are still located at, or very close to, their original site. Portable material culture is by definition less fixed in its geographic affinities, and only manufacturing evidence allows us to attribute these with confidence. New discoveries are liable to upset or contradict theories on the geographic origins of certain types of object. The dangers of assuming an origin based on mapping find-spots are demonstrated by the case of miniature pyramidal bells. These have been found on the Isle of Man (three, including two from the Peel graves), Knowth (Co. Meath), Meols (**66**), and Llanbedrgoch, together with individual finds from Scotland, Iceland and from excavations in York, Lincoln and Northampton. Little more than a decade ago, on the basis of their apparently predominant Irish

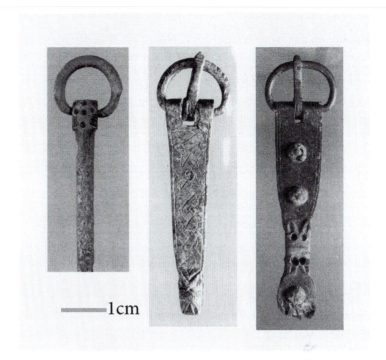

98. 'Hybrid' Irish Sea style metalwork of the tenth century: a polyhedral-headed ringed pin from Crook Street, Chester, and two buckles from Peel Castle

Sea distribution, these objects were assumed to be a western insular Viking type. However, metal-detecting activity reported to the Portable Antiquities Scheme has now added considerably to the total from the Danelaw area of eastern England, which now stands at around twenty-five new discoveries, and has cast rather a different light on their likely origins.

Nevertheless, there are signs, in metalwork in particular, that there was something approaching a distinctively 'hybrid' Irish Sea style, where objects produced in Dublin and other trading and manufacturing settlements made their way around the Irish Sea region and beyond. In Chapter 6, the silver-bossed and brambled ball-terminal or 'thistle-type' penannular brooches, which have occurred in hoards and single finds (and in one or two cases in burials), were noted. These are an adaptation of a form of ornament current in pre-Viking Ireland and Britain, perhaps most spec-tacularly represented by the ornate eighth-century Tara and Hunterston brooches (the latter, from Ayrshire, has a secondary runic inscription on the back). Two separate groups of simpler, but no less distinctive, arm-rings became forms of pre-monetary currency or 'ring money', having been produced in the Viking settlements of Ireland and Scotland.

Small woven wire balls, some of which are made of gold and silver, have been found in fur-nished graves at Peel Castle and Carlisle Cathedral, and may also represent an Irish Sea dress fashion.[22] Items of less precious metal such as copper-alloy also exhibit traits which might be termed 'Irish Sea' in origin and affinity (*98*). Similarly styled buckles and strap ends have been found at Meols, Peel, Whithorn, Llanbedrgoch and Dublin. Some have Borre-style ring-knots or ring-chains, whereas others are decorated with double-sided panels of interlace within obliquely hatched or beaded borders, and concentric roundels. The concentric roundels (some of which are pierced at the centre) are a feature difficult to explain in terms of cultural attribution, but which, interestingly, also appear on the 'Rathdown Slabs' in the hinterland of Dublin.[23] Zoomorphic strap ends with pronounced snouts and triangular ears at their terminals have been found at Dublin and Meols, suggesting that they have an Irish Sea – probably a Dublin – origin.[24] These were small personal dress items, not very valuable in themselves perhaps, but denoting contact with, and perhaps membership in, the Viking settlements of the Irish Sea region. Furnished graves at Golden Lane, Dublin, Peel Castle, and Carlisle Cathedral have produced strikingly similar pairings

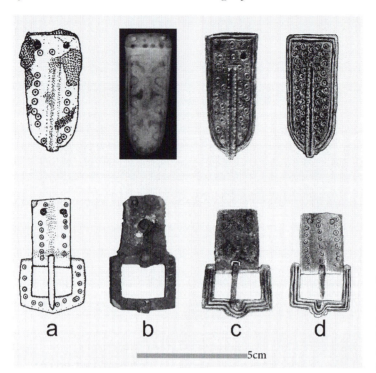

99. Strap ends and buckles:
(a) Peel; (b) Cumwhitton;
(c) Carlisle; (d) Golden
Lane, Dublin. The Xray of
the Cumwhitton strap end
(b, upper row) shows ring
and dot ornament

of square copper-alloy buckles and tongue-shaped strap ends (**99**). The Peel graves are tenth-century in date, as, very probably, are the Cumwhitton and Carlisle ones, yet the Golden Lane burial (LXXXV, above Chapter 5) is dated by radiocarbon to before the mid-ninth century. The similarities between these objects raises a serious question about the relative dating of the graves, which clearly demands further research (below, Chapter 9).

Possibly the most emblematic objects produced in the Viking-period Irish Sea region are ringed pins (**65**), which have been found across the western Viking world. They comprise a long tapering pointed shank, often deliberately bent, with a small mobile ring attached through, or hinged upon, the head. They were cast in two parts and finished by tooling and filing. By far the largest number in the Viking world comes from Dublin, where the Christchurch Place excavation is the only site so far to have produced manufacturing evidence in the form of a clay mould bearing both ring and pin matrices. As many as 263 ringed pins recovered in the series of excavations between 1962 and 1981 were studied and published by the late Tom Fanning.[25] Fanning identified a series of variants that span the period from the ninth to twelfth centuries. Some variants were concurrent in manufacture and use, but none lasted throughout, so Fanning was able to offer a broad chronology. The simplest and earliest variant, the plain-ringed loop-headed type, was clearly an adaptation of an existing Irish metalwork tradition. Loop-heads were simply wrought from the shank metal and hammered and bent over the ring to keep it in place, and have been dated by Fanning to the eighth to tenth centuries, although some examples can be dated as late as the twelfth century. Baluster-heads have fillets or collars above a drilled hole, and although slightly later than the loop-headed type, again seem to owe a great deal to Irish precedents. The tenth-century polyhedral-headed type (**98**, *left*) is more often decorated with ring and dot on the head and panels of hatching on the shank, and like its later tenth- and eleventh-century 'kidney-ringed' and crutch-headed, 'stirrup-ringed' variants, had begun to depart from native metalworking traditions and become a distinctive 'hybrid' type recognisably denoting Dublin's contribution to changing fashions.

Architecture: urban and rural

The few rural buildings excavated in Viking settlements in the Irish Sea region (above, Chapter 4) display some traits that could be described as Scandinavian. At Cherrywood, Co. Dublin, and The Braaid, Isle of Man, the proportions of the buildings echo the classic 'bow-sided' Viking longhouse type, although Llanbedrgoch Building 1 is a shorter, more compact rectilinear version perhaps indicative of the site's predominantly trading and manufacturing rather than agricultural status (*27*). Buildings excavated on the Isle of Man at Doarlish Cashen, Cronk ny Merriu, and Cass ny Hawin, display an apparently Manx-Norse preference for opposed doorways at about the three-quarter length point. Urban buildings display marked 'hybrid' traits. Dublin, Waterford and Wexford Type 1 and 2 buildings (*77*) appear to owe significant aspects of their layout (with internal roof supports, side benches and, in Type 1, a central hearth) to Scandinavian precedents, at Kaupang in particular, but in other ways they are strongly reminiscent of native Irish building traditions.[26]

Their methods of construction in particular, using wattle and split planks, are unlike the stone wall-footings and turf superstructure found in Viking buildings in the northern and western isles, suggesting that local materials and technologies were adopted and adapted from the earliest point of settlement. Choice of building materials had a major effect on the ways in which a building was used and inhabited, dictating the methods of heating, insulation, lighting and, indeed, the lifespan of the building, or the frequency or need for replacement. Such adaptation is possibly indicative of more than just pragmatism: it reveals a conscious decision not to build structures of alien material and form in Dublin, but to accommodate aspects of the Irish domestic lifestyle. Other urban structures, such as the Dublin Type 4 sunken-featured buildings (*78*), and the later cellared structures observed at Waterford (*84*), seem to offer a marked contrast in lifestyle and materials, and even though small in number, they are perhaps most likely to reflect direct importation of architectural forms from the *burhs* of Anglo-Saxon England.

Language and inscriptions

Communication must rapidly have improved as individuals and groups began to develop greater understandings of unfamiliar languages and traditions. In negotiations over war and peace, and in buying and selling, people in all circumstances instinctively find ways of making their case, with more elaborate realms of communication following later. In such situations people who had the ability to communicate in two or more languages became extremely useful, and in some situations, powerful. Old Norse, Irish and Welsh remained separate languages, albeit with some loan-words passing between them,[27] whereas Old Norse and Old English (which, as Germanic languages, were much closer to each other in linguistic origin) may have merged into a new hybrid variant in some north-western English dialects. Many individuals amidst the incomers and the people they encountered must have developed at least a basic knowledge of more than one of these languages, extending to multiple fluencies in some individuals. An interrelated 'creole' probably existed in trading communities in the market settlements and ports, and amongst people of specialist and often itinerant occupations such as seafaring, craft manufacturing, and fishing. The identity of the first fully bilingual Norse-Irish speaker is unknown to us, but he/she was probably born of mixed parentage (and possibly to an enslaved mother) as early as the turn of the eighth and ninth centuries. Few would disagree that the Old Scandinavian languages were widely understood in Dublin, the Isle of Man, and the Viking settlements of north-west England in the tenth and eleventh centuries, although debate continues as to the levels of society and proportion of the population who spoke them.

Runic inscriptions on wood and bone objects have been found in tenth- and eleventh-century Dublin, indicating a widespread use and understanding of Norse within the town, although the extent of literacy amongst the population is less clear. Most texts are very short statements of personal ownership, and several are truncated and made difficult to read by wear or damage to

100. Kirk Braddan Cross
138, Isle of Man; the
runic inscription reads:
*Hross-Ketill betrayed in a
truce his own oath-fellow*

the object on which they were carved. Barnes, Hagland and Page published twelve inscriptions
and two 'rune-like symbols' from Dublin excavations in 1996, and four (a small total) from the rest
of Ireland, including inscriptions on stones from Beginish (Co. Kerry) and Killaloe (Co. Clare),
and a silver arm-ring from Roosky (Co. Donegal). An inscription on the plain reverse side of an
interlace-decorated strap end found in 1870 in a souterrain at Greenmount, Co. Louth, near the
longphort at Annagassan (above, Chapter 2) reads 'Domnall seal's head owns this sword'.[28] Apart
from mentioning an Irish-named individual (Domnall), its find-spot suggests that the influence
of Norse runes extended to other coastal areas of strategic interest to Dublin. Another, equally
concentrated, group of runic inscriptions (thirty-one, of which twenty-six are 'substantive')[29]
occurs in the Isle of Man, which, unlike Dublin examples, are predominantly carved on stone
monuments. This is an impressive total, given that there are only around forty from the whole of
Norway. Unlike the Dublin runes, which were mostly found on tools and cheap, throwaway items,
Manx runes are mostly found on carved stone crosses, some of which are of sufficient splendour
to be linked unambiguously to elite social status.

A close link between the predominant 'short-twig' *futhark* (alphabet) of Manx and Norwegian
runes has been remarked on by a succession of runologists, yet Page also noted grammatical
slip-ups in the rendition of Norse grammar, even in the hands of the carver Gautr, who claimed,
on Kirk Michael Cross 101 (**94**), that he 'made this and all in Man'. Gautr also recorded on the
Andreas I inscription that he was the son of Bjarnar (a Norse name) from 'Kuli', a place-name
which is probably Celtic, but is otherwise unidentifiable, indicating he was a Viking descendant
born somewhere in Britain, Ireland, or indeed the Isle of Man itself. Amongst the personal names
that are mentioned on inscriptions at Kirk Michael, Maughold and Andreas are other Norse individuals (Arni, Aþisl, Sandulf, *Svarti,* 'the Black', husband of Arinbjorg) and the misdeed of Hross
Ketill ('Horse Ketil') is commemorated at Braddan (**100**). Other names, even amongst earlier
inscriptions such as those carved by Gautr, are Gaelic or Irish, including Malmury, wife of (Norse)
Aþisl but daughter of (Gaelic) Dufgal; Melbrigti and Aþakan (Norse renditions of OI *Aedhacán*
and *Máelbrigte*). Apart from showing the familial integration of Gaelic and Norse-named people in
the Isle of Man, the status of monuments on which these inscriptions are carved also indicates that
such cultural hybridity had reached the upper levels of society by the mid-tenth century. Indeed
Norse has been termed a 'prestige' language by some commentators.[30]

Dating runes is a generally inexact science; when they are not found in stratified excavated
contexts, as some in Dublin were, dating derives from an interpretation of the art-historical

affinities of other elements of decoration on the objects, structures or crosses upon which they were carved. A connection with Norway, which is manifested most impressively on the earlier runic inscriptions from the Isle of Man dating from the mid- to late tenth century, gave way to adaptations and new techniques in about 1000, which drew them away from contemporary Norwegian practice. The resurgent influence of Gaelic is seen in the re-emergence of Ogham (or Ogam) script, the incised linear alphabet that was common in Ireland and west Wales until the seventh century. At Kirk Michael and Maughold on the Isle of Man, runic inscriptions on cross slabs are accompanied by the Ogham alphabet. A short Ogham inscription was found on part of a bone comb excavated at Dublin Castle in 1961–2 (another comb, excavated at Dublin Castle in 1985–7, has a runic inscription on it), and a rare bilingual runic/Ogham inscription exists at St Flannan's Cathedral, Killaloe (Co. Clare); here both runic and Ogham script in Norse and Irish respectively exist on the same stone. Loosely dated to the early eleventh century, the inscriptions mention a Norse-named individual, Þorgrimr. Perhaps transmitted within the context of the Kingdom of the Isles, later Ogham found its way north into the Viking-settled areas of western and northern Scotland, as demonstrated by a small wooden plaque from Bornais, South Uist. In the Irish Sea region, its Viking-period reappearance seemingly did not extend beyond the Isle of Man and Ireland.[31]

Runic inscriptions in Dublin and the Isle of Man form noticeable clusters against a rather sparse background across the Irish Sea. Most of Ireland, south-west Scotland, Wales and north-west England are singularly lacking in early runic inscriptions, and only two, discovered on portable objects in the form of fine brooches, are known so far. One is on the spectacular eighth-century silver and gold Hunterston brooch from Ayrshire, and the other on one of the silver penannular brooches from Flusco Pike, Cumbria (above, Chapter 6). The former, a secondary inscription on the back of the brooch, reads (where intelligible) *Malbriþa á stilk* (Malbritha owns this, or 'owns me'); the Flusco brooch has a *futhark* on its hoop.[32] A lack of early static monumental inscriptions is surprising because in north-west England there was an existing Anglo-Saxon runic tradition, which produced some fine pre-Viking inscriptions such as on the eighth-century stone memorial to Æthelmund from Overchurch, Wirral.[33] Those few stone inscriptions which do survive in western Britain are generally interpreted as dating to the twelfth century or later, indicating the persistence of Norse language well after the Viking period, albeit in a debased form. These include a group of inscriptions found inside the cave of St Molaise on Holy Island, Arran, and on architectural stonework in Cumbrian churches at Pennington, Dearham, Bridekirk and Conishead. In Carlisle Cathedral, two inscriptions have been found on adjoining stones in the building fabric, the longer one reading: 'Dolfin scratched these runes', and the shorter one probably reads: '*aik*' ('oak'). Barnes and Page interpreted these as early twelfth-century in date. The only known possible example from Wales, an inscription on the base of a churchyard cross at Corwen (Denbighshire), which was drawn by R.A.S. Macalister in 1935 but is now unintelligible, was dismissed by Barnes and Page on the grounds that what was drawn was not diagnostically Norse.[34]

Hybridity and acculturation – the process of cultural change

People in all situations actively define their own identity and status. This happens on an individual level within families and communities, but also at a group level where a sense of common heritage and belonging, marked by linguistic and material distinctiveness, takes on the guise of ethnicity. In contrast to inherited biological traits, ethnicity can mutate and change over a single lifetime. Since the work of the Norwegian anthropologist Fredrik Barth in the 1960s,[35] there has been an increasing willingness amongst cultural historians and archaeologists to accept that ethnicity and identity are not fixed or immutable. Traditionally, Vikings, Anglo-Saxons and 'Celts' were simply regarded as 'national' or even racial categories of people, synonymous with ancestry and geographical origin – producing a view of ethnicity that is now termed the 'primordial interpretation'. This was an appropriate counterpart to the 'Culture Historical' school of archaeological thought, prominent until the 1970s, which sought to identify and classify cultures based on fixed perceptions of the objects and structures they left behind. Barth emphasised what he termed the 'instrumental' interpretation, where ethnicity could be actively moulded and changed by people themselves in response to new threats, challenges and opportunities. Groups or networks of people (such as the Vikings of the Irish Sea) who find themselves in close engagement and interaction with others of different cultural and biological origins, actively develop strategies to survive and prosper in new situations by choosing to combine elements of their own cultures with those they now encountered.

In this and many other historical situations, piracy, mercenary and trading activity produce their own hybrid cultures, as connections and interdependencies with indigenous populations grow. The term 'diaspora' has gained some currency amongst those who would see Vikings as a distinctive supra-national group of migrants with specialised political and economic prowess.[36] Their distinctiveness was based on retaining some inherited links and affinities to their ancestral homelands, or to an inherited or semi-imagined idea of those ancestries and homelands.[37] Geographic dispersal saw the migrants seek to mould their existing roles and identities to encompass new allegiances and conform to new political realities. Their gradual and piecemeal changes of religious belief and allegiance from paganism to Christianity may have been a purely theological, salvation-driven conversion for some, but the pragmatism of its social and cultural context cannot be denied. Placement of pagan burials at strategic positions within the landscape, and at Christian places, the 'transitional' burials with fewer and less obvious grave-goods, and the encompassing of pagan mythological scenes on Christian stone monuments, may all be seen as a linked series of developments. Norse remained a prestigious language, even though the grammar of inscriptions deteriorated in quality.

Against this background we see the emergence of consciously hybrid architectural and metalwork styles denoting changing tastes in domestic life and personal dress. Burial and artistic expression amongst the Viking settlers in Ireland, Cumbria, and the Isle of Man combined 'conservative' elements (mounds, weapons, heirlooms and recognisably Scandinavian artistic motifs), which commemorated their ancestry and landed authority in Scandinavia, with those that had demonstrable connections to the beliefs, practices and places familiar to the people they settled amongst. History and memory themselves are weapons. Physical and symbolic forms of commemoration act as a 'mnemonic' to stimulate the telling and re-telling of histories, which largely served the interests of contemporary present. The archaeological evidence leaves little doubt that the establishment of power and authority in the Viking settlements around the Irish Sea depended on the reinvention and manipulation of an ancestral Scandinavian past, principally by ruling families, but perhaps also by their more humble followers.

CHAPTER 9

CONCLUSION

The brief survey in the foregoing chapters has attempted to outline the evidence available, principally to historians and archaeologists, for the Viking phenomenon around the Irish Sea. The sea was an ever-present backdrop to political events, to settlement and economy, and to the changing cultures of people. A network of short, often uncomfortable, but well-known and relatively predictable sea-crossings offered unrivalled opportunities for Vikings to exploit. Was there an 'Irish Sea Province' in the Viking period? Yes and no. There were certainly closely interlinked developments around its coasts. Vikings made alliances and took lands across the region in ways that were clearly politically and economically interdependent. Opportunistic political gambles were taken when lands just a short sail across a familiar sea seemed more promising targets than those more immediately at hand. The ways in which Vikings encountered and engaged with existing populations bear considerable similarity and comparison around the Irish Sea. However, there was little obvious cultural conformity. Place-names, burial rites, traditions of sculpture and art, and the use of runes and inscriptions are far more complex and interesting in their local variations, rather than merely in serving an artificial broad-brush notion of a 'culture province'. Why did elements of Scandinavian culture and language persist (and were indeed reinvented) for so long in place-names and inscriptions, amongst people whose forebears had already lived and died in Britain and Ireland for generations? Viking ancestral and cultural affinities, which had been so powerful in the context of the land-take and establishment of trading centres in the ninth and tenth centuries, gave rise to traditions of prestige and legitimacy which were to survive throughout the eleventh, twelfth and thirteenth centuries.

Despite the roll-call of scholars who have created and pursued this subject in museums, archives, and during excavations, the overall historical picture is still partial and in many ways sketchy. This is, however, a vibrant and productive research field involving a range of scholarly disciplines. Fieldworkers, scientists and philologists continue to make groundbreaking discoveries. Many research questions remain to be tackled by future work. Three in particular have emerged most prominently in the course of writing this book. Firstly, and forming a highly charged and fascinating theme, is the archaeology of people themselves, through their bodily remains and their burial rites. Recent discoveries of furnished burials in Dublin (above, Chapter 5) have highlighted the contribution that scientific analyses may make to our understanding of the period. These have, however, also raised interesting and challenging conundrums that threaten to undermine some long-held assumptions. The message of the radiocarbon data obtained thus far is that a number of the burials might be older than we may have assumed on the basis of artefact dating alone. The very early intercept dates (dating to before 800) may yet be subject to scientific revision, but, nevertheless, appear to challenge received historical wisdom concerning the foundation of the Dublin *longphort*. Grave-goods such as the very similar sets of belt equipment found in graves across the region (**99**) also raise conflicting indications of their date of deposition. These objects occur in ninth-century burials in Dublin, yet they appear in other furnished graves in Cumbria and the Isle of Man that very probably date to the early to mid-tenth century. In order to broaden the available sample of evidence, a renewed and extended programme of AMS radiocarbon dating,[1] to cover all or most available human remains from this period in the region, is a necessary and indeed prescient next step. This should not just include inhumations from pagan furnished graves, but, for the sake of comparison, also those from contemporary unfurnished or Christian burials. Stable isotope studies are as yet in their infancy in this region but promise much for the future. We may yet use them to discover where many more of the individuals buried in graves were born and raised, and this could help us in attempting to quantify and understand the incidence of Scandinavian traits in the DNA of modern populations. The development of identity and ethnicity is a more contentious area that cannot be resolved by biological data alone. Interdisciplinary studies of history, language, and material culture continue to be vital in pursuing this theme.

Secondly, the chapters above (particularly Chapters 4 and 6) have highlighted the current lack of well-developed research priorities for landscape and settlement archaeology across the Irish Sea region. Unexpected and spectacular discoveries, such as at Llanbedrgoch, Woodstown and Cherrywood, confirm that the region is far from devoid of rich, well-defined Viking-period settlements. However, these three sites were initially found for reasons that were largely incidental, namely metal-detecting, road construction and private-sector development. Most other rural excavations in the region took place many decades ago, and their published interpretations are badly in need of revision. Archaeological material from older investigations survives in archives and museums, and as the recent publication of Meols shows, is itself potentially a rich reservoir of new information. Investigating settlement and trading sites in coastal landscapes, by understanding better the effects of sea level and climate change and the masking effect of later overburdens of windblown sand dunes, is likely to yield exciting results in future. Intensive coastal surveys are needed, such as that recently undertaken at Strangford Lough, Co. Down, and their results should be integrated regionally. More and wider research is needed into long-term landscape formation processes, the exploitation of wetlands and woodlands, and the development of upland agriculture. Viking influence was a passing, and in many places near-invisible, phase in the long-term development of the landscape. A more comprehensive research framework might succeed in identifying Viking-period occupation amidst better-understood patterns both of earlier and later settlement. It is time finally to recognise that Viking settlements were, for the most part, not islands of pure Scandinavian culture in alien territory, but portals of influence and cultural change. Burials, buildings, artefacts, and ways of exploiting natural resources, all evolved and developed in relation to the practical and cultural imperatives of living in new lands.

Thirdly, the rise of towns and urban cultures dominates the history and archaeology of the Irish Sea in the Viking period, yet the precise impetus behind this astonishing series of developments remains uncertain. How did a small, crowded and vulnerable settlement on the muddy banks of the Poddle and Liffey become within a few decades not only one of the greatest Viking trading towns in the world, but a kingdom as well? What were the intentions of the Mercians when Chester was founded in 907? What or whom was responsible for the sudden urban take-off in Waterford, Wexford and Cork in the eleventh century? The experience of living in a densely built-up environment shaped new attitudes and aspirations. The impact of urban life on the development of culture and identity cannot be underestimated. Major urban excavations in Dublin, Chester, Waterford and other places have created an enormous and diverse archive of information. Although structural site reports have in most cases been published, there remains a vast untapped reservoir of further interpretative potential in the material from these excavations. How was authority exercised, and how was this reflected in buildings, artefacts and diet? How much more can we know about the lives of women, children and the elderly? Can we begin to understand the place of marginalised people such as slaves, prisoners and the chronically diseased in urban society? How deeply and how quickly did the experience of urban life change peoples' view of themselves and their own inherited pasts? As Vikings' independent military power waned, their roles and identities were redefined, as demonstrated by the emergence of the Ostmen, after Dublin and the other Hiberno-Norse towns fell under Irish, and subsequently Anglo-Norman, political dominance (their presence is marked in the name Oxmantown, which still exists north of the Liffey in Dublin). Traditional 'culture historical' notions of identity using national terms such as Scandinavian, Irish, Welsh or English, in common with 'native' and 'foreigner', have out-lived much of their usefulness. New definitions stressing fluid urban and occupational identities, hybridity and diaspora, are now creeping into, and enlivening our discourse.

The date 1050 is as good a date as any upon which to conclude the initial story of Vikings of the Irish Sea, but it was far from the end of landed and political Scandinavian influence. The rise of Alba to become the Scottish kingdom, and the Norman Conquest in England, saw the absorption and assimilation of former Viking elites into new political realities. The raiding and principal settlement phases may have run their course by the middle of the eleventh century, but Viking-descended dynasties in the Scottish Isles and the Isle of Man, in Ireland and in Gwynedd, continued to compete with each other for power and influence. There were, especially during the later eleventh and early twelfth centuries, brief resurgences of political interest in the region from Scandinavia. Most dramatic amongst these was the attempt to impose direct Norwegian rule on the Isle of Man and Anglesey by Magnús *Berfœttr* ('Magnus Barelegs'), King of Norway from 1093 to 1103. The 'Battle of the Menai Straits' in July 1098 saw Magnús's forces confront and defeat those of the Norman earls of Chester and Shrewsbury. The King of Gwynedd at the time, who sought Norwegian help in resisting the Normans, was none other than that ultimate Irish Sea hybrid Viking, Gruffudd ap Cynan. After the victory, in which he personally slew Earl Hugh of Shrewsbury, Magnús returned to Norway but soon came back again to the Irish Sea, briefly taking the lordship of Dublin in 1102, before being ambushed and killed on the coast of Ulster in 1103. Norwegian designs on Ireland thus ended, but the Isle of Man remained part of the Kingdom of the Isles. Its affinities with the Hebrides are still evident in the name of the diocese of Sodor and Man, from Norse *Suðreyar,* 'The Southern Isles'. The Kingdom of the Isles was nominally under the Norwegian crown, but after 1103 was in practice ruled by powerful local Norse-Gaelic dynas-ties based on the west coast of Scotland, such as the Somerleds and MacSorleys. It lasted until its overlordship was settled in favour of Scotland at the Battle of Largs in 1263, and the ensuing Treaty of Perth of 1266.[2]

No contemporary documentary source attests to the 'end' of Viking power on the Irish Sea. No single historical event, such as the Battle of Clontarf in 1014, the superimposition of native Irish rule over Dublin in 1052, the Norman Conquest of England in 1066, or the Anglo-Norman Conquest of Ireland in 1170–71, can truly be said to mark the point when Viking influence ended. It lived on in the minds of people, in their speech and in their stories, for many generations. Much academic commentary on language has focused on the long decline of spoken Norse in northern England as it merged into Medieval dialects of Norman-English.[3] The descendants of Viking settlers continued to pass on words, names, stories, and indeed their genes, from genera-tion to generation. Place-names which still used Scandinavian-derived terms proliferated in the eleventh century and beyond, obfuscating and diluting the original extent of Viking place-names established in the ninth and tenth centuries. Local Anglo-Scandinavian dialects and folk traditions in areas such as Cumbria survived long enough for Victorian romanticists to study and document them, and indeed in certain ways they still echo the speech and vocabulary of a thousand years ago. Yet, as we have seen, even in the ninth and tenth centuries, ethnic distinctions were fluid and malleable. It was possible even then for people to cross ethnic lines and adopt the guise of belong-ing to a group different to their own genetic and cultural backgrounds. Vikings have often been likened to chameleons in their ability to blend into new roles, lands, and peoples. Their opportun-ism is legendary, yet we must remember that we are not referring to a single people or culture that could be expected to behave in the same predictable ways.

Vikings became half-forgotten as the Middle Ages gave way to the early modern times. It took firstly the inquisitive antiquarians of the seventeenth and eighteenth centuries, and then the scholars and collectors of the nineteenth and early twentieth centuries, to prevent them from lapsing altogether into obscurity. National histories of the early to mid-twentieth century left little room for pagan outsiders, although much good work on the sources was done by scholars such as Eilert Ekwall, A.H. Smith, A.T. Lucas and F.T. Wainwright. From the 1960s onwards, high-profile excavations, museum exhibitions, and clear, approachable texts by historians writing for a popular audience, began to turn the tables in popular perceptions. The dramatic controversies and sit-ins over the fate of the Wood Quay site in Dublin in the late 1970s (above, Chapter 7), and the televising at the same time of the rather more decorous events celebrating the 'Manx Millennium' at Tynwald on the Isle of Man,[4] projected Irish Sea Vikings into the media spotlight as never before. Since then, new discoveries at Peel Castle, Whithorn, Llanbedrgoch, Woodstown and Cumwhitton have been the subject of national news coverage in Britain, Ireland and beyond. Cumwhitton even featured on Channel 4's *Richard and Judy Show*. The voyage of the *Sea Stallion from Glendalough*, the Roskilde-built replica of the Irish-built *Skuldelev 2* warship, attracted many thousands of people to the Dublin waterfront, as it arrived from Denmark, via Orkney, in 2007 (to maintain the geographic balance, it returned to Roskilde via the English Channel in 2008).[5] Viking festivals and re-enactment societies flourish, and new pagans have reinstated their version of the 'old religion' whilst its ancient adversary, Christianity, struggles to maintain its footing in a secular age. The Internet has created a flow of information and interpretation which could hardly have been imagined only twenty years ago. This book will inevitably seem dated, probably very soon, as new discoveries come to light and the means and media of disseminating academic and popular writing change and develop yet again. However, the endless fascination embodied in its subject will undoubtedly live on and continue to flourish.

LIST OF ABBREVIATIONS

ASC	*Anglo-Saxon Chronicle*
AU	*Annals of Ulster*
CI	*Chronicle of Ireland*
MI	Middle Irish
NMRS	National Monuments Record of Scotland
OI	Old Irish
ON	Old Norse
OE	Old English
PAS	Portable Antiquities Scheme
RCHME	Royal Commission on the Historical Monuments of England

NOTES

PREFACE

1 Philpott 1990, Graham-Campbell 1992.

CHAPTER I

1 Brink 2008, 5–7.
2 Ottar: trans. Swanton 1975, 32–7; Wamers 1983.
3 Worsaae 1852; Bugge 1905; Petersen 1919; Bøe 1940; Grieg 1940; Shetelig 1940. For a review of earlier scholarship, see Harrison 2007. Studies of settlement, towns and landscapes are comparatively recent developments.
4 Wawn 2000.
5 Collingwood 1927; Townend 2009.
6 Hodges 2006.
7 For a recent and comprehensive survey, see Brink and Price 2008.
8 Etchingham 2001.
9 Redknap 2004, 143.
10 Fleure and Roberts 1915; Fox 1932.
11 Mackinder 1907.
12 Moore 1970.
13 Cunliffe 2001.
14 Cummings and Fowler 2004; Hudson 1999; Hudson 2006.
15 AU, Mac Airt and Mac Niocáill 1983, 90–91; CI, Charles-Edwards 2006, 113.
16 Whitelock 1979, 664.
17 Colgrave and Mynors 1969, 148–9; 162–3; AU, Mac Airt and Mac Niocáill 1983, 148–9; CI, Charles-Edwards 2006, 165.
18 The battle is described in Bede's Eccesiastical History, Colgrave and Mynors 1969, 140–41; Whitelock 1979, 662. A riverside earthwork enclosure at Heronbridge, near Chester, was once thought to be a Viking fortification, but recent excavations have shown it is probably earlier, and a group of inhumations have been suggested as battle casualties from AD 616, Mason 2007, 35–56.
19 A Savignac, and subsequently Cistercian, abbey was founded here in 1131, almost certainly on the site of a much earlier Mercian stronghold where Coenwulf probably died in 821 (Whitelock 1979, 185, n2); the OE –werk suffix suggests a previous fortification. The Mercian site is yet to be identified archaeologically.
20 ASC 876, Whitelock 1979, 195.
21 Charles-Edwards 2006.
22 Etchingham 2001; Hudson 2005; Downham 2007; Ó Corráin 1997; Woolf 2007.
23 Ó Floinn 1998a, 142.
24 Bowden *et al* 2008, summary in Harding and Jobling 2008; McEvoy *et al* 2006.

25 Helgason *et al* 2000.
26 Hadley 2006, 2–9.

CHAPTER 2

1 Warner 1974, 63.
2 Mac Airt 1977, 119.
3 See e.g. Cubbon 1983, 13.
4 AU, Mac Airt and Mac Niocáill 1983, 252–3; CI,Charles-Edwards 2006, 260.
5 White 2007, 57.
6 The location of this ominous incident is confirmed by the *Annals of St Neots*;Woolf 2007, 46–7.
7 Downham 2000.
8 Lucas 1966.
9 Dumville 1997.
10 AU, Mac Airt and Mac Niocaill 1983; CI, Charles-Edwards 2006, 282.
11 Etchingham 1996.
12 Lowe 2007.
13 Blindheim 1976;Wamers 1983, 1998.
14 AU, Mac Airt and Mac Niocáill 1983, 294–5; CI, Charles-Edwards 2006, 294.
15 Ó Corráin, 2001, 19.
16 *Annals of the Four Masters*, 938; Doyle 1998.
17 AU, Mac Airt and Mac Niocáill 1983, 294–5; CI, Charles-Edwards 2006, 294.
18 For detailed breakdown of historical references, see Downham 2007, 13.
19 AU, Mac Airt and Mac Niocáill 1983, 304–5; CI, Charles-Edwards 2006, 302.
20 Buckley and Sweetman 1991, nos 259 and 947; Ó Floinn 2001, 88. Further studies of Annagassan, which
   are in preparation by Eamonn P. Kelly, are awaited with interest.
21 CI, Charles-Edwards 2006, 315.
22 Kelly and Maas 1995.
23 Richards 1991.
24 Biddle and Kjølbye-Biddle 2001.
25 Kelly 1998; plan of survey: www.mglarc.com/index.php/munster
26 Gibbons 2004.
27 Sheehan 2008, 283–4.
28 *Chronicum Scotorum*, CI, Charles-Edwards 2006, 305.
29 O'Brien *et al* 2006; further reports available online at http://www.environ.ie/en/
30 Sheehan 2008, 292, illus. 6; further studies of the weights are being undertaken by P. F. Wallace.
31 Russell 2003.
32 Simpson 2005.
33 AU, Mac Airt and Mac Niocáill 1983, 294–5; CI Charles-Edwards 2006, 295.
34 Ó Corráin 2001, 19.
35 AU, Mac Airt and Mac Niocáill 1983, 308-9; CI, Charles-Edwards 2006, 305.
36 Downham 2007, 15.
37 Ó Corráin 1997.
38 Valante 2008, 68–9.
39 Wamers 1998.
40 Smyth 1977, 1979.
41 Dumville 2005.
42 Downham 2007, 14.
43 Clancy 2008 summarises the arguments.
44 Dumville 1997, Downham 2007, 17.

CHAPTER 3

1 Rhodri Mawr, King of Gwynedd (844–78).
2 *Annales Cambriae*, Dumville 2002, 11–12.
3 Whitelock 1979, 526–7, no. 90; Sawyer 1968, 207.
4 Davies 1990, 69.
5 ASC, 893–4, Whitelock 1979, 204.
6 Redknap 2000, 30.
7 Woolf 2007, 109–10.
8 Downham 2007, 182–4.
9 Hill 1997, 162–4.
10 *Chronicum Scotorum*, Woolf 2007, 108–10.
11 Ó Corrain 2001, 21.
12 Brooke 1991; Clancy 2008.
13 Downham 2007, 165 ff.
14 Woolf 2007, 129.
15 *Chronicum Scotorum*, Woolf 2007, 129.
16 Higham 1992, 26–9.
17 *Annales Cambriae*, Dumville 2002, 14.
18 Redknap 2004, 146.
19 Wainwright 1948.
20 Higham 1992.
21 Griffiths 2001.
22 ASC, Whitelock 1979, 218 and 305; Downham (2007, 99) cautiously points out that there is another Farndon in Mercia, in Nottinghamshire.
23 Whitelock 1979, 287.
24 AU, Mac Airt and Mac Niocáill 1983, 361–3.
25 ASC, Whitelock 1979, 218.
26 ASC, Whitelock 1979, 219–20.
27 Dodgson 1957; Cavill *et al* 2000; Halloran 2005; Cavill 2008. An excellent recent account of the battle and its historical context, in more detail than is possible here, can be found in Woolf 2007, 158–76.
28 Cavill *et al* 2004.
29 ASC, Whitelock 1979, 222.
30 Redknap 2000, 43.
31 Etchingham 2001, 179.
32 Whitelock 1979, 228.
33 ASC, Whitelock 1979, 237.
34 Downham 2007, 52.
35 AU, Mac Airt and Mac Niocáill 1983, 444–5.
36 Jones 1910; Evans 1990.

CHAPTER 4

1 Fellows-Jensen 1985, 22–23; Roberts 1990.
2 Fellows-Jensen 1983.
3 Megaw 1978; Gelling 1991; Abrams and Parsons 2004.
4 Fellows-Jensen 2001, 2003.
5 Wainwright 1943, 1975; Harding 2007.
6 Etchingham 1994.
7 Gelling 1995.
8 Oftedal 1976, 131; Bradley 1988, 56–8; Bradley 2009.

9 Fellows-Jensen 1985.
10 Coates 1998.
11 'Frenchman's Farm', Dodgson 1972, 287; alternatives are the ON personal names Franki or Frakki.
12 See e.g. Thomson 2008, 51–4.
13 Ekwall 1922, Fellows-Jensen 1985.
14 Whitelock 1979, 546–51; Sawyer 1968, nos 407, 396 and 397.
15 Fellows-Jensen 1985, 417.
16 Fellows-Jensen 1985, 21.
17 Ormerod (ed. Helsby) 1882, II, 518; also quoted by Dodgson 1957, 306. Pantos (1999) reconstructs the Hundred of Caldy.
18 Dodgson 1957.
19 Harding 2007.
20 Gelling 1995.
21 Sawyer and Thacker 1987.
22 Davies 1949, 214–9
23 Welsh: 'stone of the field of Saint Cwyfan', the Hiberno-Norse saint Cóemgen (Kevin, of Glendalough) to which the church at Dyserth was formerly dedicated.
24 Griffiths 2006.
25 Kenyon 1991, 140 ff.
26 Whitelock 1979, 586–7, no. 125.
27 Higham 1993, 114.
28 ON Toki-stoð, 'Toki's staithe or landing place'; Wainwright 1946 and Fellows-Jensen 1985.
29 Farrar and Brownbill 1906, 37.
30 Grant 2002.
31 Edmonds, forthcoming.
32 Winchester 1985; Winchester 1987, 14–22.
33 Angus Winchester, pers. comm.
34 Fellows-Jensen 1985, 406, Table 22.
35 Fellows-Jensen 1985, 290–91. Some of the Eden names are post-Norman Conquest in date. See note 1.
36 Bailey 1980, 85 ff.
37 Fellows-Jensen 1985, 265.
38 Graham-Campbell and Batey 1998, 109.
39 Graham-Campbell and Batey 1998, 251.
40 Oram 1995, 135.
41 Fellows-Jensen 1991, 92–3.
42 Graham-Campbell and Batey 1998, 96.
43 Grant 2005.
44 Bradley 1988; Bradley 2009.
45 Downham, forthcoming.
46 Etchingham 1994, 32-3.
47 Barrow 1975.
48 See e.g. Moore 1999 for the Isle of Man.
49 Reilly 1988.
50 Marstrander 1937.
51 Megaw 1978.
52 Wilson 2008, 90–92.
53 Marwick 1935.
54 Swift 2004.
55 Excavated by Bersu and Gelling, more recent summaries in Johnson 1999 and Wilson 2008.
56 Longley 1991.
57 Crawford-Coupe 2005.
58 McErlean 1983.

59 Armstrong *et al* 1950–52, 288–95.
60 Andersen 2006.
61 Darvill 2004.
62 Keen 1925–9.
63 Fellows-Jensen 1985, 288; Fellows-Jensen 1991, 87.
64 National Monuments Record of Scotland NY08SW3.
65 Driscoll 2004.
66 National Monuments Record of Scotland NX97NE5; Coles 1893, 117–8; Piggott and Simpson 1970, 65.
67 Ó Floinn 1998a, 135; see also Harrison 2005.
68 Duffy 1997.
69 Armstrong *et al* 1950–52, 267.
70 Dodgson 1972, 232; Pantos 1999.
71 Swainson Cowper 1891; Higham 1985, 36, pl. IV.
72 Quartermaine and Krupa 1994.
73 See e.g. Wilson 2008, 125.
74 Munch *et al* 2003
75 Skre 2007; 2008b.
76 Storli 2000; illustrated in Griffiths 2004, 134.
77 Warner 2004, Fitzpatrick 2004a.
78 FitzPatrick 2004b.
79 Hartnett and Eogan 1964.
80 Ó Néill 2000.
81 Fleure and Dunlop 1942; Gelling 1964.
82 Johnson 1999.
83 Gelling 1970.
84 Wilson 2008, 93–5.
85 Freke 2002, 132–9.
86 King 2004; Coggins 2004.
87 Dickinson 1985.
88 RCHME Westmorland 1936.
89 Newman and Brennand 2007, 80.
90 Cowell and Innes 1994; Hodgkinson *et al* 2000.
91 E.g. Higham 2004a; 2004b, 308–9.
92 Bewley 1987.
93 Clifford Jones, pers. comm.
94 Philpott in prep.
95 Philpott and Adams, forthcoming.

CHAPTER 5

1 Petersen 1919; Petersen 1928. A corpus of Viking graves in Ireland is in preparation by Stephen Harrison.
2 O'Brien *et al* 2006.
3 Simpson 2005.
4 Telford *et al* 2004.
5 O'Donovan 2008.
6 Harrison 2001.
7 See e.g. Graham-Campbell 1976, 40. Stephen Harrison has recently compared the weapons from the College Green burials with those from Kilmainham/Islandbridge, suggesting there were strong similarities.
8 Ó Floinn 1998a.
9 Coffey and Armstrong 1910; O'Brien 1998.
10 Wilde 1866. An eminent physician and antiquarian, father of Oscar.

11 Henry (ed.) 1995, 60–64.
12 For a discussion of the dates of specific types of oval brooch and swords, see Ó Floinn 1998a, 138.
13 Walsh 1998.
14 O'Brien 1992.
15 Wallace 2004.
16 Ó Floinn 1998a, 144.
17 Coffey 1902.
18 Ó Floinn 1998b.
19 Warner 1974.
20 Ó Floinn 1998a, 146–7.
21 Briggs 1974.
22 Graham-Campbell 1976, 59–61.
23 Ó Floinn 1998a, 146.
24 Raftery 1961.
25 Sheehan 1988.
26 Gibbons and Kelly 2003.
27 O'Kelly 1956; Sheehan *et al* 2001.
28 Conolly and Coyne 2005, 68–74.
29 Kermode 1907.
30 Wilson 2008, 37.
31 Kermode 1930; Wilson 2008, 37, n.39.
32 Walsh 1998.
33 Bersu and Wilson 1966.
34 Fanning 1983.
35 Bersu and Wilson 1966, 45–62.
36 For a translation see Jones 1984, 425 ff, or Foote and Wilson 1970, 408–11; also quoted at length by
     Wilson 2008, 25–26.
37 R.D. Teare of London University quoted in Bersu and Wilson 1966, 47–8.
38 Graham-Campbell and Batey 1998, 118–22.
39 Williams 2006, 175.
40 Bersu and Wilson 1966, 13.
41 Tarlow 1997
42 Wilson 2008, 27, 38.
43 Cubbon 1983, 18.
44 Harrison 2007.
45 Freke 2002.
46 Graham-Campbell and Archibald in Freke 2002.
47 Graham-Campbell, in Freke 2002, 66–69.
48 Price 2002, 160–61.
49 J. Graham-Campbell, pers. comm.
50 Edwards 1998 and Redmond 2007 provide surveys of north-west England and Redknap 2004 of Wales.
51 Rooke 1792. Aspatria is probably named after Gospatric, a Hiberno-Norseman whose son, Waltheof, was
     Earl of Allerdale in the later eleventh century.
52 Abramson 2000.
53 Hodgson 1832, Cowen 1934, 1948, Graham-Campbell 1995a, 74.
54 Edwards 1970.
55 Graham-Campbell and Batey 1998, 108.
56 Edwards 1992, 48.
57 Griffiths, Philpott and Egan 2007, 71–77.
58 Smith 1932; information on rediscovery of skeleton from Nancy Edwards (pers. comm.).
59 Lawlor 1925, 72–3.
60 Graham-Campbell and Edwards 2008.

61 Graham-Campbell and Batey 1998, 109.

62 Adams, Lupton and Simpson 2004; OA North 2008.

63 Richardson 1996.

64 Grieg 1940, 13; Graham-Campbell 1999, 11–15.

65 Wilson 1984, pls. 56–59.

66 Redknap 2000, 97–8.

67 Potter and Andrews 1994.

68 Keevill 1989; Keevill 2008.

69 Lynn 1997.

70 Hill 1997, 189.

CHAPTER 6

1 AU, Mac Airt and Mac Niocáill 1983, 284–5; CI, Charles-Edwards 2006, 286. Ard Cainachta is the coastal district of Brega.

2 Holm 1986.

3 Doherty 1980, 72.

4 Charles-Edwards 1993, 478–85.

5 Ryan 1982.

6 Pirie 1986, 82.

7 Edwards 1998, 46.

8 Graham-Campbell 1995b, 4; Graham-Campbell and Batey 1998, 109.

9 Metcalf 1992; Metcalf 1995, 4.

10 Dolley 1955, 8.

11 Dolley 1965, 1966 for Ireland, see p. 132 for Limerick; Bornholdt 1999 for the Isle of Man.

12 Sheehan 1998 with additions. Sheehan has recently developed a five-level classification for Viking silver hoards from Ireland; see Sheehan 2007.

13 Metcalf 1992, 95.

14 Sheehan 1998, 173; Kenny 1987.

15 Kruse 1992.

16 Wallace 1987b, 206–7.

17 Graham-Campbell and Philpott, forthcoming.

18 Graham-Campbell 1983, 62–8; Graham-Campbell and Batey 1998, 238–9.

19 Graham-Campbell 1992, 109-10; Richardson 1996.

20 Richardson 1996; Treasure Annual Report 2005/6, 101.

21 Sheehan 2008.

22 Downham 2003b, 25.

23 Graham-Campbell 1987; 1992; quoted from 1998, 108.

24 Edwards 1998, 66.

25 Archibald 1992.

26 Graham-Campbell 1992; Graham-Campbell, forthcoming.

27 Blunt *et al* 1989, 104.

28 Illustrated in Edwards 1992, 53. The silver went missing during the upheavals of the English Civil War later in the seventeenth century. A silver pyx existed for many years in the Roman Catholic church at Little Crosby, which was reputedly made of metal from the hoard; it was stolen in the 1970s.

29 Mack 1967.

30 Webster, Dolley and Dunning 1953; Turner 1944; Hill 1920.

31 Boon 1986, 14.

32 Blackburn 1996.

33 Hill 1997, 332–47 and 397–400.

34 Graham-Campbell 1983, 55, Figures 2 and 3.

35 Metcalf 1992, 93.

36 King 2004.

37 Redknap 2000, 82.

38 Graham-Campbell and Batey 1998, 109.

39 Information from Portable Antiquities Scheme: www.finds.org

40 Youngs and Herepath 2001, Youngs 2002.

41 Thompson Watkin 1883; O'Sullivan 1993, 30; Edwards 1998, 39.

42 Redknap 2000, 23; Redknap 2007, 54–5.

43 Hume 1863.

44 Griffiths, Philpott and Egan 2007.

45 McGrail and Switsur 1979.

46 Parts of what was probably a modest-sized clinker-built boat, which were discovered by workmen in 1938 under the Railway Inn, Meols, have recently been publicised as being a possible Viking boat or even a ship; this is highly speculative, and the 'boat' could have been considerably more recent in date.

47 Cook and Besly 1990, 229, pl. 22, no. 81.

48 Cowell and Philpott 1993.

49 Redknap 2000; 2004.

50 Hudson 2005, 120.

51 Loyn 1976, 18–21.

52 Griffiths 1992.

53 Skinner and Bruce-Mitford 1940; Laing and Laing 1987.

54 McErlean *et al* 2003, 78–87.

CHAPTER 7

1 Skre 2008b.

2 Blindheim 1976.

3 Skre 2008c.

4 Hilberg 2008.

5 Feveile 2008.

6 Skre 2008a.

7 Skre 2007, 214–7.

8 Simpson 2000.

9 Lynch and Manning 2001; Simpson 2000.

10 Bradley 1984.

11 Wallace 1992, 5.

12 Walsh 2001; see also Scally 2002 and Hayden 2002 for further work on the defences.

13 Wallace 1987a, 276–7.

14 Wallace 2001, 40.

15 Murray 1983; Wallace 1992, 7–23.

16 Wallace 2008, 435.

17 Geraghty 1996.

18 Wallace 1987b, 203.

19 Wallace 1998.

20 Hencken 1942, 1950.

21 Valante 2008, 179.

22 Larsen 2001, 131.

23 James 1978.

24 Wallace 1987b, 219–20.

25 Wallace 1986, 210–11.

26 Meyer 1892.

27 Wallace 1986; 1987b.
28 Hall 1994.
29 Wallace 1992, 75–7.
30 Ward 1994.
31 Griffiths 2001.
32 Mason 1985.
33 C. Walsh, in Hurley and Scully 1997, 45–53.
34 Ward 1994.
35 Graham-Campbell 1985.
36 Mason 1985, 21.
37 Thacker 1987, 257; Thacker 2003.
38 Sawyer and Thacker 1987, 342–3.
39 Whitelock 1979, 212–3.
40 Redknap 2000, 40–41.
41 Richards 1962.
42 Thacker 1982.
43 Sivier 2002, 33.
44 Pelteret 1995, 59; Mason 1990, 289–94.
45 Hurley and Scully 1997.
46 T. Barry in Hurley and Scully 1997, 13.
47 Hurley and Scully 1997, 20.
48 Bourke 1995.
49 Cleary and Hurley 2003, 151–60.
50 C. Walsh in Hurley and Scully 1997, 45.
51 Lynn 1988.
52 Hill 1997, 209–31.
53 Hill 1987.
54 Hill 1997, 55.

CHAPTER 8

 1 Nelson 1997, 36.
 2 The 'Vale of York' Hoard, dated to *c.* 927, and found in 2007, was buried in a very similar cup. Both hoards
    are mentioned at: www.britishmuseum.org
 3 The South Great George Street excavation project osteologist noted that Burial F196 had been disturbed
    or moved during decomposition, as its right arm was laid across the body, out of its normal position (an
    alternative possibility that the right arm had been severed before or at death, was also suggested); see
    Simpson 2005, 38.
 4 Williams 2006, 179 ff; Thäte 2007.
 5 Dumville 1997.
 6 Abrams 1997.
 7 Price 2002, 75–6.
 8 Smith 1967; Fellows-Jensen 1985, 47.
 9 A silver Thor's Hammer amulet recently found 'near Carlisle' is likely to be a fake or reproduction
    (J. Graham-Campbell, pers. comm.)
10 Dolley 1965, 22.
11 Andrén 2005.
12 Wilson 2008, 80–83.
13 Bailey 1980, 125–31; Bailey and Cramp 1988, 102–3.
14 Lang 1984.
15 Llanddewi-aber-Arth (Ceredigion) and Castledermot (Co. Kildare).

16 Bailey and Whalley 2006.

17 Bailey 1980, 136.

18 Bailey 1980, 176–82.

19 Lang 1988.

20 Redknap 2000, 55.

21 Henri 1967.

22 Graham-Campbell 2002, 71.

23 Johnson 2004, 42, illustrates an example from Tully Church, Co. Dublin.

24 Thomas 2000, 246.

25 Fanning 1994.

26 Mytum 2003.

27 Byrne 2003, appendix.

28 Barnes, Hagland and Page 1997.

29 Page 1983; Wilson 2008, 75–8.

30 See e.g. Wilson 2008, 75.

31 Forsyth 2007.

32 Barnes and Page 2006.

33 Bailey 2010.

34 Barnes and Page 2006.

35 Barth 1969.

36 See e.g. Jesch 2008.

37 Downham, forthcoming; Glørstad, forthcoming.

CHAPTER 9

1 Accelerated Mass Spectrometry.

2 MacDonald 1997.

3 Parsons 2001; Townend 2002.

4 The Manx government decided in the 1970s that the year 979 marked the beginning of the island's political tradition. The Queen presided over the 'thousandth' Tynwald Ceremony on 5 July 1979.

5 Nicholl 2009.

BIBLIOGRAPHY

Abrams, L. (1997) 'The Conversion of the Scandinavians of Dublin', *Anglo-Norman Studies* XX, 1–29

Abrams, L. and Parsons, D.N. (2004) 'Place-names and the History of Scandinavian Settlement in England', in Hines, J., Lane, A. and Redknap, M. (eds) *Land, Sea and Home, Settlement in the Viking Period*, Society for Medieval Archaeology, Monograph 20, Maney, Leeds, 379–431

Abramson, P. (2000) 'A re-examination of a Viking Age burial at Beacon Hill, Aspatria', *Transactions of the Cumberland and Westmorland Antiquarian and Archaeological Society*, Vol. C, 79–88

Adams, P., Lupton, A. and Simpson, F. (2004) 'Cumbrian Heritage', *British Archaeology* 79, 28–31

Andersen, P.S. (2006) *Det siste norske landnåmet i Vesterled: Cumbria – Nordvest England*, Oslo

Andrén, A. (2005) 'Behind heathendom: Archaeological Studies of Old Norse Religion', *Scottish Archaeological Journal* 27 (2), 105–38

Archibald, M.M. (1992) 'Dating Cuerdale: the evidence of the coins', in Graham-Campbell, J.A. (ed.) *Viking Treasure from the North West, the Cuerdale Hoard in its Context*, National Museums and Galleries on Merseyside, Liverpool, 15–20

Armstrong, A.M., Mawer, A., Stenton, F. and Dickins, B. (1950–52) *The Place-names of Cumberland*, English Place-Name Society XX–XXII, Cambridge University Press, Cambridge

Bailey, R.N. (1980) *Viking Age Sculpture in Northern England*, Collins, London

Bailey, R.N. and Cramp, R. (1988) 'Cumberland, Westmorland and Lancashire North-of-the-Sands', *British Academy Corpus of Anglo-Saxon Stone Sculpture*, Vol. II, Oxford University Press, Oxford

Bailey, R.N. and Whalley, J. (2006) 'A miniature Viking-Age hogback from the Wirral', *Antiquaries Journal*, 86, 345–56

Bailey, R.N. (2010) 'Lancashire and Cheshire' *British Academy Corpus of Anglo-Saxon Stone Sculpture* Vol. IX, Oxford University Press, Oxford

Barnes, M. (1992) 'Norse in the British Isles', in Faulkes, A. and Perkins, R. (eds) *Viking Revaluations*, Viking Society for Northern Research, London, 55–84

Barnes, M., Hagland, J.R. and Page, R.I. (1997) *The Runic Inscriptions of Viking Age Dublin*, Medieval Dublin Excavations 1962–81, Series B Volume 5, Royal Irish Academy, Dublin

Barnes, M. and Page, R.I. (2006) *The Scandinavian Runic Inscriptions of Britain,* Institute of Nordic Languages, Uppsala

Barrow, G.W.S. (1975) 'The Pattern of Lordship and Feudal Settlement in Cumbria', *Journal of Medieval History,* 1, 117–138

Barth, F. (1969) *Ethnic Groups and Boundaries: The social organisation of culture difference*, Little Brown, Boston

Bersu, G. (1949) 'A Promontory fort on the Shore of Ramsey Bay, Isle of Man', *Antiquaries Journal* 29, 62–79

Bersu, G. and Wilson, D. M. (1966) *Three Viking Graves in the Isle of Man*, Society for Medieval Archaeology, Monograph 1, London

Bewley, R.H. (1987) 'Ewanrigg', *Current Archaeology* 103, 232–3

Biddle, M. and Kjølbye-Biddle, B. (2001) 'Repton and the "great heathen army"', 873–4, in Graham-Campbell, J., Hall, R., Jesch, J. and Parsons, D. (eds) *Vikings and the Danelaw*, Oxbow, Oxford, 45–96

Blackburn, M. (1996) 'Hiberno-Norse and Irish Sea imitations of Cnut's *Quatrefoil* Type', *British Numismatic Journal* 66, 2–20

Blindheim, C. (1976) 'A Collection of Celtic (?) bronze objects fround at Kaupang (Skiringssal), Vestfold', Norway', in Almqvist, B. and Green, D. (eds) *Proceedings of the Seventh Viking Congress, Dublin 1973*, Dublin, 9–27

Blunt, C.E., Stewart, B.H.I.H. and Lyon, C.S.S. (1989) *Coinage in Tenth-Century England*, British Academy, Oxford

Bøe, J. (1940) 'Norse Antiquities in Ireland', in Shetelig, H. (ed.) *Viking Antiquities in Great Britain and Ireland*, Part III, Aschehoug, Oslo

Boon, G.C. (1986) *Welsh Hoards*, National Museum of Wales, Cardiff

Bornholdt, K. (1999) 'Myth or Mint: The evidence for a Viking-Age coinage from the Isle of Man', in Davey, P. J. (ed.) *Recent Archaeological Research on the Isle of Man*, British Archaeological Reports, British Series 278, Oxford, 199–220

Bourke, E. (1995) 'Life in the sunny south-east. Housing and domestic economy in Viking and Medieval Wexford', *Archaeology Ireland* 9:3, 33–6

Bowden, G.R., Balaresque, P., King, T.E., Hansen, Z., Lee, A.C., Pergl-Wilson, G., Hurley, E., Roberts, S. J., Waite, P., Jesch, J., Jones, A.L., Thomas, M.G., Harding, S.E. and Jobling, M. (2008) 'Excavating Past Population Structures by Surname-based Sampling: the Genetic Legacy of the Vikings in North-west England', *Molecular Biology and Evolution* 25(2), 301–309

Bradley, J. (ed.) (1984) *Viking Dublin Exposed*, O'Brien Press, Dublin

Bradley, J. (1988) 'The Interpretation of Scandinavian settlement in Ireland', in Bradley, J. (ed.) *Settlement and Society in Medieval Ireland, Studies Presented to F.X. Martin*, Boethius Press, Kilkenny, 49–78

Bradley, J. (2009) 'Some reflections on the problem of Scandinavian settlement in the hinterland of Dublin during the ninth century', in Bradley, J, Fletcher, A. J. and Simms, A. (eds), *Dublin in the Medieval World: Studies in Honour of Howard B. Clarke*, Four Courts Press, Dublin, 39–62

Briggs, C.S. (1974) 'A boat burial from Co. Antrim', *Medieval Archaeology* XVIII, 158–60

Brink, S. (2008) 'Who were the Vikings?', in Brink, S. and Price, N. (2008) *The Viking World*, Routledge, 4–7

Brooke, D. (1991) 'Gall-Gaidhil and Galloway', in Oram, R. and Stell, G.P. (eds) *Galloway, Land and Lordship*, Scottish Society for Northern Studies, Edinburgh

Buckley, V. and Sweetman, P. D. (1991) *An Archaeological Survey of County Louth*, Dublin

Bugge, A. (1905) *Vesterlandenes inflydelse paa Nordboernes, kultur, levesæt og samfundsforhold i Vikiingetiden*, Christiania

Bu'Lock, J.D. (1958) 'Pre-Norman Crosses of West Cheshire and the Norse settlements around the Irish Sea', *Transactions of the Lancashire and Cheshire Antiquarian Society* 68, 1–11 (reprinted in Cavill *et al* 2000)

Byrne, F. J. (2003) 'The Viking Age', with appendix 'Old Norse Borrowings into Irish', in Ó Cróinín, D. (ed.) *A New History of Ireland 1: Prehistoric and Early Ireland*, Oxford University Press, Oxford, 609–34

Cavill, P. (2008) 'The site of the battle of Brunanburh: manuscripts and maps, grammar and geography', in Padel, O. and Parsons, D. (eds) *A commodity of good names: essays in honour of Margaret Gelling*, Donnington, 303–19

Cavill, P., Harding, S. and Jesch, J. (2000) *Wirral and its Viking Heritage*, English Place-Name Society, Nottingham

Cavill, P., Harding, S. and Jesch, J. (2004) 'Revisiting *Dingesmere*', *Journal of the English Place-Name Society* 36, 25–38

Charles, B.G. (1934) *Old Norse relations with Wales,* Cardiff

Charles-Edwards, T.M. (1993) *Early Irish and Welsh Kinship,* Oxford University Press, Oxford

Charles-Edwards, T.M. (trans.) (2006) *The Chronicle of Ireland*, 2 vols, Liverpool University Press, Liverpool

Clancy, T.O. (2008) 'The Gall-Ghàidheil and Galloway', *Journal of Scottish Name Studies* 2, 19–50

Cleary, R.M. and Hurley, M. (eds) (2003) *Excavations in Cork City 1984–2000*, Cork, Cork City Council

Coates, R. (1998) 'Liscard and Irish Names in Northern Wirral', *Journal of the English Place-Name Society* 30, 23–26

Coffey, G. 1902 'A Pair of Brooches and Chains of the Viking Period found recently in Ireland', *Journal of the Royal Society of Antiquaries of Ireland* XXXII, 71–73

Coffey, G. and Armstrong, E. (1910) 'Scandinavian Objects found at Islandbridge and Kilmainham', *Proceedings of the Royal Irish Academy* 28C, 107–22

Coggins, D. (2004) 'Simy Folds, Twenty Years on', in Hines, J., Lane, A. and Redknap, M. (eds) *Land, Sea and Home, Settlement in the Viking Period*, Society for Medieval Archaeology, Monograph 20, Maney, Leeds, 325–34

Coles, F.R. (1893) 'The motes, forts, and doons in the east and west divisions of the Stewartry of Kirkcudbright', *Proceedings of the Society of Antiquaries of Scotland 27*, 117–8

Colgrave, B. and Mynors, R.A.B. (trans.) (1969) *Bede's Ecclesiastical History of the English-Speaking Peoples*, Oxford University Press, Oxford

Collingwood, W.G. (1927) *Northumbrian Crosses of the Pre-Norman Age*, Faber and Gwyer, London

Collingwood, W.G. (1928) 'Early Monuments of West Kirby', in Brownbill, J. (ed.) *West Kirby and Hilbre, a Parochial History*, Henry Young, Liverpool, 14–26 (reprinted in Cavill *et al* 2000)

Conolly, M. and Coyne, F. (2005) *Underworld, death and burial in Cloghermore Cave, Co. Kerry*, Bray

Cook B.J. and Besly E.M. (1990) 'Coin Register 1989', *British Numismatic Journal* 59 (for 1989), 221–33

Cowell, R. and Innes, J. (1994) 'The Wetlands of Merseyside', *North West Wetlands Survey* 1, Lancaster

Cowell, R. and Philpott, R. (1993) 'Some Finds from Cheshire reported to Liverpool Museum', *Cheshire Past* 3, 10–11

Cowen, J.D. (1934) 'A Catalogue of Objects of the Viking period in the Tullie House Museum, Carlisle', *Transactions of the Cumberland and Westmorland Antiquarian and Archaeological Society* 2, series 34, 166–87

Cowen, J.D. (1948) 'Viking Burials from Cumbria', *Transactions of the Cumberland and Westmorland Antiquarian and Archaeological Society* 2, series 48, 73–6

Crawford-Coupe, G. (2005) 'The Archaeology of Burton Point', *Journal of the Chester Archaeological Society* 80, 71–90

Cubbon, A.M. (1983) 'The Archaeology of the Vikings in the Isle of Man', in Fell, C., Foote, P., Graham-Campbell, J. and Thomson, R. (eds) *The Viking Age in the Isle of Man*, London, 13–26

Cummings, V. and Fowler, C. (eds) (2004), *The Neolithic of the Irish Sea, Materiality and Traditions of Practice*, Oxbow, Oxford

Cunliffe, B. (2001) *Facing the Ocean, the Atlantic and its Peoples 8000 BC–AD 1500*, Oxford University Press, Oxford

Darvill, T. (2004) 'Tynwald Hill and the 'things' of power', in Pantos, A. and Semple, S. (eds) *Assembly Places and Practices in Medieval Europe*, Four Courts Press, Dublin, 217–32

Davies, E. (1949) *The Prehistoric and Roman Remains of Flintshire*, Lewis, Cardiff

Davies, W. (1990) *Patterns of Power in Early Wales*, Clarendon Press, Oxford

Dickinson, S. (1985) 'Bryant's Gill, Kentmere, another "Viking-Period" Ribblehead?', in Baldwin, J.R. and Whyte, I.D. (eds) *The Scandinavians in Cumbria*, Scottish Society for Northern Studies, Edinburgh, 83–88

Dodgson, J. McN. (1957) 'The background to Brunanburh', *Saga Book of the Viking Society* 14, 303–16. (reprinted in Cavill *et al* 2000)

Dodgson, J. McN. (1972) *The Place-Names of Cheshire. Part IV: The Place-Names of Broxton Hundred and Wirral Hundred*, English Place-Name Society 47, Cambridge University Press, Cambridge

Doherty, C. (1980) 'Exchange and Trade in Early Medieval Ireland', *Journal of the Royal Society of Antiquaries of Ireland* 110, 67–89

Dolley, M. (1955) 'The Mint of Chester (Part I)', *Journal of the Chester and North Wales Architectural and Archaeological Society* 42, 1–20

Dolley, M. (1965) *Viking Coins of the Danelaw and Dublin*, British Museum, London

Dolley, M. (1966) *Hiberno-Norse Coins in the British Museum*, Sylloge of Coins of the British Isles, London

Downham, C. (2000) 'An imaginary Viking-raid on Skye in 795?', *Scottish Gaelic Studies* 20, 192–6

Downham, C. (2003a) 'The Vikings in Southern Uí Néill to 1014', *Peritia* 17–18, 233–55

Downham, C. (2003b) 'England and the Irish Sea Zone in the Eleventh Century', Anglo-Norman Studies XXVI, 55–73

Downham, C. (2004) 'The Historical Importance of Viking-Age Waterford', *Journal of Celtic Studies* 4, 71–96

Downham, C. (2007) *Viking Kings of Britain and Ireland to AD 1014*, Dunedin Press, Edinburgh

Downham, C. (2009) '"Hiberno-Norwegians" and "Anglo-Danes": Anachronistic Ethnicities in Viking Age England', *Mediaeval Scandinavia* 19 (2009) 139–69

Downham, C. (forthcoming 2010) 'Non-Urban settlements of Vikings in Ireland before 1014', in Bolton, T. and Steinsland, G. (eds) *Proceedings of the conference on Irish-Norse relations 800–1200 held in Oslo on 5 November 2005*, Oslo

Doyle, I. (1998) 'The Early Medieval Activity at Dalkey Island, Co. Dublin, A Reassessment', *Journal of Irish Archaeology* IX, 89–103

Driscoll, S.T. (2004) 'The Archaeological Context of assembly in early Medieval Scotland – Scone and its comparanda', in Pantos, A. and Semple, S. (eds) *Assembly Places and Practices in Medieval Europe,* Four Courts Press, Dublin, 73–94

Duffy, S. (1997) 'Ireland's Hastings: The Anglo-Norman Conquest of Dublin', *Anglo-Norman Studies* XX, 69–85

Dumville, D.N. (1997) *The Churches of North Britain in the First Viking-Age,* Whithorn Lecture, Whithorn

Dumville, D.N. (trans.) (2002) *Annales Cambriae AD 682–954: Texts A–C in Parallel,* Cambridge, Department of Anglo-Saxon Norse and Celtic, University of Cambridge

Dumville, D.N. (2005) 'Old Dubliners and New Dubliners in Ireland and Britain, a Viking-Age story', in Duffy, S. (ed.) *Medieval Dublin* VI, Dublin, 78–93

Edmonds, F. (forthcoming) 'History and Names', in Graham-Campbell, J.A. and Philpott, R.A. (eds) *The Huxley Viking Hoard: Scandinavian Settlement in the North West,* National Museums Liverpool

Edwards, B.J.N. (1970) 'The Claughton Burial', *Transactions of the Historic Society of Lancashire and Cheshire* 121, 109–16

Edwards, B.J.N. (1992) 'The Vikings in North-West England: the Archaeological Evidence', in Graham-Campbell, J. (ed.) *Viking Treasure from the North West, the Cuerdale Hoard in its Context,* National Museums and Galleries on Merseyside, Liverpool, 43–62

Edwards, B.J.N. (1998) *Vikings in North West England, The Artifacts,* Centre for North-West Regional Studies, Lancaster

Ekwall, E. (1922) *The Place-Names of Lancashire,* Manchester University Press, Manchester

Etchingham, C. (1994) 'Evidence of Scandinavian Settlement in Wicklow', in Hannigan, K. and Nolan, W. (eds) *Wicklow – History and Society: Interdisciplinary Essays in the History of an Irish County,* Dublin, 113–38

Etchingham, C. (1996) *Viking Raids on the Irish Church Settlements in the Ninth Century: A Reconsideration of the Annals,* Maynooth Monograph Series, Maynooth

Etchingham, C. (2001) 'North Wales, Ireland and the Isles, the Insular Viking Zone', *Peritia* 15, 145–87

Evans, S.D. (1990) *A Medieval Prince of Wales: the Life of Gruffudd ap Cynan,* Lampeter

Fanning, T. (1983) 'Hiberno-Norse Pins in Man', in Fell, C. *et al* (eds) *The Viking Age in the Isle of Man, Selected Papers from the Ninth Viking Congress,* Viking Society for Northern Research, London, 27–36

Fanning, T. (1994) 'Viking age ringed pins from Dublin', *National Museum of Ireland, Medieval Dublin Excavations 1962–81, Ser B,* 4, Royal Irish Academy, Dublin

Farrar, W. and Brownbill, J. (1906) *Victoria History of the County of Lancashire,* Vol. 1, London

Fellows-Jensen, G. (1983) 'Scandinavian Settlement in the Isle of Man and North-West England: the place-name evidence', in Fell, C., Foote, P., Graham-Campbell, J. and Thomson, R. (eds) *The Viking Age in the Isle of Man,* London, 37–52

Fellows-Jensen, G. (1985) *Scandinavian Settlement Names in the North-West,* C.A. Reitzels Forlag, Copenhagen

Fellows-Jensen, G. (1991) 'Scandinavians in Dumfriesshire and Galloway, the place-name evidence', in Oram, R.D. and Stell, G. (eds) *Galloway, Land and Lordship,* Scottish Society for Northern Studies, Edinburgh, 77–95

Fellows-Jensen, G. (2001) 'The Mystery of the –bý names in Man', *Nomina* 24, 33–46

Fellows-Jensen, G. (2003) 'How old are the Scandinavian place-names in Man?', *Proceedings of the Isle of Man Natural History and Antiquarian Society* 11, 3, 423–36

Feveile, C. (2008) 'Ribe', in Brink, S. and Price, N. (eds) *The Viking World,* Routledge, 126–30

FitzPatrick, E. (2004a) 'Royal Inauguration Mounds in Medieval Ireland, Antique Landscape and Tradition', in Pantos, A. and Semple, S. (eds) *Assembly Places and Practices in Medieval Europe,* Four Courts Press, Dublin, 44–72

FitzPatrick, E. (2004b) *Royal inauguration in Gaelic Ireland c. 1100–1600,* Boydell, Woodbridge

Fleure, H.J. and Roberts, E.J. (1915) 'Archaeological problems of the West Coast of Britain', *Archaeologia Cambrensis* 70, 405–20

Fleure, H.J. and Dunlop, M. (1942) 'Glendarragh Circle and Alignments, The Braaid, I.o.M.', *Antiquaries Journal* XXII, 39–53

Flynn, P. (1997) Excavations at St Michael, Workington, *Church Archaeology* 1, 43–4

Foote, P. and Wilson, D.M. (1970) *The Viking Achievement,* London

Forsyth, K. (2007) 'An ogham-inscribed plaque from Bornais, South Uist', in Ballin-Smith, B., Taylor, S. and Williams, G. (eds) *West over Sea. Studies in Scandinavian sea-borne expansion and settlement before 1300. A Festschrift in honour of Dr Barbara E. Crawford,* Leiden: Brill, 460–77

Fox, C. (1932) *The Personality of Britain*, Cardiff

Freke, D. (2002) *Excavations on St Patrick's Isle, Peel, Isle of Man, 1982–88: Prehistoric, Viking, Medieval and Later,* Liverpool University Press, Liverpool

Gelling, M. (1991) 'The place-names of the Isle of Man', in Ureland, P. Sture and Broderick, G. (eds) *Language Contact in the British Isles,* Tübingen, 141–55

Gelling, M. (1995) 'Scandinavian Settlement in Cheshire', in Crawford, B.E. (ed.) *Scandinavian Settlement in Northern Britain,* Leicester, 187–94

Gelling, P. S. (1964) 'The Braaid Site', *Journal of the Manx Museum* 6, 201–5

Gelling, P. S. (1970) 'A Norse Homestead at Doarlish Cashen, Kirk Patrick, Isle of Man', *Medieval Archaeology* 14, 74–82

Geraghty, S. (1996) *Viking Dublin, Botanical Evidence from Fishamble Street,* Medieval Dublin Excavations 1962–81, Series C Volume 2, Royal Irish Academy, Dublin

Gibbons, E.K. and Kelly, E.P. (2003) 'A Viking Age Farmstead in Connemara', *Archaeology Ireland,* Spring 2003, 28–32

Gibbons, M. (2004) 'The longphort phenomenon in Early Christian and Viking Ireland', *History Ireland* 12, 3

Glørstad, Z.T. (forthcoming 2010) 'Homeland – Strange Land – New Land. Material and Theoretical Aspects of Defining Norse Identity in the Viking Age', in Bolton, T. and Steinsland, G. (eds) *Proceedings of the conference on Irish-Norse relations 800–1200 held in Oslo on 5 November 2005,* Oslo

Graham-Campbell, J. (1976) 'The Viking Age Silver Hoards of Ireland', in Almqvist, B. and Greene, D. (eds) *Proceedings of the Seventh Viking Congress, Dublin 1973,* Royal Irish Academy, Dublin, 39–70

Graham-Campbell, J. (1983) 'The Viking-Age Silver Hoards of the Isle of Man', in Fell, C., Foote, P., Graham-Campbell, J. and Thomson, R. (eds) *The Viking Age in the Isle of Man,* London, 53–80

Graham-Campbell, J.A. (1985) 'Two Scandinavian disc brooches of Viking-age date from England', *Antiquaries Journal* LXV, 448–9

Graham-Campbell, J.A. (1987) 'Some Archaeological Reflections on the Cuerdale Hoard', in Metcalf, D. M. (ed.) *Coinage in Ninth-Century Northumbria,* British Archaeological Reports, British Series 180, Oxford, 329–44

Graham-Campbell, J.A. (ed.) (1992) *Viking Treasure from the North West, the Cuerdale Hoard in its Context,* National Museums and Galleries on Merseyside, Liverpool

Graham-Campbell, J.A. (1995a) 'The Irish Sea Vikings, raiders and settlers', in Scott, T. and Starkey, E. (eds) *The Middle Ages in the North West,* Leopard's Head Press, Oxford, 59–83

Graham-Campbell, J.A. (ed.) (1995b) *The Viking-Age Gold and Silver of Scotland,* National Museums of Scotland, Edinburgh, 16–25

Graham-Campbell, J.A. (1998) 'The Early Viking Age in the Irish Sea Area', in Clarke, H. B., Ní Mhaonaigh, M. and Ó Floinn, R. (eds) *Ireland and Scandinavia in the Early Viking Age,* Dublin, 104–30

Graham-Campbell, J.A. (1999) *Whithorn and the Viking World,* Whithorn Lecture, Whithorn Trust, Whithorn

Graham-Campbell, J.A. (2002) 'Tenth-century graves: the Viking-Age artefacts and their significance', in Freke, D. (ed.) *Excavations on St Patrick's Isle, Peel, Isle of Man, 1982–88: Prehistoric, Viking, Medieval and Later,* Liverpool University Press, Liverpool, 83–98

Graham-Campbell, J.A. (forthcoming) *The Cuerdale Hoard and Related Viking-Age Silver and Gold, from Britain and Ireland, in the British Museum,* British Museum, London

Graham-Campbell, J.A. and Batey, C.E. (1998) *Vikings in Scotland, An Archaeological Survey,* Edinburgh University Press, Edinburgh

Graham-Campbell, J.A. and Edwards, B.J.N. (2008) 'An Eighteenth-century Record of a Lancashire Viking Burial', *Transactions of the Lancashire and Cheshire Antiquarian Society* 104, 151–8

Graham-Campbell, J.A. and Philpott, R.A. (eds) (forthcoming) *The Huxley Viking Hoard: Scandinavian Settlement in the North West,* National Museums Liverpool

Grant, A. (2002) 'A New Approach to the Inversion Compounds of North-West England', *Nomina* 20, 65–90

Grant, A. (2005) 'The Origin of the Ayrshire *Bý* names', in Gammeltoft, P. (ed.) *Cultural Contacts in the North Atlantic Region: The Evidence of Names,* Lerwick, 127–40

Grieg, S. (1940) 'Viking Antiquities in Scotland', in Shetelig, H. (ed.) *Viking Antiquities in Great Britain and Ireland*, Part II, Aschehoug, Oslo

Griffiths D. (1992) 'The Coastal Trading Ports of the Irish Sea', in Graham-Campbell, J. (ed.) *Viking Treasure from the North West, the Cuerdale Hoard in its Context*, National Museums and Galleries on Merseyside, Liverpool, 63–72

Griffiths D. (1994) 'Trade and the late Saxon port', in Ward S.W. *Excavations at Chester, Saxon Occupation within the Legionary Fortress, Sites Investigated 1963–81,* Chester Archaeological Service, Monograph 7, Chester, 124–28

Griffiths D. (1996) 'The maritime economy of the Chester region in the Anglo-Saxon Period', in Carrington P. (ed.) *Where Deva Spreads her Wizard Stream. Trade and the Port of Chester,* Chester City Council, Chester, 49–60

Griffiths, D. (2001) 'The North-West Frontier', in Hill, D. and Higham, N. (eds) *Edward the Elder 899–924,* Manchester University Press, Manchester, 167–87

Griffiths D. (2003) 'Markets and productive sites: a view from Western Britain', in Pestell T. and Ulmschneider K. (eds) *Markets in Early Medieval Europe,* Windgather Press, Bollington, 62–72

Griffiths D. (2004) 'Settlement and Acculturation in the Irish Sea Region', in Hines, J., Lane, A. and Redknap, M. (eds) *Land, Sea and Home, Settlement in the Viking Period,* Society for Medieval Archaeology Monograph 20, Maney, Leeds, 125–38

Griffiths D. (2006) 'Maen Achwyfan and the Context of Viking Settlement in North-East Wales' *Archaeologia Cambrensis* 155, 143–62

Griffiths, D., Philpott, R.A. and Egan, G. (2007) *Meols, The Archaeology of the North Wirral Coast,* Oxford University School of Archaeology Monograph Series 68, Oxford

Hadley, D.M. (2006) *Vikings in England, Settlement, Society and Culture,* Manchester University Press, Manchester

Hall, R.A. (1994) *Viking Age York,* Batsford/English Heritage, London

Halloran, K. (2005) 'The Brunanburh Campaign: A Reappraisal', *Scottish Historical Review* 84, 133–48

Harding, S. (2007) 'The Wirral Carrs and Holms', *Journal of the English Place-Name Society* 39, 45–57

Harding, S. and Jobling, M. (2008), 'Looking for Vikings in North West England', *British Archaeology* 103 (2008), 22–25

Harrison, S.H. (2001) 'Viking Graves and Grave Goods in Ireland', in Larsen, A–C (ed.) *The Vikings in Ireland,* Roskilde, 61–75

Harrison, S.H. (2005) 'College Green – A Neglected 'Viking' Cemetery at Dublin', in Mortensen, A. and Arge, S.V. (eds) *Viking and Norse in the North Atlantic, Select Papers from the Proceedings of the Fourteenth Viking Congress, Tórshavn, 19–30 July 2001,* Annales Societatis Scientarium Faeroensis Supplementum XLIV, Tórshavn, 329–39

Harrison, S.H. (2007) 'Separated from the Foaming Maelstrom: Landscapes of Insular "Viking Burial", in Semple, S. (ed.) *Anglo-Saxon Studies in Archaeology and History* 14, 173–82

Harrison, S.H. (forthcoming) *A Corpus of Viking Graves and Grave Goods from Ireland,* National Museum of Ireland/ Royal Irish Academy, Dublin

Hartnett, P. and Eogan, G. (1964) 'Feltrim Hill, Co. Dublin, a Neolithic and Early Christian Site', *Journal of the Royal Society of Antiquaries of Ireland* 94, 1–37

Hayden, A. (2002) 'The excavation of pre-Norman defences and houses in Werburgh Street, Dublin: a summary', in Duffy, S. (ed.) *Medieval Dublin* III, 44–66

Helgason, A., Sigurðardóttir, S., Gulcher, J., Ward, R. and Stefánsson, K. (2000) 'MtDNA and the origin of the Icelanders: Deciphering signals of recent population history', *American Journal of Human Genetics* 66, 999–1016

Hencken, H.N. O'N. (1942) 'Ballinderry Crannog No. 2', *Proceedings of the Royal Irish Academy* 47, C, 1–76

Hencken, H.N. O'N. (1950) 'Lagore Crannog: an Irish Royal residence of the seventh to tenth centuries AD, *Proceedings of the Royal Irish Academy* 53, C, 1–248

Henri, F. (1967) *Irish Art during the Viking Invasions 800–1020 AD,* Methuen, London

Henry, D. (ed.) (1995) *Viking Ireland, Jens Worsaae's accounts of his visit to Ireland 1846–47,* Pinkfoot Press, Balgavies

Higham, M.C. (1995) 'Scandinavian settlement in north-west England, with a special study of *Ireby* names', in

Crawford, B.E. (ed.) *Scandinavian Settlement in Northern Britain*, Leicester, 195–205

Higham, N.J. (1985) 'The Scandinavians in North Cumbria, Raids and Settlement in the later Ninth to mid Tenth Centuries', in Baldwin, J.R and Whyte, I.D. (eds) *The Scandinavians in Cumbria*, Scottish Society for Northern Studies, Edinburgh, 37–51

Higham, N.J. (1992) 'Northumbria, Mercia and the Irish Sea Norse', in Sea', in Graham-Campbell, J. (ed.) *Viking Treasure from the North West, the Cuerdale Hoard in its Context*, National Museums and Galleries on Merseyside, Liverpool, 21–30

Higham, N.J. (1993) *The Origins of Cheshire*, Manchester University Press, Manchester

Higham, N.J. (2004a) 'Viking-age Settlement in the North-western Countryside, lifting the veil', in Hines, J., Lane, A. and Redknap, M. (eds) *Land, Sea and Home, Settlement in the Viking Period*, Society for Medieval Archaeology, Monograph 20, Maney, Leeds, 297–311

Higham, N.J. (2004b) *A Frontier Landscape, The North West in the Middle Ages*, Windgather Press, Bollington

Hilberg, V. (2008) 'Hedeby, An Outline of its Research History', in Brink, S. and Price, N. (eds) *The Viking World*, Routledge, 101–11

Hill, G.W. (1920) 'A find of Coins of Eadgar, Eadweard II and Æthelred II at Chester', *Numismatic Chronicle* 4, series 20, 141–65

Hill, P. (1987) *Whithorn 2, Excavations 1984–1987*, Interim Report, Whithorn Trust

Hill, P. (1997) *Whithorn and St Ninian, The Excavation of a Monastic Town, 1984–91*, Sutton, Stroud

Hodges, R. (2006) *Goodbye to the Vikings*, Duckworth, London

Hodgkinson, D., Huckerby, E., Middleton, C. and Wells, C. (2000) 'The Lowland Wetlands of Cumbria', *North West Wetlands Survey* 6, Lancaster

Hodgson, C. (1832) 'An Account of some antiquities found in a cairn, near Hesket-in-the-Forest, Cumberland', *Archaeologia Aeliana* 2, 106–9

Holm, P. (1986) 'The Slave Trade of Dublin, Ninth to Twelfth Centuries', *Peritia* 5, 317–45

Hudson, B. (1999) 'The Changing Economy of the Irish Sea Province AD 900–1300', in Smith, B. (ed.) *Britain and Ireland 900–1300*, Cambridge University Press, Cambridge, 39–66

Hudson, B. (2005) *Viking Pirates and Christian Princes, Dynasty, Religion and Empire in the North Atlantic*, Oxford University Press, Oxford

Hudson, B. (2006) *Irish Sea Studies 900-1200*, Four Courts Press, Dublin

Hume, A. (1863) *Ancient Meols, or some Account of the Antiquities found near Dove Point on the Sea Coast of Cheshire*, John Russell Smith, London

Hurley, M.F. and Scully, O.M.B. (1997) *Late Viking Age and Medieval Waterford, Excavations 1986–1992*, Waterford Corporation, Waterford

James, D. (1978) 'Two Medieval Arabic accounts of Ireland', *Journal of the Royal Society of Antiquaries of Ireland* 108, 5–9

Jesch, J. (2008) 'Myth and Cultural Memory in the Viking Diaspora', *Viking and Medieval Scandinavia* 4, 221–6

Johnson, A. (1999) 'A View from the Hills – Some thoughts on the Reoccupation of Promontory Forts and the Possible Origins of the Manx Farmstead', *Proceedings of the Isle of Man Natural History and Antiquarian Society* XI, 1997–99, 1, 52–66

Johnson, R. (2004) *Viking Age Dublin*, Irish Treasures Series, Town House, Dublin

Jones, A. (1910) *The History of Gruffudd ap Cynan, the Welsh Text*, Manchester University Press, Manchester

Jones, G. (1984) A History of the Vikings, Oxford University Press, Oxford

Keen, J.J. (1925–9) *The Place-Names of the Isle of Man with their origins and history* (6 vols), Douglas

Keevill, G. (1989) *Carlisle Cathedral Excavations 1988, Interim Report*, Carlisle Diocesan Registry

Keevill, G. (2008) 'Excavations at Carlisle Cathedral in 1985', *Transactions of the Cumberland and Westmorland Antiquarian and Archaeological Society* 3 ser, VIII, 35–61

Kelly, E.P. and Maas, J. (1995) 'Vikings on the Barrow', *Archaeology Ireland* 9, no. 3, 30–32

Kelly, E.P. (1998) 'A Viking Longphort near Athlunkard, Co. Clare', *Archaeology Ireland* 12, no. 4, 13–16

Kenny, M. (1987) 'The Geographical Distribution of Irish Viking-Age Coin Hoards' *Proceedings of the Royal Irish Academy* 87C 8, 507–25

Kenyon, D. (1991) *The Origins of Lancashire*, Manchester University Press, Manchester

Kermode, P.M.C. (1907) *Manx Crosses*, London, re-published 1994 by Pinkfoot Press, Balgavies

Kermode, P.M.C. (1930) 'A Ship Burial in the Isle of Man', *Antiquaries Journal* X, 126–33

King, A. (2004) 'Post Roman Upland Architecture in the Craven Dales and the Dating Evidence', in Hines, J., Lane, A. and Redknap, M. (eds) *Land, Sea and Home, Settlement in the Viking Period*, Society for Medieval Archaeology, Monograph 20, Maney, Leeds, 335–44

Kruse, S.E. (1992) 'Metallurgical Evidence of Silver Sources in the Irish Sea Province', in Graham-Campbell, J. (ed.) *Viking Treasure from the North West, the Cuerdale Hoard in its Context*, National Museums and Galleries on Merseyside, Liverpool, 73–88

Laing, L.R. and Laing, J. (1987) 'The Early Christian Period Settlement at Ronaldsway, Isle of Man, a Reappraisal', *Proceedings of the Isle of Man Natural History and Antiquarian Society* IX, 3, 389–415

Lang, J.T. (1984) 'The hogback. A Viking colonial monument', *Anglo-Saxon Studies in Archaeology and History* 3, 86–176

Lang, J.T. (1988) '*Viking-Age Decorated Wood: A Study of its Ornament and Style*', Medieval Dublin Excavations 1962–81, Series B Volume 1, Royal Irish Academy, Dublin

Larsen, A-C (ed.) (2001) *The Vikings in Ireland*, Viking Ship Museum, Roskilde

Lawlor, H.C. (1925) *The Monastery of St Machaoi*, Belfast

Longley, D. (1991) 'The excavation of Castell, Porth Trefadog, a coastal promontory fort in North Wales', *Medieval Archaeology* 35, 64–85

Lowe, C.E. (2007) 'Image and Imagination: the Inchmarnock 'Hostage Stone', in Ballin-Smith, B., Taylor, S. and Williams, G. (eds) *West over Sea. Studies in Scandinavian sea-borne expansion and settlement before 1300. A Festschrift in honour of Dr Barbara E. Crawford,* Brill, Leiden, 53–67

Loyn, H.R. (1976) *The Vikings in Wales*, Dorothea Coke Memorial Lecture, London

Lucas, A.T. (1966) 'Irish-Norse Relations, Time for a Reappraisal?' *Journal of the Cork Archaeological and Historical Society* 71, 62–75

Lynch, A. and Manning, C. (2001) 'Excavations at Dublin Castle 1985–7', in Duffy, S. (ed.) *Medieval Dublin* II, Dublin, 169–204

Lynn, C.J. (1988) 'Ulster's Oldest Wooden Houses', in Hamlin, A. and Lynn, C.J. (eds) *Pieces of the Past*, HMSO, Belfast, 44–7

Mac Airt, S. (trans.) (1977) *The Annals of Inisfallen*, Dublin Institute for Advanced Studies, Dublin

Mac Airt, S. and Mac Niocáill, G. (trans.) (1983) *The Annals of Ulster to 1131*, Dublin Institute for Advanced Studies, Dublin

MacDonald, R.A. (1997) *The Kingdom of the Isles, Scotland's Western Seaboard c. 1100–c. 1336*, Scottish Historical Review, Monograph Series 4, East Linton

Mack, R.P. (1967) 'The St Johns Church, Chester, Hoard of 1862', *British Numismatic Journal* 36, 36–9

Mackinder, H.J. (1907) *Britain and the British Seas*, Clarendon Press, Oxford

Marstrander, C. (1937) 'Treen og Keeill', *Norsk Tidsskrift for Sprogvidenskab* 8, 287–500, Oslo

Marwick, H. (1935) 'Leidang in the West or the Norse Fleets of Orkney and the Isle of Man', *Proceedings of the Orkney Antiquarian Society* XIII, 15–31

Mason, D.J.P. (1985) *Excavations at Chester, 26–42 Lower Bridge Street, the Dark Age and Saxon Periods*. Grosvenor Museum Archaeological Excavation and Survey Reports 3, Chester

Mason, D. (2007) *Chester AD 400–1066*, Tempus, Stroud

Mason, E. (1990) *St Wulfstan of Worcester, c. 1008–1095*, Blackwell, Oxford

Maund, K. (1991) *Ireland, Wales and England in the Eleventh Century*, Studies in Celtic History 12, Boydell, Woodbridge

Maund, K. (2000) *The Welsh Kings, The Medieval Rulers of Wales*, Sutton, Stroud

McErlean, T. (1983) 'The Irish Townland System of Landscape Organisation' in Reeves-Smyth, T. and Hammond, F. (eds) *Landscape Archaeology in Ireland*, British Archaeological Reports, British Series 116, Oxford, 315–39

McErlean, T., McConkey, R. and Forsythe, W. (2003) *Strangford Lough: An Archaeological Survey of the Maritime Cultural Landscape*, Northern Ireland Monographs 6, Blackstaff, Belfast

McEvoy B., Brady, C., Moore L.T., Bradley D.G. (2006) 'The scale and nature of Viking settlement in Ireland from Y-chromosome admixture analysis', *European Journal of Human Genetics* 14, 1288–1294

McGrail S. and Switsur R. (1979) 'Medieval logboats of the River Mersey – a classification study', in McGrail

S. (ed.) *The Archaeology of Medieval Ships and Harbours in Northern Europe*, British Archaeological Reports, International Series 66, Oxford, 93–115

Megaw, B.R.S. (1978) 'Norseman and Native in the Kingdom of the Isles, A Reassessment of the Manx Evidence', in Davey, P.J. (ed.) *Man and Environment in the Isle of Man*, British Archaeological Reports, British Series 54, Oxford, 265–314

Metcalf, D.M. (1992) 'The Monetary Economy of the Irish Sea Province' in Graham-Campbell, J. (ed.) *Viking Treasure from the North West, the Cuerdale Hoard in its Context*, National Museums and Galleries on Merseyside, Liverpool, 89–106

Metcalf, D.M. (1995) 'The Monetary Significance of Scottish Viking-Age Coin Hoards, with a short commentary', in Graham-Campbell, J. (ed.) *The Viking-Age Gold and Silver of Scotland*, National Museums of Scotland, Edinburgh, 16–25

Meyer, K. (trans.) (1892) *Aislinge Meic Conglinne, the Vision of Mac Conglinne*, Longman, London

Moore, D. (ed.) (1970) *The Irish Sea Province in Archaeology and History*, Cambrian Archaeological Association, Cardiff

Moore, R.H. (1999) 'The Manx Multiple Estate: evidence for undertones in the Manx land-system', in Davey, P.J. (ed.) *Recent Archaeological Research on the Isle of Man*, British Archaeological Reports, British Series 278, Oxford, 171–82

Morris, M. (ed.) (1983) *Medieval Manchester*, Greater Manchester Archaeology Unit, Manchester

Munch, G.S., Johansen, O.S. and Roesdahl, E. (eds) (2003) *Borg in Lofoten, A Chieftain's Farm in North Norway*, Tapir Press, Trondheim

Murray, H. (1983) *Viking and Early Medieval Buildings in Dublin*, British Archaeological Reports, British Series 119, Oxford

Myhre, B. (1992) 'The Beginning of the Viking Age' in Faulkes, A. and Perkins, R. (eds) *Viking Revaluations*, Viking Society for Northern Research, London, 182–204

Mytum, H. (2003) 'The Vikings and Ireland: Ethnicity, Identity and Culture Change', in Barrett, J. H. (ed.) *Contact, Continuity and Collapse, the Norse Colonization of the North Atlantic*, Brepols, 113–37

Nelson, J. (1997) 'The Frankish Empire', in Sawyer, P.H. (ed.) *The Oxford Illustrated History of the Vikings*, Oxford University Press, Oxford, 19–47

Newman, R. and Brennand, M. (2007) 'The Early Medieval Period Research Agenda' in Brennand, M. (ed.) *Research and Archaeology in North-West England, An Archaeological Research Framework for North–West England Volume 2*, Archaeology North West 9, 73–94

Nicholl, T. (2009) 'From Roskilde to Dublin, the story of the *Sea Stallion from Glendalough*', in Duffy, S. (ed.) *Medieval Dublin* IX, Dublin, 213–50

OA North (2008) *Townfoot Farm, Cumwhitton, Cumbria*, Post Excavation Assessment Report, Oxford Archaeology North, Lancaster

O'Brien, E. (1992) 'A Reassessment of the "great sepulchral mound" containing a Viking burial at Donnybrook, Dublin', *Medieval Archaeology* 36, 170–3

O'Brien, E. (1998) 'The Location and Context of Viking Burials at Kilmainham and Islandbridge, Dublin', in Clarke, H. B., Ní Mhaonaigh, M. and Ó Floinn, R. (eds) *Ireland and Scandinavia in the Early Viking Age*, Dublin, 203–221

O'Brien, R., Quinney, P. and Russell, I. (2006) 'Preliminary Report on the Archaeological Excavation and Finds Retrieval Strategy of the Hiberno-Scandinavian Site of Woodstown 6, County Waterford' *Decies* 61, 13–122

Ó Corráin, D. (1997) 'Ireland, Wales, Man and the Hebrides', in Sawyer, P.H. (ed.) *The Oxford Illustrated History of the Vikings*, Oxford University Press, Oxford, 83–109

Ó Corráin, D. (2001) 'The Vikings in Ireland', in Larsen, A-C (ed.) *The Vikings in Ireland*, Roskilde, 17–27

Ó Donnabháin, B. and Hallgrímsson, B. (2001) 'Dublin: the biological identity of the Hiberno-Norse town', in Duffy, S. (ed.) *Medieval Dublin* II, Dublin, 65–87

O'Donovan, E. (2008) 'The Irish, the Vikings and the English: new archaeological evidence from excavations at Golden Lane, Dublin', in Duffy, S. (ed.) *Medieval Dublin* VIII, 36–130

Ó Floinn, R. (1998a) 'The Archaeology of the Early Viking Age in Ireland', in Clarke, H. B., Ní Mhaonaigh, M. and Ó Floinn, R. (eds) *Ireland and Scandinavia in the Early Viking Age*, Dublin, 131–65

Ó Floinn, R. (1998b) 'Two Viking Burials from Co. Wicklow', in Corlett, C. and O'Sullivan, A. (eds) *Wicklow Archaeology and Society* I, 29–35

Ó Floinn, R. (2001) 'Irish and Scandinavian Art in the Early Medieval Period', in Larsen, A-C (ed.) *The Vikings in Ireland,* Roskilde, 87–97

Oftedal, M. (1976) 'Scandinavian place-names in Ireland', in Almqvist, B. and Greene, D. (eds) *Proceedings of the Seventh Viking Congress, Dublin 1973,* Royal Irish Academy, Dublin, 125–33

O'Kelly, M. (1956) 'An island settlement at Beginish, Co. Kerry', *Proceedings of the Royal Irish Academy* C, 57, 159–94

Ó Néill, J. (2000) 'Excavation of a rural Norse settlement at Cherrywood, Co. Dublin', http://www.mglarc. com/index.php, updated 25 May 2009

Oram, R.D. (1995) 'Scandinavian Settlement in South-West Scotland, with a special study of Bysbie', in Crawford, B.E. (ed.) *Scandinavian Settlement in Northern Britain,* Leicester, 127–40

Ormerod, G. (1882) *A History of the County Palatine of Chester,* (2nd ed., Helsby, T.), Routledge, London

O'Sullivan, D. (1993) 'Sub-Roman and Anglo-Saxon Finds from Cumbria', *Transactions of the Cumberland and Westmorland Antiquarian and Archaeological Society* 93, 25–42

Page, R.I. (1983) 'Manx Rune Stones', in Fell, C., Foote, P., Graham-Campbell, J. and Thomson, R. (eds) *The Viking Age in the Isle of Man,* London, 133–46

Pantos, A. (1999) 'Meeting Places in *Wilaveston* Hundred, Cheshire', *Journal of the English Place-Name Society* 31, 91–112

Parsons, D.N. (2001) 'How long did the Scandinavian language survive in England? Again', in Graham-Campbell, J., Hall, R., Jesch, J. and Parsons, D. (eds) *Vikings and the Danelaw,* Oxbow, Oxford, 45–96, 299–312

Pelteret, D.A.E. (1995) *Slavery in Early Medieval England,* Boydell, Bury St Edmunds

Petersen, J. (1919) *De norske vikingesverd. En typologisk-kronologisk studie over vikingetidens vaaben,* Kristiania

Petersen, J. (1928) *Vikingetidens Smykker,* Stavanger

Petersen, J. (1940) 'British Antiquities of the Viking Period found in Norway', in Shetelig, H. (ed.) *Viking Antiquities in Great Britain and Ireland,* Part V, Aschehoug, Oslo

Philpott, F. (1990) *A Silver Saga,* National Museums and Galleries on Merseyside, Liverpool

Philpott, R.A. (in prep) *Excavations on a Medieval Site at Hoylake Road, Moreton, Wirral, 1987–8,* National Museums Liverpool

Philpott, R.A. and Adams, M.H. (forthcoming 2010) *Irby, Wirral: Excavations on a Late Prehistoric, Romano-British and Medieval Site, 1987–96,* National Museums Liverpool

Piggott, S. and Simpson W. D. (1970) *An Illustrated Guide to Ancient Monuments: Volume VI, Scotland,* Edinburgh

Pirie, E.J.E. (1986) 'Finds of 'sceattas' and 'stycas' of Northumbria, in Blackburn M.A.S. (ed.) *Anglo-Saxon Monetary History,* Leicester University Press, Leicester, 67–90

Potter, T.W. and Andrews, R.D. (1994) 'Excavation and Survey at St Patrick's Chapel and St Peter's Church, Heysham, Lancashire 1977–78', *Antiquaries Journal* LXXIV, 54–134.

Price, N. S. (2002) *The Viking Way, Religion and War in Late Iron Age Scandinavia,* Aun 31, Uppsala

Quartermaine, J. and Krupa, M. (1994) *Thingmount, Little Langdale, Cumbria,* Archaeological Survey Report Commissioned by the National Trust, Lancaster University Archaeological Unit, Lancaster

Raftery, J. (1961) 'A Viking burial in Co. Galway', *Journal of the Galway Archaeological and Historical Society* 29, 1960–61, 3–6

RCHME (1936) *An Inventory of the Historical Monuments in Westmorland,* Royal Commission on the Historical Monuments of England, HMSO, London

Redknap, M. (2000) *Vikings in Wales, An Archaeological Quest,* National Museums and Galleries of Wales, Cardiff

Redknap, M. (2004) 'Viking Age Settlement in Wales and the Evidence from Llanbedrgoch', in Hines, J., Lane, A. and Redknap, M. (eds) *Land, Sea and Home, Settlement in the Viking Period,* Society for Medieval Archaeology, Monograph 20, Maney, Leeds, 139–75

Redknap, M. (2007) 'Crossing Boundaries, Stylistic Diversity and External Contacts in Early Medieval Wales and the March: Reflections on Sculpture and Metalwork', in Sims-Williams, P. and Williams, G.A. (eds) *Crossing Boundaries/Croesi Ffiniau, Proceedings of the XII International Congress of Celtic Studies, 24–30 August 2003,* Aberystwyth, 22–86

Redknap, M. (2008) 'The Vikings in Wales', in Brink, S. and Price, N. (eds) *The Viking World*, Routledge, 410–10

Redmond, A.Z. (2007) *Viking Burial in the North of England*, British Archaeological Reports, British Series 429, Oxford

Reilly, P. (1988) *Computer Analysis of an Archaeological Landscape, Medieval Land Divisions on the Isle of Man*, British Archaeological Reports, British Series 190, Oxford

Richards, M. (1962) 'Norse Place-Names in Wales', in Ó Cuív, B. (ed.) *Proceedings of the First International Congress of Celtic Studies, Dublin, 6–10 July 1959,* Dublin, 51–60

Richards, J.D. (1991) *Viking Age England*, English Heritage/Batsford

Richardson, C. (1996) 'A find of Viking-period silver brooches and fragments from Flusco, Newbiggin, Cumbria', *Transactions of the Cumberland and Westmorland Antiquarian and Archaeological Society* 96, 35–44

Roberts, B.K. (1990) 'Late *–by* names in the Eden Valley, Cumbria', *Nomina* XIII, 25–40

Rooke, H. (1792) 'Druidical and other remains in Cumberland', *Archaeologia* 10, 105–13

Russell, I.R. (2003) *Report on Archaeological Excavation of Woodstown 6*, NRA/Waterford City Council

Ryan, M. (1982) 'Some archaeological comments on the occurrence and use of silver in pre-Viking Ireland', in Scott, B.G. (ed.) *Studies on Early Ireland: essays in honour of M. V. Duignan*, Belfast 45–50

Sawyer, P.H. (1968) *Anglo-Saxon Charters, An Annotated List and Bibliography*, Royal Historical Society, London

Sawyer, P.H. (1970) 'The Vikings and the Irish Sea', in Moore, D. (ed.) (1970) *The Irish Sea Province in Archaeology and History*, Cambrian Archaeological Association, Cardiff, 86–92

Sawyer P.H. and Thacker A.T. (1987) 'Domesday Survey', in Harris B.E. and Thacker A.T. (eds) *A History of the County of Chester, Vol. I.* Oxford University Press for Institute of Historical Research, London, 293–370

Scally, G. (2002) 'The earthen banks and walled defences of Dublin's north-east corner', in Duffy, S. (ed.) *Medieval Dublin* III, Dublin, 11–33

Sheehan, J. (1988) 'A Reassessment of the Viking Burial from Eyrephort, Co. Galway', *Journal of the Galway Archaeological and Historical Society* 41, 1987–8, 60–72

Sheehan, J. (1998) 'Early Viking Age Silver Hoards from Ireland and their Scandinavian Elements', in Clarke, H.B., Ní Mhaonaigh, M. and Ó Floinn, R. (eds) *Ireland and Scandinavia in the Early Viking Age*, Dublin, 166–202

Sheehan, J. (2007) 'The Form and Structure of Viking-Age Silver Hoards: the evidence from Ireland', in Graham-Campbell, J.A. and Williams, G. (eds) *Silver Economy in the Viking Age*, Left Coast Press, Walnut Creek, 149–62

Sheehan, J. (2008) 'The *Longphort* in Viking Age Ireland, *Acta Archaeologica* 79, 282–95

Sheehan, J., Stumann-Hansen, S. and Ó Corráin, D. (2001) 'A Viking Age maritime haven, a reassessment of the island settlement at Beginish, Co. Kerry', *Journal of Irish Archaeology* 10, 93–119

Shetelig, H. (ed.) (1940) *Viking Antiquities in Great Britain and Ireland*, Ascheoug, Oslo

Simpson, L. (2000) 'Forty Years a-digging, a preliminary synthesis of archaeological investigations in Medieval Dublin', in Duffy, S. (ed.) *Medieval Dublin* I, Dublin, 11–68

Simpson, L. (2005) 'Viking Warrior Burials in Dublin: is this the longphort?', in Duffy, S. (ed.) *Medieval Dublin* VI, Dublin, 11–62

Sivier, D. (2002) *Anglo-Saxon and Norman Bristol*, Tempus, Stroud

Skinner, F. G. and Bruce-Mitford, R.L.S. (1940) 'A Celtic Balance Beam of the Christian Period', *Antiquaries Journal* XX, 87–102

Skre, D. (ed.) (2007) *Kaupang in Skiringssal*, Kaupang Excavation Project Publication Series Volume 1, Norske Oldfunn XXII, Aarhus

Skre, D. (2008a) 'The development of Urbanism in Scandinavia', in Brink, S. and Price, N. (eds) *The Viking World*, Routledge, 83–93

Skre, D. (2008b) 'Kaupang – Skíringssalr', in Brink, S. and Price, N. (eds) *The Viking World*, Routledge, 112–20

Skre, D. (ed.) (2008c) *Means of Exchange, Dealing with Silver in the Viking Age*, Kaupang Excavation Project Publication Series Volume 2, Norske Oldfunn XXIII, Aarhus

Smith, A.H. (1967) *The Place-Names of Westmorland* , English Place-Name Society 17–18, Cambridge University Press, Cambridge

Smith, F.G. (1932) 'Talacre and the Viking Grave', *Proceedings of the Llandudno, Colwyn Bay and District Field Club* 17, 42–50

Smyth, A.P. (1977) 'The Black Foreigners of York and the White Foreigners of Dublin', *Saga Book of the Viking Society* 19, 1974–77, 101–17

Smyth, A.P. (1979) *Scandinavian Kings of York and Dublin*, Dublin

Stocker, D. (2000) 'Monuments and Merchants: Irregularites in the Distribution of Stone Sculpture in Lincolnshire and Yorkshire in the Tenth Century', in Hadley, D. M. and Richards, J. D. (eds) *Cultures in Contact, Scandinavian Settlement in England in the Ninth and Tenth Centuries*, Brepols, 179–212

Storli, I. (2000) 'Barbarians of the North, Reflections on the establishment of courtyard sites in North Norway', *Norwegian Archaeological Review* 33.2, 81–103

Swainson-Cowper, H. (1891) 'A Law Ting at Fell Foot, Little Langdale, Westmorland', *Transactions of the Cumberland and Westmorland Antiquarian and Archaeological Society* 11, 1–6

Swanton, M.J. (1975 and later editions) *Anglo-Saxon Prose*, Dent, London

Swift, C. (2004) 'Royal Fleets in Viking Ireland, the evidence of *Lebor na Cert,* AD 1050–1150', in Hines, J., Lane, A. and Redknap, M. (eds) *Land, Sea and Home, Settlement in the Viking Period*, Society for Medieval Archaeology, Monograph 20, Maney, Leeds, 188–206

Tarlow, S. (1997) 'The Dread of Something after Death: Violation and Desecration on the Isle of Man in the Tenth Century', in Carman, J. (ed.) *Material Harm: Archaeological Studies of War and Violence*, Cruithne, Glasgow, 133–42

Telford, R.J., Heegaard, E and Birks, H.J.B. (2004) 'The Intercept is a poor estimate of a calibrated radiocarbon age', *The Holocene* 14, 2, 296–8

Thacker, A.T. (1982) 'Chester and Gloucester: Early Ecclesiastical Organization in Two Mercian Burhs', *Northern History* XVIII, 199–211

Thacker, A.T. (1987) 'Anglo-Saxon Cheshire', in Harris B.E. and Thacker A.T. (eds) *Victoria History of the County of Chester Volume 1*, Oxford University Press for Institute of Historical Research, London, 237–92

Thacker, A.T. (1988) 'Early Medieval Chester: the historical background', in Hodges R. and Hobley B. (eds) *The Rebirth of Towns in the West,* CBA Research Report 68, London, 119–24

Thacker, A.T. (2003) 'Early Medieval Chester', in Lewis, C.P. and Thacker, A.T. (eds) *Victoria History of the County of Chester Volume 5*, Boydell for Institute of Historical Research, Woodbridge, 16–33

Thäte, E. S. (2007) *Monuments and Minds: Monument Re-Use in Scandinavia in the Second Half of the First Millennium AD,* Acta Archaeologica Lundensia 4, 27, Lund

Thomas, G. (2000) 'Anglo-Scandinavian Metalwork from the Danelaw', in Hadley, D.M. and Richards, J.D. (eds) *Cultures in Contact, Scandinavian Settlement in England in the Ninth and Tenth Centuries*, Brepols, 237–55

Thompson Watkin, W. (1883) *Roman Lancashire,* Thomas Brakell, Liverpool (reprinted in 1969 by S. R. Publishers Ltd)

Thomson, W. (2008) *The New History of Orkney*, Revised edition, Birlinn, Edinburgh

Townend, M. (2002) 'Viking Age England as a Bilingual Society', in Hadley, D.M. and Richards, J.D. (eds) *Cultures in Contact, Scandinavian Settlement in England in the Ninth and Tenth Centuries*, Brepols, 89–101

Townend, M. (2009) *The Vikings and Victorian Lakeland, the Norse Medievalism of W.G. Collingwood and his contemporaries,* Cumberland and Westmorland Antiquarian and Archaeological Society, Carlisle

Treasure Annual Report (2005/6) British Museum, Department of Culture Media and Sport, London

Turner, T.M. (1944) 'A find of coins of Eadred, Edwig and Eadgar at Chester', *British Numismatic Journal* 24, 47–9

Valante, M.A. (2008) *The Vikings in Ireland, Settlement, Trade and Urbanization*, Four Courts Press, Dublin

Wainwright, F.T. (1943) 'Wirral Field Names', *Antiquity* 27, 57–66

Wainwright, F.T. (1946) 'The Scandinavians in West Lancashire', *Transactions of the Lancashire and Cheshire Antiquarian Society* 58, 71–116

Wainwright, F.T. (1948) 'Ingimund's Invasion', *English Historical Review* 63, 145–69

Wainwright, F.T. (1975) 'The Field-Names of Amounderness Hundred', in Finberg, H.P.R. (ed.) *Scandinavian England*, Phillimore, Chichester, 229–79

Wallace, P.F. (1985) 'The Archaeology of Viking Dublin', in Clarke, H.B. and Simms, A. (eds) *The Comparative History of Urban Origins in Non-Roman Europe*, British Archaeological Reports, International Series 255i, Oxford, 103–45

Wallace, P.F. (1986) 'The English presence in Viking Dublin', in Blackburn M.A.S. (ed.) *Anglo-Saxon Monetary History*, Leicester University Press, Leicester, 201–21

Wallace, P.F. (1987a) 'The Layout of Later Viking Age Dublin: Indications of its regulation and problems of continuity', in Knirk, J. (ed.) *Proceedings of the Tenth Viking Congress, Larkollen, Norway 1985*, Oslo, 271–85
Wallace, P.F. (1987b) 'The Economy and Commerce of Viking Age Dublin', in Düwel, K. *et al* (eds)
   *Unterschungen zu Handel und Verkehr der vor- und frühgeschichtlichen Zeit in Mittel- und Nordeuropa, 4 Der Handel
   der Karolinger- und Wikingerzeit,* Gottingen, 200–45
Wallace, P.F. (1992) *The Viking Age Buildings of Dublin,* Medieval Dublin Excavations 1962–81, Series A Volume
   1 (2 vols), Royal Irish Academy, Dublin
Wallace, P.F. (1998) 'Line Fishing in Viking Dublin: contemporary explanation for archaeological evidence', in
   Manning, C. (ed.) *Dublin and beyond the Pale,* Bray, 3–18
Wallace, P.F. (2001) 'Ireland's Viking Towns', in Larsen, A-C (ed.) *The Vikings in Ireland,* Roskilde, 37–50
Wallace, P.F. (2004) 'A woman of importance in ninth-century Finglas', *Archaeology Ireland,* Autumn 2004, 7
Wallace, P.F. (2008) 'Archaeological Evidence for the different expressions of Scandinavian settlement in
   Ireland', in Brink, S. and Price, N. (eds) *The Viking World,* Routledge, 434–8
Walsh, A. (1998) 'A Summary Classification of Viking Age Swords in Ireland', in Clarke, H. B., Ní Mhaonaigh,
   M. and Ó Floinn, R. (eds) *Ireland and Scandinavia in the Early Viking Age,* Dublin, 222–35
Walsh, C. (2001) 'Dublin's southern town defences, tenth to fourteenth centuries: the evidence from Ross
   Road', in Duffy, S. (ed.) *Medieval Dublin* II, 88–127
Wamers, E. (1983) 'Some ecclesiastical and secular insular metalwork found in Norwegian Viking Graves',
   Peritia 2, 277–306
Wamers, E. (1998) 'Insular Finds in Viking Age Scandinavia and the State Formation of Norway', in Clarke, H.
   B., Ní Mhaonaigh, M. and Ó Floinn, R. (eds) *Ireland and Scandinavia in the Early Viking Age,* Dublin, 37–72
Ward S.W. (1994) *Excavations at Chester, Saxon Occupation within the Legionary Fortress, Sites Investigated 1963–81,*
   Chester Archaeological Service, Monograph 7, Chester
Warner, R. (1974) 'Re-provenancing of two important Viking Period Penannular Brooches', *Ulster Journal of
   Archaeology* 36–7, 1973–4, 58–70
Warner, R. (2004) 'Notes on the Inception and Development of the royal mound in Ireland', in Pantos, A. and
   Semple, S. (eds) *Assembly Places and Practices in Medieval Europe,* Four Courts Press, Dublin, 27–43
Wawn, A. (2000) *The Vikings and the Victorians, Inventing the Old North in Nineteenth-Century Britain,* Brewer,
   Woodbridge
Webster, G., Dolley, R.H.M. and Dunning, G. (1953) 'A Saxon Treasure Hoard found at Chester', *Antiquaries
   Journal* XXXIII, 22–32
White, R. (2007) *Britannia Prima,* Tempus, Stroud
Whitelock, D. (1979) *English Historical Documents, Volume 1,* Eyre Methuen, London
Wilde, W.R. (1866) 'On the Scandinavian antiquities lately discovered at Islandbridge, near Dublin', *Proceedings
   of the Royal Irish Academy* 10, 14
Williams, H. (2006) *Death and Memory in Early Medieval Britain,* Cambridge University Press, Cambridge
Wilmott, T. (2001) *Birdoswald Roman Fort, 1800 Years on Hadrian's Wall,* Tempus, Stroud
Wilson, D.M. (1984) *Anglo-Saxon Art from the seventh century to the Norman Conquest,* British Museum, London
Wilson, D.M. (2008) *The Vikings in the Isle of Man,* Aarhus University Press, Aarhus
Winchester, A.J.L. (1985) 'The Multiple estate: A framework for the Evolution of Settlement in Anglo-Saxon
   and Anglo-Scandinavian Cumbria', in Baldwin, J.R. and Whyte, I.D. (eds) *The Scandinavians in Cumbria,*
   Scottish Society for Northern Studies, Edinburgh, 89–102
Winchester, A.J.L. (1987) *Landscape and Society in Medieval Cumbria,* John Donald, Edinburgh
Woolf, A. (2007) *From Pictland to Alba 789–1070,* The New Edinburgh History of Scotland, Edinburgh
   University Press, Edinburgh
Worsaae, J.J.A. (1852) *An Account of the Danes and Norwegians in England, Scotland and Ireland,* John Murray,
   London
Youngs, S. (2002) 'Cumbria, Arnside' in Geake H. (ed.) 'Medieval Britain and Ireland 2001', *Medieval Archaeology*
   46, 129–30
Youngs, S. and Herepath, N. (2001) 'Cumbria, Arnside' in Geake H. (ed.) 'Medieval Britain and Ireland 2000',
   Medieval Archaeology 45, 237–8

INDEX